VISUAL QUICKPRO GUIDE

# MACROMEDIA COLDFUSION MX

## DEVELOPMENT WITH DREAMWEAVER MX

Sue Hove
Marc Garrett
Ben Forta

Peachpit Press

Visual QuickPro Guide

# Macromedia ColdFusion MX Development with Dreamweaver MX
Sue Hove, Marc Garrett and Ben Forta

## Peachpit Press
1249 Eighth Street
Berkeley, CA 94710
510/524-2178
800/283-9444
510/524-2221 (fax)

Find us on the World Wide Web at: http://www.peachpit.com
To report errors, please send a note to errata@peachpit.com
Published by Peachpit Press in association with Macromedia Press
Peachpit Press is a division of Pearson Education

Macromedia Press Editor: Angela C. Kozlowski
Development Editor: Barb Terry
Technical Editor: Jay Kellett
Production Coordinator: Lisa Brazieal
Copy Editor: Barb Terry
Indexer: Joy Dean Lee
Proofreader: Annie M. Quinn
Compositor: Christi Payne
Cover Design: The Visual Group

ISBN 0-321-15802-4

9 8 7 6 5 4 3 2

Printed and bound in the United States of America

# Dedication

To Shumona-Marc

# Bio

Sue Hove is Macromedia's Director of Instructor Readiness in their Education Services department. She has spent the last six years working with Allaire Corp. and then Macromedia, Inc., in helping to write instructor-led courses, online training offerings and the developer certification exam questions. She also delivers trainings to customers as well as certifies instructors worldwide to ensure high quality training programs. Prior to joining Allaire, Sue used her formal computer science training working for vendors such as AT&T, Informix, Powersoft and Sybase with a speciality in relational database design, maintenance and connectivity. Sue now lives in Holmes, Pennsylvania and welcomes your email at sue@hove.com.

**Marc Garrett**, founder of Smart Element, builds web applications for small businesses and foundations. Over 30,000 developers have downloaded Marc's Dreamweaver extensions. A Macromedia Associate Partner, Marc also runs since1968.com, which features conversations with industry leaders in Web design and development. Marc lives in Singapore and New York.

# Acknowledgements

First of all, I must thank my significant other, Joe Batchelor, for putting up with my midnight writing sessions and grumpy mornings for months as I wrote this book. I'd like to recognize my co-auther, Marc, for jumping in head first in the middle of this book's writing to replace a dropped-out author—he's done a great job pulling it together from very far away. Thanks to Donnie Robinson, who allowed me to collaborate on the instructor-led training on this subject, to help me better formulate the content of this book, and who is also a very dear friend. I'd like to give a special thanks to Ben Forta, for allowing me to get involved in this book and for helping me grow as a writer, as well as Angela, my ever-efficient editor who encouraged me to greater confidence. Thanks to all.

—*Sue Hove*

Thanks first to my parents for always believing in me. Thanks also to my parents-in-law, Laboni, and Sabeel for their support.

My appreciation to Barb Terry, who improved my writing with each suggestion, and Jay Kellett, who saved me from professional embarrassment not once, but twice. Thanks also to Sue Hove and Ben Forta at Macromedia, for including me on such an exciting project. Special thanks to Neil Robertson-Ravo for his permission to use his excellent extension, the Flash Expression Panel, in this book.

Internet books don't exist without Internet software: Thanks to Macromedia for assembling such a great suite of products.

Last but not least, to Angela Kozlowski at Peachpit, who may not have anticipated the breadth, urgency, and quirkiness of the questions I am capable of foisting on an editor: Thank you.

—*Marc*

# TABLE OF CONTENTS

TABLE OF CONTENTS

# INTRODUCTION

If you're reading this book, then you're probably a Web page designer or an HTML (Hypertext Markup Language) developer who has reached the limit of what you can do with HTML. You've done an impressive job of creating attractive and informative Web sites using Dreamweaver MX. However, you now hunger for more—for the ability to take your Web sites to the next level. Perhaps you have been maintaining a site of hundreds or thousands of pages, and you are tired of manually updating the information. Or perhaps you have written many Web sites and you're finding patterns in both the types of information you publish and the layout of those pages, and you want the site to be faster to build and easier to maintain. The answer is to evolve your Web site into a *Web application*.

Macromedia's ColdFusion MX application server can supply the functionality of a Web application, and Macromedia Dreamweaver MX can help you build it—faster.

## Top Five Reasons for Web Applications

1. Enable users to input information to be captured and stored by the Web application.

2. Allow collaboration between users, such as with message boards and calendar applications.

3. Secure content based on user authentication.

4. Develop an online catalog for e-commerce to accept and process orders while leveraging existing database data.

5. Allow others to update content without knowledge of HTML—to build an application to maintain the Web site.

# What Can HTML Do?

A Web site is comprised of HTML pages. Contrary to popular belief, HTML is not a programming language.

HTML is the set of markup symbols or codes in a file intended for display on a browser using the World Wide Web. The markup tells the Web browser how to display a Web page's words and how to bring in the linked images.

## The limitations of HTML

HTML cannot get information from a database or other source and display it on a Web page. It cannot perform programming logic to determine whether some text or image should be displayed on the page. HTML by itself can't change anything; its pages are static. Why would you even want to do these things?

Consider an example of an intranet Web site for a Human Resources department. One piece of functionality of this site is to display a detail page of information of each employee in the company. In order to remain consistent, each page that displays an employee record should have the same layout. Each employee can be described with a name, address, contact information, a picture, and department information. If you had a company with hundreds of employees, you'd have to create hundreds of HTML pages with the same basic layout, but each page would have different information.

### Internet, Intranet, and Extranet

You know the Internet to be a massive communication network based on standard protocols, on which the Web is just one application. An intranet is nothing more than a private Internet in which security is usually critical and Web sites are behind a secure firewall. An extranet is a hybrid of the two, a private intranet that also allows secure log-in access to people outside the company, such as customers and vendors.

## Those static HTML Web pages

A Web site is considered static when the only way the pages change is by *manually altering* the HTML and text. The players in this game are the Web server and the Web browser. The process that the Web uses to retrieve and display HTML pages is as follows:

1. The user requests the page by typing a URL in a browser, clicking on a link, or submitting a form.

2. The browser requests an HTML page (.htm or .html extension) from the Web server, using HTTP (Hypertext Transfer Protocol).

3. The Web server sends the page to the browser in the form of HTML.

4. The browser interprets the HTML and displays the page to the user. The browser may also interpret certain client-side scripting languages, such as JavaScript.

**WHAT CAN HTML DO?**

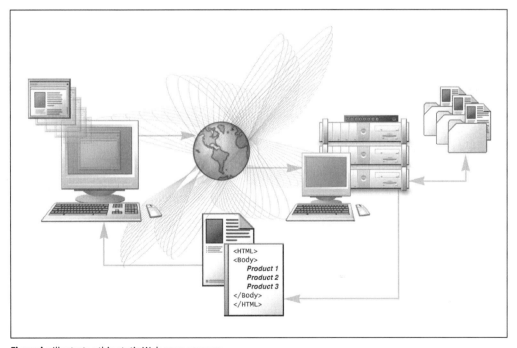

**Figure i.1** Illustrates this static Web page process.

# What Are These Sexy Web Applications?

In the previous example about an employee intranet, imagine instead that you had a database that contained a listing of all employees and their related information. This database may be maintained from another internal application, or may be maintained through a different Web application. You want to leverage the existing database to display information about each employee on your Web site in real-time. Also, you wanted each user to be securely connected by logging in and salary information displayed only for direct managers and HR employees to see (**Figure i.2**). Each of these requirements for a Web application is called a business rule, or business logic.

Connecting to a database and displaying database data, as well as any type of conditional display of information, exceeds the capabilities of a static Web site and requires a dynamic Web application. The site is dynamic because not only can it create each employee page on the fly, but it can use information from the database when the page is requested—and can change when the database changes.

## Enter stage right: Application servers

When you take the static HTML page environment and add an application server, you can introduce dynamic elements into your pages—be it programming logic and/or database connectivity. HTML cannot do either of these, so you need a programming language to help you.

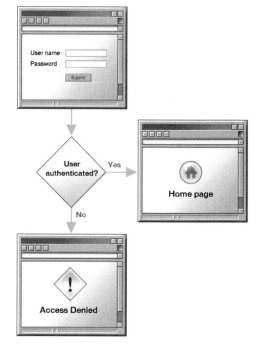

**Figure i.2** Web applications can perform programming logic, such as user authentication.

This is where the generic term of application server enters the scene. An application server is a piece of software that is installed and connected to the Web server. This application server is invoked whenever the Web server deems it needs to process a requested file (based on the file extension) and processes the business logic programmed into the requested page.

## Dynamic application server pages

When you add an application server into the mix, the process for serving Web pages changes to the following steps:

1. The user requests the page by typing a URL in a browser.

2. The browser requests the page from the Web server using HTTP (Hypertext Transfer Protocol).

*continues on next page*

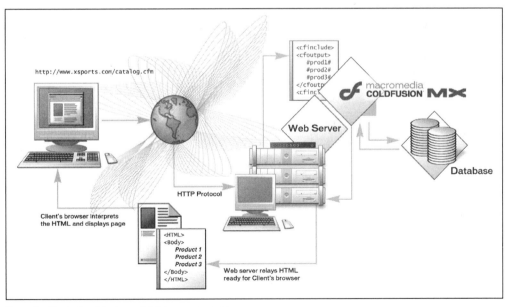

**Figure i.3** Illustrates this dynamic Web page process.

3. The Web server detects that the page is dynamic and passes the page to the application server for processing. In most cases, the Web server recognizes a page that needs to be processed by the extension of the page. It is not usually named with a .htm or .html extension.

4. The application server takes the page and searches it for work to do—performing programming logic or database connectivity.

5. The application server resolves all the work it has to do and sends back an HTML page to the Web server.

6. The Web server sends the page to the browser in the form of HTML.

7. The browser interprets the HTML and displays the page to the user. The browser can also interpret certain scripting languages, such as JavaScript.

## Enter ColdFusion MX

An earlier section defined a Web application and an application server. ColdFusion MX is one such application server. ColdFusion has proven to be a fast, efficient, secure, and highly scalable platform on which to build Web applications. And indeed, tens of thousands of organizations and hundreds of thousands of developers worldwide use ColdFusion every day to help shape the future of the Web.

Macromedia ColdFusion MX is a commercial product and comes in three versions:

◆ ColdFusion MX Server Professional Edition

◆ ColdFusion MX Server Enterprise Edition

◆ Macromedia ColdFusion MX for J2EE Application Servers

### J2EE Application Servers

Java 2 Enterprise Edition (J2EE) application servers allow organizations to develop large-scale web applications, usually for mission critical functions. These systems are fast and stable, but usually quite expensive. If your organization has already implemented such a system, you can use Macromedia ColdFusion MX for J2EE Application Servers to develop ColdFusion application that will run within that environment.

## The language of ColdFusion

ColdFusion pages are named with a .cfm extension, unlike html, which usually ends with .htm or .html. CFML (ColdFusion Markup Language) lets you create dynamic Web pages. The CFML tags signal the ColdFusion MX application server to perform specific operations. Each tag identifies a particular operation, such as setting a variable, running a database query, outputting results, or including a block of code from another file. CFML tags can be freely mixed with HTML tags in the page (**Figure i.4**).

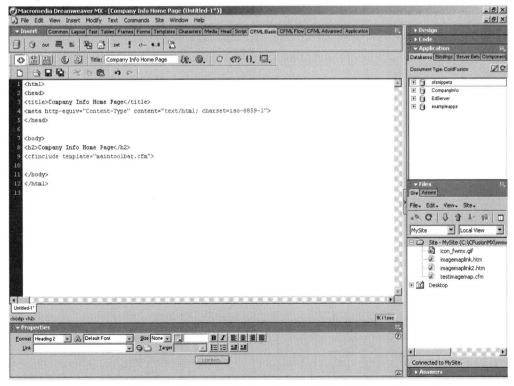

**Figure i.4** ColdFusion tags all begin with the letters cf and look very much like HTML tags. This <cfinclude> tag includes the toolbar on this page when it is requested—thus allowing the same toolbar to be included on many pages but maintained in just one place.

## The advantages of ColdFusion

Despite all that power, ColdFusion's claim to fame has always been ease of use. ColdFusion is so easy to learn that most users are writing code in hours, not in days, weeks, or months. With each successive version, ColdFusion becomes even more powerful and even easier to use.

There are many reasons to use ColdFusion MX:

◆ Intuitive server scripting

◆ Short learning curve

◆ Powerful server-side features

◆ Performance and scalability

◆ Support for open standards, including J2EE and .NET

# What Did MX Do to Dreamweaver?

Macromedia Dreamweaver MX is a combined collaboration of the renowned visual layout tools of Dreamweaver 4, the code generation features of Dreamweaver Ultradev 4, and the rapid application development environment for code-editing support using Macromedia HomeSite.

## The power of Dreamweaver MX

For the first time, every member of your development team—designers, developers, and programmers—can work in a single integrated environment to create, build, and manage Web sites and Internet applications. The code generation features of Dreamweaver MX can help you to create ColdFusion pages quickly and can gently help you understand the programming language of CFML when you're ready for it.

Some of the powerful features are listed below:

◆ Flexible workspace that is extensible and customizable

◆ Site setup wizard

◆ Enhanced templates

◆ Supercharged CSS

◆ Layout/code quick-starts

◆ Accessibility for disadvantaged users, as per Section 508 compliance

◆ Code hints and precise code control

◆ Tag editors for HTML, CFML, ASP.NET, PHP, and JSP

## Code Editors Versus Visual Editors

Code editors are tools used to create and edit Web pages. They enable you to write HTML and "get in the code," because every tag is composed by hand. Code editors don't conceal the code, but present it to you as you edit. There are many different general-purpose editors on the market, including simple word processing programs and even Notepad.

Visual editors are code-scripting tools used to create Web pages. Unlike code editors, visual editors separate you from the HTML and eliminate the need for working directly in the source code. They also provide you with tools to make your Web page development easy. For example, common visual editor tools let you drag and drop elements, like images, on a page and generate the underlying HTML code. Dreamweaver MX is a visual editor, but also has a sophisticated code editing view to give you the best of both approaches to creating HTML.

## The power of RAD

Dreamweaver offers server behaviors and application objects, both rapid application development (RAD) tools. These can help you build sophisticated Web applications without having to write much, if any, server-side code. RAD tools include, but are not limited to, the following list:

◆ Information display pages, which enable you to display data from database tables at the time the browser requests that page.

◆ Master/Detail pages, which organize and display database data in a clickable, drill-down format.

◆ Search pages, which allow you to create interfaces so that users can find the data they need—and not more than they need—in the database.

◆ Insert and update pages, which allow you to insert new information into database tables and update existing rows.

◆ Security constructs, which allow you to build pages that are secure and require a user log in.

## Cross-platform issues

Dreamweaver MX runs on both the Macintosh and Windows operating systems. However, ColdFusion MX runs only on Windows and specific Unix systems, such as Linux. For this reason, the configuration for developing and testing pages is different for each platform, and we address those differences in this book. Also, we identify the differences in mouse actions, in menus, and in the workspace environment you will be working in. This book points out each step for both the Macintosh and Windows platforms when they differ.

# Who Should Read This Book?

Web designers, Web developers and application programmers can now use Dreamweaver MX. Web designers work in HTML and graphically layout and design the pages and images.

If you've purchased this book (or are evaluating it for purchase), then you probably have created HTML pages, either with a visual development environment like Dreamweaver or a coding-centric vision of HomeSite. You have a strong knowledge of HTML and can create Web pages, understanding the interaction between the Web server and the Web browser. You've created enough static pages to be bored by them and annoyed by the level of administrative support you have to give to the pages and sites that you have created. You may have little to no programming experience, but having some certainly is helpful to have as you read this book.

This book introduces novice to seasoned Web designers to the application-programming world of ColdFusion by using the code generation features of Dreamweaver MX.

# How Should You Use This Book?

Like all Visual QuickStart Guides, this book takes you out of simply reading and into creating ColdFusion pages with Dreamweaver MX as soon as possible. The book uses straightforward language and step-by-step instructions to complete common tasks of Web application developers, without a lot of background noise. Whenever possible, we make each task or set of tasks independent of others so that, after you set up your initial environment, you can jump to a specific task that you are interested in performing. If you want to be thorough, you can also read this book from cover to cover, but you should be able to jump into a task that you need to perform.

This book uses the following elements to help you navigate this book easily:

◆ Tips help you get extra information about a task you are performing.

◆ Sidebars are useful and (hopefully) interesting information that relates to the topic, but you may skip them if you want to move right to the task at hand.

◆ Numbered steps help you complete tasks in a no-nonsense manner.

◆ Information that you are requested to type is shown in bold.

## Files and Folders

Since this book is designed so that you can jump into a specific task instead of reading each chapter sequentially, we do not get too specific on naming your files nor advocating a folder structure for your web application. It is recommended, however, that you plan the structure of your web application folders before you get started writing code. While working through this book you may wish to create a subfolder for each chapter, so you can return to those files at a later time to refresh

your knowledge. If you store all your work in one folder, be sure to name each file uniquely so you do not overwrite your previous work.

## Section I: CFML code generation

The first section of this book is an introduction to ColdFusion programming by showing off the rapid interface development capabilities of Dreamweaver MX to build commonly used interfaces for dynamic data on the Web. You will do very little, if any, actual coding; Dreamweaver MX generates all the code for you.

## Section II: Gentle CFML hand-coding

As you become more comfortable with the environment and with ColdFusion, the second part of this book gently introduces you to the Code view of a ColdFusion developer so you can expand your knowledge and build more robust Web applications.

## Appendix

In the appendix, you learn about installing both Dreamweaver MX and ColdFusion MX. Dreamweaver MX may be installed on either Windows or Macintosh operating system machines. ColdFusion MX can be installed only on Windows machines.

## ColdFusion MX Development with Dreamweaver MX: Visual Quickstart Guide Web site

The companion Web site for this book contains example applications, database files, CSV files, errata, reviews, buying, links to useful resources, and more.

Visit
http://www.forta.com/books/0321158024

# GETTING STARTED

Before you generate Macromedia ColdFusion pages, you need to set up your Macromedia Dreamweaver MX environment. In this chapter, you launch Dreamweaver, perhaps for the first time, and select the workspace layout of Dreamweaver when you're using Windows.

Next, all work in Dreamweaver begins with creating a site. Easy-to-use site creation wizards can help you define the startup information about your site.

After you define your site, you're ready to start building Web pages. This chapter shows you how to create pages based on templates, introduces you to a way to "paint" your pages in Design view, and takes you all the way through saving and browsing your pages. When you get this process of page creation and editing down, you can create all your Web site pages.

# Launching Dreamweaver

Launching Dreamweaver on Windows computers for the first time is a different experience than launching Dreamweaver on Macintosh computers. Starting with Dreamweaver MX, there is a new look and feel on Windows computers to the workspace, the environment you work in.

For Windows users, Dreamweaver has three different views available to work in, as shown in **Figure 1.1**. For Macintosh users, only the Dreamweaver 4 workspace is available, and thus this dialog does not appear on first use.

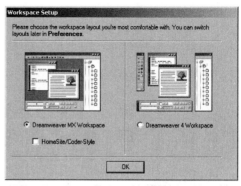

**Figure 1.1** The Dreamweaver MX Workspace has three Setup options in Windows.

## To choose an initial workspace in Windows:

◆ Choose Dreamweaver MX Workspace for an all-in-one workspace with grouped and docked panels on the right of the interface (**Figure 1.2**).

   *or*

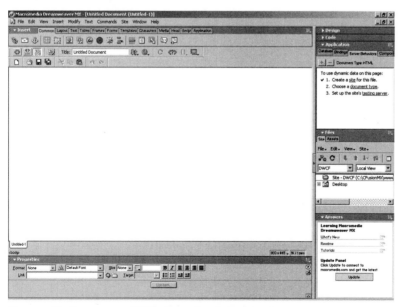

**Figure 1.2** The Dreamweaver MX Workspace has docked panels.

LAUNCHING DREAMWEAVER

**Figure 1.4** The Dreamweaver 4 Workspace has floating panels.

◆ Choose Dreamweaver MX Workspace and the HomeSite/Coder-Style checkbox for a workspace with grouped and docked panels on the left side and with Code view as the initial view (**Figure 1.3**).

*or*

◆ Choose Dreamweaver 4 Workspace for a floating workspace with floating panels (**Figure 1.4**).

## ✔ Tip

■ Why does Dreamweaver offer three different workspace options and which would appeal most to you? Dreamweaver 4 functionality was combined with ColdFusion Studio, the powerful code-editing environment chosen by ColdFusion developers. Experienced ColdFusion developers might be most comfortable with the MX workspace and Homesite/Coder-style interface. However, new users to either Dreamweaver MX or ColdFusion MX would benefit from the MX workspace because it's friendlier to beginner developers.

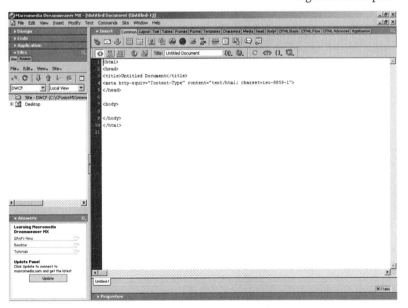

**Figure 1.3** The Dreamweaver MX Workspace with the HomeSite/Coder-Style option has docked panels, but they are in the left side of the interface and the initial view is Code view.

**LAUNCHING DREAMWEAVER**

**3**

# Changing the Workspace

After you've worked in Dreamweaver a bit, you may decide that you've chosen the wrong type of workspace; another type may be more comfortable or more productive for you. Changing the workspace is not difficult.

## To change your workspace in Windows:

1. Choose Edit > Preferences to change the workspace you've selected to another one (**Figure 1.5**).

2. In the Preferences dialog, select the General category, and then, in Document Options, click the Change Workspace button.

   Dreamweaver opens the Workspace Setup dialog.

3. Change your workspace selection.

4. Click OK.

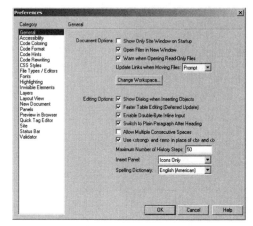

**Figure 1.5** Use the General panel of the Preferences dialog to change your workspace.

**Figure 1.6** Each Web site will have a root folder, in which all files and subfolders will reside.

# Creating a Site in Dreamweaver

All pages that you create have to be part of a site. A site, as defined in Dreamweaver, is a folder that contains all the subfolders and files that make up a Web site.

A root folder is the top-level directory of a Web site. This folder will contain all related subfolders and files. Each Web site will have its own root folder, as depicted in **Figure 1.6**. After you have created a site, you can view the folder structure of your site in the Site panel.

If you are running Dreamweaver on a Macintosh, you must install ColdFusion on a Windows computer in order to develop and test your pages. Create your root directory under the Webroot on the Windows computer. See the Appendix for more information about installing ColdFusion.

If you do not already have a folder with the files you plan on putting on a Web site, then you can allow Dreamweaver to create the root folder for you as part of the site creation process.

## Webroot Location

When you create your root folder for your Web site, you must take care to create it in a directory that is accessible by your Web server. All Web site software has a folder known as the Webroot. The Webroot is the central location of all Web sites on a computer (by default).

For the built-in Web server that comes with ColdFusion, which is the assumed configuration in this book, the default Webroot is C:\CFusionMX\wwwroot.

## To define a new Web site:

1. In Dreamweaver, choose Site > New Site. The Site Definition dialog appears.

2. If the Basic tab is not already selected, click it to begin using the Site Definition wizard (**Figure 1.7**).

3. In the text box, assign a unique name that encompasses the meaning of the Web site.

   We are setting the name of the site to DWCF to represent the site files created in this book. Dreamweaver will use the name of the site as a default root folder name in a subsequent step.

4. Click Next.

   The Editing Files, Part 2 panel appears (**Figure 1.8**).

5. Select the Yes radio button to indicate you will use a server technology, and, from the drop-down menu, select ColdFusion as the server technology you will use.

6. Click Next.

   Editing Files, Part 3 prompts you to choose how you want to work with files during development.

7. Select one of the editing options.

   ▲ On a Windows computer, select the Edit and test locally option.

   *or*

   ▲ On the Macintosh, select the Edit directly on remote testing server using local network option.

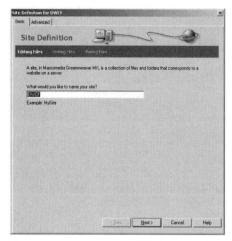

**Figure 1.7** Use the Basic tab of the Site Definition wizard to begin to define your Web site.

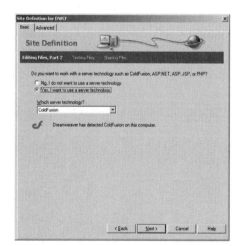

**Figure 1.8** Select your server technology in the Editing Files, Part 2 panel.

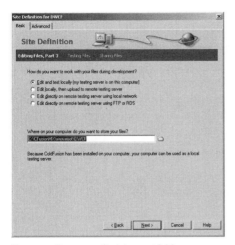

**Figure 1.9** Browse to find the root folder.

**Figure 1.10** Test the URL to ensure you can access your Web server.

**Figure 1.11** If your site fails the testing of the URL, check that your Web server is installed correctly and is running.

**8.** If you already have a root folder for your Web site, browse to find your root folder.

If you want Dreamweaver to create the root folder for you, either accept the default folder name (taken from the site name) and move through the wizard, or change the name of the root folder and continue (**Figure 1.9**).

**9.** Click Next.

The Testing Files panel prompts you to input the URL to the root of your Web site.

**10.** Enter the URL to your computer by doing one of the following:

▲ On a Windows computer, type

`http://localhost:8500/dwcf`

where *dwcf* is the name of the root folder you created.

▲ On a Macintosh, type

`http://servername:8500/dwcf`

You cannot specify *localhost* as the Web server, since your ColdFusion application server resides on a remote Windows computer.

**11.** Click the Test URL button to ensure that you can access your Web server.

When you are successful, you receive the message shown in **Figure 1.10**.

When you are unsuccessful, you receive the error message shown in **Figure 1.11**. This error means that you cannot connect to your Web server and that it is not functioning properly. Please refer to the appendix for more information on installation.

**12.** After the Web server URL tests successfully, click OK.

*continues on next page*

CREATING A SITE IN DREAMWEAVER

**13.** Click Next.

The next section of the wizard on Windows (for a local setup) prompts you to indicate whether you'd like to use a remote testing server (**Figure 1.12**). Macintosh users editing files remotely using the local network will find this step is skipped.

**14.** Select the No radio button and click Next.

The summary of options displays (**Figure 1.13**).

**15.** Click Done.

**16.** View your site and files in the Site panel. (If this panel is not displayed, choose Window > Site.)

The Site panel shows the new local root folder for your current site and the integrated file browser for viewing all your local and networked disks (**Figure 1.14**).

## ✔ Tips

■ If you cannot test the URL with *localhost* (http://*localhost*:8500/*dwcf*), try replacing *localhost* with 127.0.0.1 or the actual name of the server.

■ To revisit your site settings, choose Site > Edit Sites and select the site to modify.

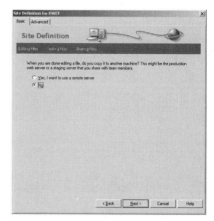

**Figure 1.12** Specify a remote server.

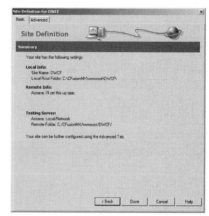

**Figure 1.13** A summary of setup options are displayed so you can go back and change them if you wish.

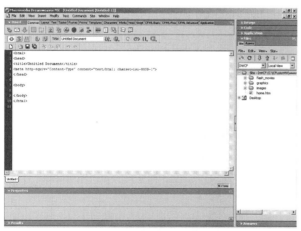

**Figure 1.14** The Site panel displays all sites and all folders and files within a site.

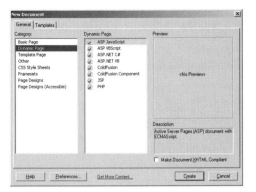

**Figure 1.15** When you select the Dynamic Page category, the section to the right changes.

# Creating Your First Page

Now that you have a site defined, you are ready to start developing your first Web page. The process of creating a Web site page is to create a new document; insert text, links, and images CFML tags; title the page; save it; and then test it by browsing to it. You can use this iterative process for creating all your Web pages.

## To create a new page:

**1.** Choose File > New.

The New Document dialog appears.

**2.** In the General tab of the New Document dialog (**Figure 1.15**), select the Dynamic Page category.

The middle section of the dialog changes to Dynamic Page.

**3.** In the Dynamic Page section of the New Document dialog, select ColdFusion and click Create.

## The Types of Servers

Dreamweaver defines three types of servers when it comes to sites:

◆ **Local servers** contain files that individual Web site developers create on their computers. Macintosh computers cannot have ColdFusion installed, and thus developers using those computers will not be able to test their pages locally.

◆ **Testing servers** are centralized computers on which teams of developers can upload their files that are part of a bigger Web site. This server must have ColdFusion installed so that files can be tested.

◆ **Remote servers** are the live servers on which Internet users or a company's intranet users can surf the final Web pages in the site. Dreamweaver helps you to automatically upload files and create folders on the remote server.

CREATING YOUR FIRST PAGE

## To title and save your page:

1. Select the text Untitled Document in the Title text box of the Document toolbar (**Figure 1.16**).

   If you don't see the Document toolbar, choose View > Toolbars > Document.

2. Type a new, meaningful name for the page, such as **DWCF Home Page**.

3. Choose File > Save and select the location for this file under the site root folder.

   All ColdFusion pages must have a .cfm extension. Because you've chosen Cold-Fusion as your application server, Dream-weaver automatically assigns a .cfm extension when you omit an extension.

## ✔ Tips

- ■ Always name each page. A page title primarily identifies a document and is displayed in the browser's title bar and as the bookmark or favorite name.

- ■ It is best to name your files in lowercase, just in case you are using (or will use in the future) a Web server on a Unix computer, which is case-sensitive. Also, do not use spaces or special characters and do not begin your page name with a number—use letters, numbers, and the underscore character.

CREATING YOUR FIRST PAGE

## Connection Strategies

Dreamweaver offers four different ways to develop your Web site pages:

- ◆ **Edit and test locally** allows you to build your pages on your personal computer. You can use this option only if you have ColdFusion MX locally installed so that you can test your pages.

- ◆ **Edit locally and upload to a remote server** allows you to develop locally and then deploy to a remote server when you request it.

- ◆ **Edit directly on remote server using a local network connection** allows you to bypass storing files locally and saves all files on the remote computer.

- ◆ **Edit directly on remote server using FTP** (File Transfer Protocol) **or RDS** (Remote Development Service) allows you to save your files on a remote computer using the FTP or the RDS, which is unique to ColdFusion.

**Figure 1.16** Set the title of the page in the Document toolbar.

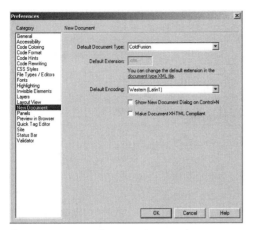

**Figure 1.17** To set preferences when creating a new document, use the Preferences dialog and the New Document category.

# Setting Document Preferences

There are two settings that you might find useful for creating new documents. One preference is to set the default document type when you choose to create a new document (the default is HTML). The second is to bypass the New Document dialog when creating a new page. This way, when using Ctrl+N (Windows) or Command+N (Macintosh) keyboard shortcuts you will not have to view and accept the document type.

### To set new document preferences:

1. Open the preferences window.
   - ▲ In Windows, choose Edit > Preferences.

   *or*

   - ▲ On a Macintosh OS X operating system, choose Dreamweaver > Preferences.

2. In the Category list on the left, select New Document (**Figure 1.17**).

3. Drop down the Default Document Type menu and select ColdFusion.

4. Uncheck the option Show New Document Dialog on Control+N (Windows) or Command+N (Macintosh).

5. Click OK.

## Home Pages

Every Web server uses the concept of a home page: names of pages that are registered with the Web server to be detected automatically and served when a user browses to the directory housing those pages. By default, Microsoft Internet Information Server (IIS) uses a page name of default.htm. You can use your Web server administration tools to add other file names. Typical home pages for ColdFusion applications are home.cfm and index.cfm.

# Testing Your Page

In any type of programming environment, it's always best to iteratively develop and test your pages. Testing frequently allows you to test smaller parts of your pages, which makes finding problems easier.

You will want to test using any browser type that you expect your users to have. Dreamweaver helps you as you develop your pages to ensure they are compatible across different browsers and versions.

In Preferences, you can specify which browsers you would like to use to preview your pages. To simplify the preview process, Dreamweaver has keyboard shortcuts for viewing your pages in two different browsers, called the primary and secondary browsers, although you can specify many different preview browsers.

One additional preference setting that is required for any dynamically processed page is to turn off the use of temporary files for browsing. This requires that all ColdFusion pages be saved prior to testing in a browser.

## To set browser preferences:

1. Specify preview browsers.

   ▲ In Windows, choose Edit > Preferences.

   *or*

   ▲ On a Macintosh OS X operating system, choose Dreamweaver > Preferences.

2. In the Category list on the left, select Preview in Browser (**Figure 1.18**).

   Dreamweaver displays a Preview in Browser section on the right side of the dialog.

3. In the Preview in Browser section, click the plus (+) button to add a browser to the list.

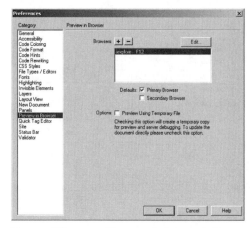

**Figure 1.18** You can set browser preferences in the Preferences dialog by using the Preview in Browser category.

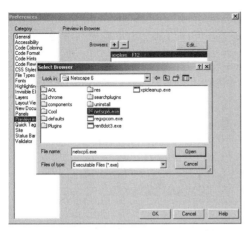

**Figure 1.19** Browse to find the executable file for the browser you wish to register.

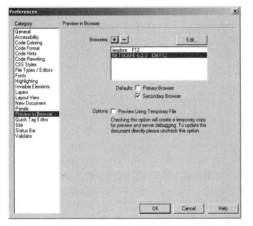

**Figure 1.20** After you select the browser executable, you will see the browser in the list.

**4.** In the Add Browser dialog, click Browse (Windows) or Choose (Macintosh) to find the browser application (**Figure 1.19**).

**5.** Specify the status of the browser.

Select the Primary Browser checkbox to enable the shortcut of pressing F12 to launch this browser when previewing your pages.

Select the Secondary Browser checkbox to enable the shortcut of pressing Ctrl+F12 (Window) or Command+F12 (Macintosh) to launch this browser.

**6.** Be sure the Preview Using Temporary File option is unchecked.

**7.** Click OK.

You will see the browser registered (**Figure 1.20**).

### ✔ Tips

- Dreamweaver attempts to automatically detect and register your primary browser, so you may not have to select this browser upon first use.

- Unlike static HTML pages, pages that contain dynamic elements such as ColdFusion tags must be saved prior to browsing.

- You can directly edit the browser list by selecting File > Preview in Browser > Edit Browser List.

TESTING YOUR PAGE

## To browse your page:

1. Choose File > Preview in Browser.

2. Select a browser from the submenu
   (**Figure 1.21**).

## ✔ Tips

■ You can also select the preview browsers
by pressing F12 for the primary browser
or Ctrl+F12 (Window) or Command+F12
(Macintosh) for the secondary browser.

■ You can use the globe icon on the
Document toolbar to quickly browse
your pages as well. If you do not see your
Document toolbar, choose View >
Toolbars > Document to toggle it on.

■ You can define up to 20 browsers, all
accessible from the Preview in Browser
menu.

■ It's a good idea to preview in the
browsers that you expect, or minimally
in Microsoft Internet Explorer 4.0,
Netscape Navigator 4.0, and at least
one text-only browser, such as Lynx.

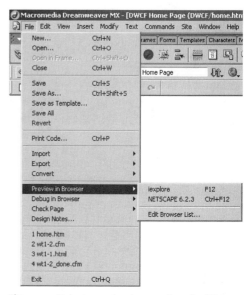

**Figure 1.21** Select a preview browser by using File >
Preview in Browser.

# DATA SOURCES

A ColdFusion MX application can have many different sources of data to generate dynamic pages. Information can come from simple text files as well as very organized, enterprise-level relational databases. These data sources are the backbone of a Web application.

This chapter introduces you to the types of data sources with which ColdFusion can communicate. The chapter also gives you an overview of the most common form of data source—the relational database. While ColdFusion makes it easy to learn how to use database data and Dreamweaver makes it even easier to create data-driven ColdFusion pages, you must still have some basic knowledge about relational database concepts and techniques.

The language of a relational database is SQL (Structured Query Language). Therefore, in this chapter you will also learn the basics of using SQL to communicate with a database.

# Understanding ColdFusion Data Sources

A data source is simply a set of structured information that ColdFusion can connect to, get information from, and perhaps write information into. ColdFusion can connect to a variety of data sources (**Figure 2.1**). Sources of data can include, but are not limited to:

◆ Text files

◆ Excel spreadsheets

◆ Relational databases

◆ LDAP (Lightweight Directory Access Protocol) directories

◆ Verity document collections

By far the most common source of data is the relational database.

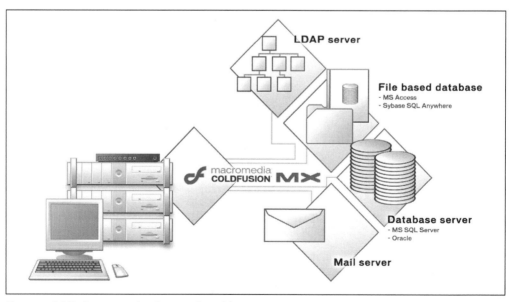

**Figure 2.1** ColdFusion can get data from a variety of data sources.

## Relational database management systems

You may have heard of an RDBMS, or DBMS. *RDBMS* stands for the Relational Database Management System. The *relational database* is really only a concept, and RDBMS is the software that allows you to create and manage physical databases. There are several software vendors that have their own version of a relational database. Some of the RDBMS software vendors are

◆ Oracle

◆ Sybase

◆ IBM's DB2

◆ Microsoft's SQL Server

Microsoft also has a flat-file database, Access, which can emulate a relational database in most cases. As far as ColdFusion is concerned, each of these databases supply information and can accept information using the same language, SQL, which we will discuss later in this chapter. For the most part, each of these databases looks the same to ColdFusion.

UNDERSTANDING COLDFUSION DATA SOURCES

# Understanding Relational Databases

A database is an organized collection of data, like a file cabinet that stores information in an orderly fashion. In the case of databases, however, the information is stored electronically and not in paper form. Databases exist solely to manage data.

## Database elements

Relational databases are made up of a collection of information vital to an organization. Some characteristics and terms regarding relational databases are these:

◆ Databases are made up of one or more related tables (**Figure 2.2**).

◆ Each table stores information about one "thing," be it a person, place, event, idea—any object. For example, if you were selling products on the Web, you might have a table to hold product information (**Figure 2.3**).

◆ Tables consist of information that describes the object and that information is stored in columns and rows of data. The Product table contains a row for each product and three pieces of information (columns) about each product (**Figure 2.4**).

◆ Each table must have a column or set of columns that uniquely identifies every row; this unique identity is known as the primary key (**Figure 2.5**). The primary key is usually a sequential number that is system-generated each time you input a row of data.

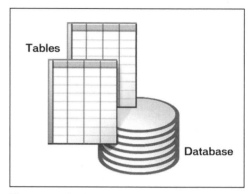

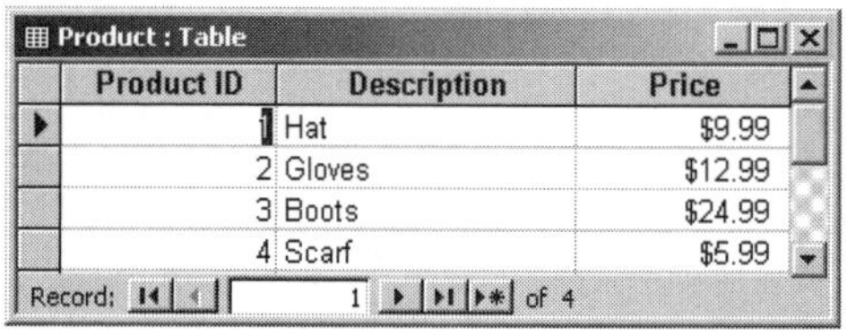

**Figure 2.2** A database contains a set of related tables.

**Figure 2.3** Each table contains information about one object, here a Product.

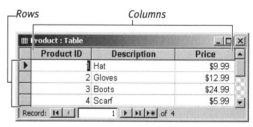

**Figure 2.4** Each table contains information in rows and columns.

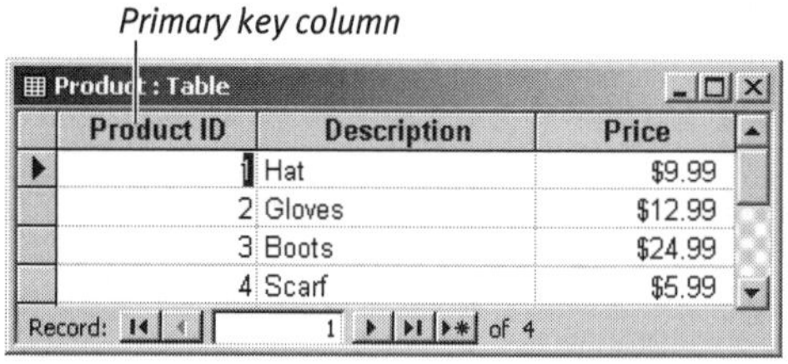

**Figure 2.5** Each table must have a column or set of columns that make each row unique—known as the primary key—here a sequential ProductID.

**Figure 2.6** A Product is obtained through a Supplier—both tables are created to store this information.

| Suppliers : Table | | | |
|---|---|---|---|
| **Supplier ID** | **Supplier Name** | **Contact Name** | **Phone Numbe** |
| 1 | Bernie's Hats | Bernie Bernard | (800) 555-1212 |
| 2 | Sue's Outdoor Gear | Sue Howe | (610) 555-1938 |

Record: 1 of 2

| Product : Table | | | |
|---|---|---|---|
| **Product ID** | **Description** | **Price** | **SupplierID** |
| 1 | Hat | $9.99 | 1 |
| 2 | Gloves | $12.99 | 2 |
| 3 | Boots | $24.99 | 2 |
| 4 | Scarf | $5.99 | 2 |

Record: 5 of 5

**Figure 2.7** Because a Product can be supplied through only one Supplier, the SupplierID is copied into the Product table.

## Learning more

This book covers how to access and use databases, but not how to create them. We are trying to give you an idea of why they exist and how they might have been created. Getting an expert to design your database tables is key to any successful application that's driven by database data.

## Relational data

Most people are now familiar with storing information into spreadsheets that contain rows and columns of data. This is very similar to data stored in a database. The difference between spreadsheets and databases and what makes a database relational is that commonly repeated values are usually grouped and broken off into additional smaller tables. The resulting tables are then related to each other through the use of keys, which are unique values that identify each row in a table. This process, called *normalization*, allows databases to store more information in less space and to function more quickly.

For example, perhaps you want to store information about the manufacturer who supplies each product. A manufacturer is an object in its own right—it has an address, a contact name, and phone number—all information that you may need to get in touch with the supplier. A relational database sets this up as two objects—a Product and a Supplier (**Figure 2.6**).

Assuming each product can be supplied through only one manufacturer, the relationship is created by migrating the SupplierID into the Product table to create the relationship (**Figure 2.7**). This relationship supports the business rules of:

- A Product can have only one Supplier (one SupplierID) but must have a supplier specified.

- A Supplier can supply many Products.

This example illustrates a one-to-many relationship, the most common relationship found in relational databases. In a one-to-many relationship, the primary key from the "one" table (here Supplier) is copied into the "many" table (here Product) to enforce the relationship. Each time you want a product, you can simply get the SupplierID and look up the rest of the supplier information. The SupplierID column in the Product table is known as a foreign key. Separating these two entities enables you to remove the redundancies of supplier information that would occur if that information was put into each product record.

## ✔ Tip

- In this example, the primary key columns are named for the table and an ID suffix, meaning that they are sequential numbers. You do not have to name the corresponding foreign key the same, but it's helpful to determine relationships for application developers.

## The role of columns

Each piece of product information, such as the name, description, and price, is stored in a separate column in the table. A column, by design, must contain only one piece of information. In the Supplier table, for example, the address can be broken up into many bits of information, such as the following:

- Address line 1

- Address line 2

- City

- State

- ZIP code

Having all those bits of information in a single column is not considered good design for a database column.

## Breaking up data

You should separate information into individual pieces so that you can retrieve that information later on. For instance, you might want to retrieve all patients in one city or in a particular state. If this information were stored together in one column, retrieving the individual pieces would be very difficult, if not impossible. Also, you may want to display information in sorted order, such as by state, which would be very difficult if it were all stored together.

Each column has an associated datatype. A *datatype* defines what type of data the column can contain. For example, a product price should be a valid monetary value and not just any value. You can restrict the type of data for the product price column by specifying the correct datatype.

Different DBMSs have different data types, but the main ones are textual values, numbers, dates, currency, and automatically-generated numbers. Check the documentation for your DBMS to find out what datatypes it supports.

# Looking at SQL

When ColdFusion pulls information from a data source, or pushes information into a data source, it uses SQL. SQL, which stands for Structured Query Language, is a language designed specifically for communicating with databases. Standard SQL is governed by the ANSI standards committee and is thus called ANSI SQL.

The SQL language is made up of three types of statements:

- **Data definition**, which allows you to create objects in a database, such as database tables.

- **Data manipulation**, which allows you to retrieve, insert, modify, and remove information from a table or set of tables.

- **Data control**, which allows you to set permissions for the database or for individual tables and columns.

In this book, we concentrate only on data manipulation statements. With these statements, you can maintain the data in your database using ColdFusion applications. The four main data manipulation statements in SQL are:

- **INSERT** for inserting a row into a table

- **SELECT** for retrieving a row or rows from a table or set of tables

- **UPDATE** for updating a row or rows into a table

- **DELETE** for deleting a row or rows from a table

The most common operation in a Web application is to query and retrieve data from a database table for display on a Web page. A simple **SELECT** statement to retrieve all rows from the Product table is shown below:

```
SELECT ProductID, Description, Price
→ FROM Product
```

To merge together the Product and Supplier tables to form a complete result of each Product and its Supplier, you would have to add the Supplier table to the **FROM** clause, and specify how the tables are joined together in a **WHERE** clause, as in the following:

```
SELECT SupplierName ProductID,
→ Description, Price
FROM Product, Supplier
WHERE Supplier.SupplierID =
→ Product.SupplierID
```

You will be learning about each of these types of statements in upcoming chapters, when you need them.

## ANSI SQL

ANSI (American National Standards Institute) is the main organization for fostering the development of technology standards in the United States. One such standard is for SQL. All major RDBMS' support ANSI SQL but may have extensions to the language specifically for their RDBMS. These extensions make each system a little different to use, especially when implementing their advanced features. As you learn more about SQL and your database, you may want to check your documentation to find out what types of advanced features it offers.

# Choosing a Database

There are many different sources of data from which you can choose once you start to create your ColdFusion applications. The easiest solution is to take an existing repository of data and connect your ColdFusion application to it. However, if you do not currently have the data in electronic format, if you're looking to move it from a file or spreadsheet into a better performing relational database, you will want to carefully search to find the right database for the job.

## Starting with a file

If you're just starting out and you want a database that is quick and easy to set up, your natural choice probably is Microsoft Access, which comes installed with Microsoft Office Professional. Access allows you to "paint" database tables quickly and easily using graphical tools. Access is just one of several file-based databases that you can choose from; dBase Plus is another option.

Some benefits of using a file-based database such as Access include:

◆ Creating tables and relationships is quick and relatively easy.

◆ Getting information into these databases is made easy through the creation of forms, as well as import features to get information from a wide variety of data sources.

◆ Databases are files, which can be more easily moved to other machines.

◆ Getting access to the database is easy, as login information usually goes through a single login.

### Getting More Information

Here is a list of URLs to find out more information about the databases discussed here.

◆ DB2:
http://www3.ibm.com/software/data/db2/

◆ Oracle:
http://www.oracle.com/ip/deploy/database/oracle9i/

◆ Microsoft Access and SQL Server:
http://www.microsoft.com

◆ MySQL:
http://www.mysql.com/

◆ Sybase:
http://www.sybase.com/products/databaseservers

◆ Informix:
http://www3.ibm.com/software/data/informix/ids

# When it's time to upsize

You know it's time to find a new database solution when you have a concern about one or more of the following issues:

◆ **Performance**. When traffic on your Web site increases substantially and many users are attempting to access the database at the same time, Microsoft Access may incur errors as well as performance problems.

◆ **Scalability**. When data requires more than two gigabytes of storage space, it has outgrown the size of an acceptable Microsoft Access database. Even before two gigabytes, response time may not be acceptable in the Web environment.

◆ **Availability**.When visitors to your site experience interruptions in service, consider upsizing. Access databases are files; therefore, any maintenance on them, such as backups, interrupt service to your Web users. Backups must be performed while no users are using the database.

◆ **Security**. Because Access is a file, it can be easier to hack into it than into a real relational database, which first obtains authentication from the server before anyone can use it.

◆ **Recoverability**. File-based databases have one major limitation: if your system crashes, all changes are lost since the last full copy of the file. Most relational databases, on the other hand, have elaborate checkpoints where you can perform backups of critical information.

# Upsizing to a server-based RDBMS

Once you've made a decision to upsize to a real relational database, you have several popular vendors to choose from, with varying degrees of support for the above five concerns. Popular vendors include the following:

◆ IBM's DB2

◆ Oracle

◆ Microsoft's SQL Server

◆ MySQL AB's MySQL

◆ Sybase

◆ IBM's Informix

CHOOSING A DATABASE

# CONNECTING TO A DATABASE

**3**

A ColdFusion MX application can have many different sources of data from which to generate dynamic pages. Information can come from simple text files as well as very organized, enterprise-level relational databases. These data sources are the backbone of a Web application.

Dreamweaver MX enables you to browse your database information from within its Databases panel. Dreamweaver also allows you to launch the ColdFusion MX server Administrator so that you can define and maintain all connections to any data source used by the server.

# Connecting ColdFusion MX to Databases

ColdFusion MX connects to databases using JDBC. JDBC provides a standard way to connect to virtually any database in a uniform way.

## JDBC

JDBC (which is not really an acronym but generally thought of as Java Database Connectivity) is an API (application programming interface) for connecting programs written in Java to popular databases (Java is the underlying language of CFML). JDBC works like a translator to turn a standard database language, SQL, into the native language needed to talk to any of a vast array of databases.

### What is an API?

An API (**application program interface**) is the specific method prescribed by a computer operating system or by an application program by which a programmer writing an application program can make requests of the operating system or another application.

### JDBC is a Translator

As an analogy to JDBC drivers, consider that you work in international sales, and you have several other countries in your territory. You need to get the same message to all countries, but you can't speak the native languages. You might call upon a translator to take your English and translate it into the local languages. In this case, you are speaking the same language, but it is translated into many other languages to communicate with your customers. This is what JDBC does for databases.

## JDBC Driver Types

ColdFusion MX allows you to connect to any of the following databases, among others:

◆ DB2 Universal database

◆ Informix

◆ Microsoft Access

◆ Microsoft SQL Server

◆ MySQL

◆ Oracle

◆ Sybase

If your database is not in that list and you would like to find out if there is an available JDBC driver, use the JDBC driver locator found on java.sun.com:

```
http://industry.java.sun.com/products/
jdbc/drivers
```

### What are Drivers?

A **driver** is a program that interacts with a particular device or special (frequently optional) kind of software. The driver contains the special knowledge of the device or special software interface that programs using the driver do not. In personal computers, a driver is often packaged as a dynamic link library (DLL) file.

CONNECTING COLDFUSION MX TO DATABASES

# Creating a Data Source

To connect to a database you must first specify how to connect to it in a data source. This *data source*, often referred to as a DSN, or data source name, is a profile, or collection of connection information. JDBC connects to many types of databases, and each database requires specific information to enable connection; therefore, there is different information needed to connect to each. Connection information that might be required includes

◆ The path and file name of the database

◆ The username and password

◆ The server on which the database resides

Using the ColdFusion Administrator, you can define how to connect to the database you are trying to use. This definition is stored as a data source for reference in your CFML pages.

## Data Sources Are Profiles

As an analogy to a data source, consider how you log into your Macintosh or Windows systems. You input your name and password, but you don't have to specify your home directory (where your files are stored by default). When you log in, there is a profile of information that you can customize just for you. This profile is stored with your login information so that you can use it each time you log in. The same is true for the data source. You can specify the login information once, and then refer to the profile each time you want to connect to the database using CFML.

# Viewing Data Sources in Dreamweaver MX

You can view all the data sources that have been created on the server associated with your Dreamweaver site by using the Application panels group. Inside this group of panels resides the Databases panel, which allows you to connect to, create connections to, and view the data in your database. You must first go through a process of setting up your testing server in order to create these connections.

Dreamweaver needs the services of a testing server to generate and display dynamic content while you work. The testing server can be your local computer, a development server, a staging server, or a production server. The server must be able to process the kind of dynamic pages you plan to develop, which in this case means it must have ColdFusion MX installed.

**Figure 3.1** The Application panel contains the Databases panel where you can view and create data sources.

In order to allow Dreamweaver MX to view data sources that you have defined, you must specify a password for the ColdFusion Remote Development Services (RDS). This password was prompted for when you installed ColdFusion MX. Using this password, you can also have Dreamweaver MX help you generate SQL queries against the database.

## To specify the testing server:

1. Select the Application panel group and the Databases panel of that group (**Figure 3.1**).

   On the Databases panel, you will see the five steps required before you can view the data sources that are defined on the ColdFusion MX server specified in the site definition.

   Because you created the site in Chapter 2, you have completed the first two steps of the process. These steps have a checkmark next to them to indicate the status. The third step in the process is to set up the site's testing server.

   *continues on next page*

**2.** Click the testing server hyperlink.

The Site Definition for DWCF dialog in Advanced mode appears. The Testing Server section of the site setup will be displayed.

**3.** Change the Access value to Local/Network (**Figure 3.2**).

**4.** Ensure that the path to your Testing Server Folder is set correctly.

 ▲ For Windows, ensure it is the local directory for /dwcf. ColdFusion MX is installed on the same machine as your Web server (C:\CFusionMX\wwwroot\DWCF\)

 ▲ For Macintosh, ensure it is the network path to the ColdFusion MX server machine where your files reside. This connection may be made through a local path if your network is configured properly. If your network is not configured for local file access to the testing server, you can use Remote Development Services (RDS) to connect to the testing server, or FTP. To do this, change the Access setting in the dialog and make sure all of the appropriate settings are filled in correctly. You may need the IP address of the testing server, which can be attained through various Windows utilities, such as Programs > Accessories > System Tools > System Information. Your IP address can be found under Components > Network > Adapter.

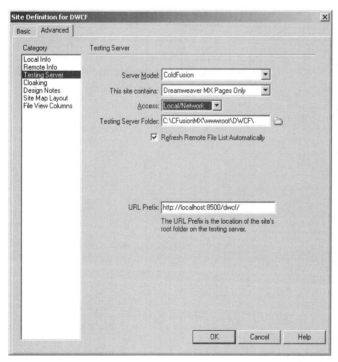

**Figure 3.2** Set up the testing server using the Advanced Site Setup dialog.

## Remote Development Services

RDS is a way that you can use Dreamweaver MX to connect to a ColdFusion MX server in order to view defined data sources and file structures. The target RDS server must have ColdFusion MX installed and running in order for this to work. Also, you must supply the password for RDS that was assigned during installation of the server.

5. Set the URL prefix:
   ▲ For Windows, use `http://localhost:8500/dwcf/`.
   ▲ For Macintosh, use the same URL except substitute *localhost* with the IP address or server name of the Windows server running ColdFusion MX `http://servername:8500/dwcf/`

6. Click OK.
   The dialog should close and you should see a checkmark next to the third step in the Databases panel.

### To specify the RDS login:

1. Click the RDS Login hyperlink in the Databases panel.
   You will receive a dialog to input the password for ColdFusion Remote Development Services (**Figure 3.3**).

2. Enter the RDS password that you assigned when you installed ColdFusion MX.

3. Click OK.
   You will receive a dialog telling you that Dreamweaver MX is loading the database schema. Once this process is complete, you should see a list of all data sources set up for your ColdFusion MX server to use.

**Figure 3.3** Step 4 of the process for displaying database connections is to specify the RDS login.

# Browsing Databases with Dreamweaver MX

Once you have completed the process for Dreamweaver MX to connect to the ColdFusion MX server, you can browse all defined data sources on that server. Operations that you can perform are

◆ View each defined data source.

◆ View all tables, views, and stored procedures in each data source.

◆ Click the plus sign (+) next to the Tables to see all tables for the data source.

◆ View the columns and their datatypes for each table.

◆ View the data in each table in read-only mode.

### To view the tables in a data source:

1. Click the plus sign next to a data source to see the browse-able list of objects, and click the plus sign next to Tables to view available tables.

2. Click the plus sign next to each table to see the columns and their datatypes within a table (**Figure 3.4**).

3. Click the Refresh icon on the Databases panel to refresh the view of the data sources, tables, and columns if you altered any of these objects since opening Dreamweaver (**Figure 3.5**).

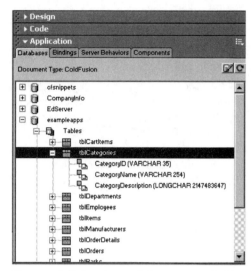

**Figure 3.4** Drill down into each data source and table to view all columns and their datatypes.

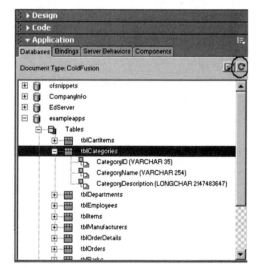

**Figure 3.5** Click Refresh if you have made any changes to the data sources or the tables since you last launched Dreamweaver MX.

## To view the data in a table:

1. Right-click on any table name and choose View Data (**Figure 3.6**).

2. Use the Previous 25 and Next 25 buttons to page through the rows if the table has more than 25 rows.

3. When you're finished browsing the data, click OK to close the window.

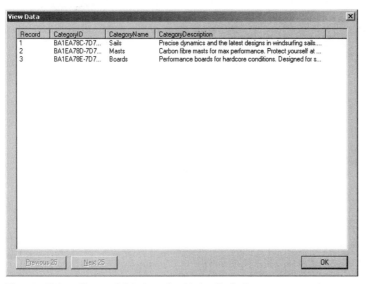

**Figure 3.6** View all rows of data in each table by displaying 25 rows at a time.

# Creating a Data Source

Dreamweaver helps you create and maintain your data source connections. The Databases panel enables you to launch the ColdFusion Administrator, where you specify all settings about the ColdFusion MX server, as well as define your data sources. Remember that you may be required to input the password that you assigned during installation.

From within the ColdFusion Administrator, you can create and modify your data sources. After you create a data source, ColdFusion MX will automatically verify that the connection is valid. You also have the ability to test one or all of your data sources whenever you change the system configuration.

## To create and verify a data source:

1. Click the Modify Data Sources button on the Databases panel (**Figure 3.7**).

   The ColdFusion Administrator will launch in a Web browser.

2. If you specified a password for the administrator during installation, input this password and click Login (**Figure 3.8**).

   The home page of the ColdFusion Administrator is displayed.

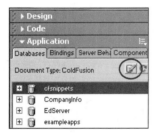

**Figure 3.7** The Modify Data Sources button launches the ColdFusion Administrator.

**Figure 3.8** Input the password you assigned when you installed ColdFusion MX server.

**Table 3.1**

| Microsoft Access Connection Parameters | |
| --- | --- |
| **PARAMETER** | **DESCRIPTION** |
| Data source name | Name of the data source you will use in applications. Must not contain spaces or special characters. |
| Description | Optional description of the data source. |
| Database File | The path and filename of the Access database (.mdb file). |
| Default Login | The default login information for Access. This value should be set to admin. |
| Password | The default login password. By default, this should be blank. |

**3.** In the Data & Services side menu, select the Data Sources option (**Figure 3.9**). From this interface, you can now add new data sources or modify existing ones.

**4.** Click on the name (a hyperlink) to select the exampleApps data source.

This will show you the connection information for connecting to a Microsoft Access database through a connection to an ODBC driver. This database gets installed during the ColdFusion MX server installation steps.

**Table 3.1** describes the connection parameters required to connect to a Microsoft Access database.

Other connection parameters exist, but they aren't required.

*continues on next page*

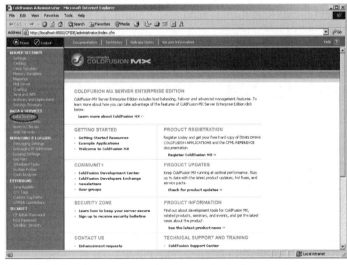

**Figure 3.9** Select the Data Sources option to maintain the server data sources.

CREATING A DATA SOURCE

**5.** Click Update to close the data source definition window.

**6.** After you create a data source, ColdFusion automatically tests the connection. It will show you either an OK or Error message in the Status column, as seen in **Figure 3.10**. If you receive a failed status, you should go back and fix it before proceeding (**Figure 3.11**). Most likely, you haven't selected the correct database file.

If you wish to retest a connection at any time, click the Verify icon next to the data source that you would like to verify.

*or*

Click the Verify All Connections button. ColdFusion MX will attempt to test each connection and will return the status of the connection in the Status column.

## ✔ Tip

- The default location of the ColdFusion Administrator is http://localhost:8500/CFIDE/administrator/index.cfm. You can also launch the administrator from the ColdFusion MX server machine by choosing Start > Programs > Macromedia ColdFusion MX > Administrator.

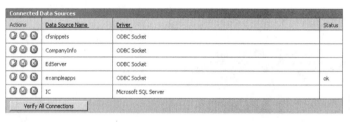

**Figure 3.10** After creating a data source, ColdFusion tests to be sure that the connection was successful.

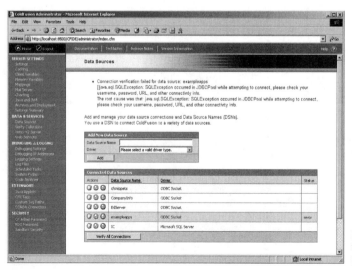

**Figure 3.11** A failure to connect to the data source yields an error message.

# RETRIEVING DATABASE DATA

In the previous chapter, you learned how to create a connection to the database using the Databases panel in the Application panel group. Now that you have a connection, you can retrieve data from the database. In this chapter, you explore the Bindings panel of the Application panel group to create a query against database tables. You learn how to query one database table and join tables together to retrieve a recordset of data to be used in the next chapter for display. There are two different ways to create a query, a simple and an advanced way, and you learn both of these in this chapter.

# Creating a Simple Query

Structured Query Language, abbreviated as SQL (sometimes pronounced "sequel"), provides a unified language for communicating with a vast array of commercial databases on the market today. The SQL statement for retrieving information is the SELECT statement. The most basic syntax of the SELECT statement is as follows:

```
SELECT {column list}
FROM {table}
```

This statement returns each column as defined in the column list from the table specified in the FROM clause. To return the first and last name values in the Employee table (named tblEmployees in the database that we are using), for example, you use the following SQL statement:

```
SELECT FirstName, LastName
FROM tblEmployees
```

Dreamweaver MX has two built-in options for creating these queries: simple and advanced recordset (or query) builders. These builders are actually dialogs that enable you to build the SELECT statement using options and text entries. Both of these options are found on the Bindings panel of the Application panel group.

## To create a simple query:

1. Create a new page, title it **Employee List**, and save it as **EmployeeList.cfm** in the DWCF site top folder.

2. Open the Application panel group's Bindings panel.

3. Click the plus sign (+) icon and choose Recordset (Query), shown in **Figure 4.1**.

   The simple recordset builder displays (**Figure 4.2**).

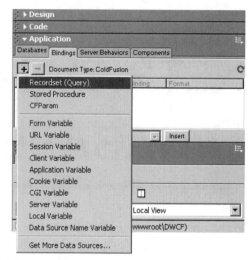

**Figure 4.1** The Application panel group's Bindings panel can help you create recordsets.

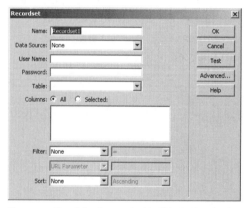

**Figure 4.2** The default recordset builder is the simple recordset builder.

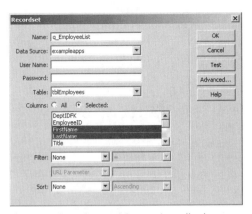

**Figure 4.3** If you do not wish to retrieve all columns, choose the Selected radio button then select one or more columns using your mouse.

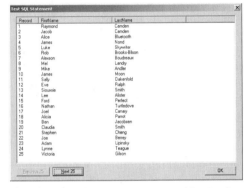

**Figure 4.4** Always test a query to ensure it's returning the data that you wish to retrieve.

## Naming Conventions

Good coding practices dictate that you should follow consistent naming conventions for creating any type of data, including queries. One such convention might be to prefix all queries with q_ to ensure that within your ColdFusion code you recognize this variable is a query recordset.

**4.** Select the data source that you wish to retrieve information from in the Data Source drop-down list, exampleapps in this task.

**5.** Name the recordset with a meaningful name, such as **q_EmployeeList**.

**6.** If the database you're connecting to requires a login and password, specify that information in the User Name and Password textboxes.

The exampleapps database does not require a username or password.

**7.** Select a table that you'd like to retrieve information from, here the tblEmployees table.

Once you select a table, Dreamweaver displays the columns in that table in the Columns section of the dialog.

**8.** Click a radio button to specify whether you'd like to retrieve All or Selected columns, and if you choose Selected, use your mouse to select one or more columns to retrieve (**Figure 4.3**).

Here, only the FirstName and LastName columns are selected.

**9.** Click the Test button to test the query.

The Test SQL Statement window opens. In this case, you will see all rows from the tblEmployees table and only the first and last names of each employee (**Figure 4.4**).

If your query returns more than 25 rows, the window displays only 25 at a time, and you can use the Previous 25 and Next 25 buttons at the bottom of the window to move through the full recordset.

*continues on next page*

CREATING A SIMPLE QUERY

**10.** Click OK to close the Test SQL Statement window.

**11.** When you're satisfied with the query, click OK to create the query and close the simple recordset builder window.

When the recordset window closes, Dreamweaver places the query inside the open document and lists it in the Recordset list in the Bindings panel (**Figure 4.5**).

## Recordsets and CFML

After you create a recordset and close the recordset builder, Dreamweaver puts the query into the page. The `<cfquery>` tag performs the query in ColdFusion, and thus Dreamweaver puts it into the page. This tag surrounds all SQL statements and indicates to ColdFusion to take the SQL, send it to the database, and get back any results from the database.

If you are in Design view, then you will not see a difference on the page as of yet. It is not until you display the contents of the query to a page that you will see the results.

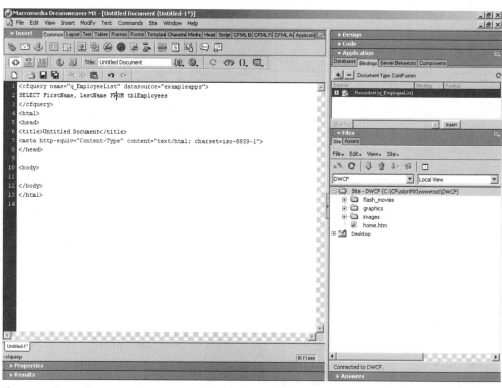

**Figure 4.5** All recordsets created on a page are listed in the Bindings panel.

**12.** Click the Document toolbar's Show Code and Design Views icon to display the code (**Figure 4.6**).

Changing the view enables you to see the query that was created.

**13.** Save your page.

## ✔ Tips

- If you manually type a query (instead of using the builder to create a recordset), Dreamweaver MX automatically detects it in your open page and displays it in the Bindings panel.

- In addition to the Bindings panel, you can use the Insert bar's Application toolbar and the Server Behaviors panel of the Application panel group to create a recordset.

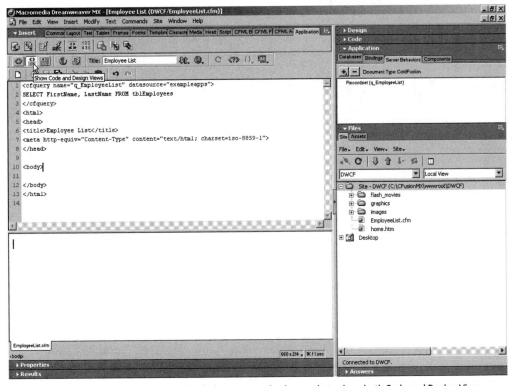

**Figure 4.6** To view the query that was created, change your viewing mode to show both Code and Design View.

# Updating a Simple Query

In this fast-paced world, the structure of a database changes almost as soon as a query is finished. Being able to update queries is critical. Fortunately, Dreamweaver makes that process simple.

### To update a simple query:

1. Open the page with the recordset, here EmployeeList.cfm, which was created in the last section.

2. In the Bindings panel, select the recordset to update, in this case q_EmployeeList.

3. Double-click on the recordset.

   The simple recordset builder displays with the values of the recordset defaulted.

4. Modify the columns selected and test the recordset to ensure it is successful. When you're satisfied, click OK to update the recordset.

If you update and change the name of the recordset, Dreamweaver brings up a dialog (**Figure 4.7**) that lets you know that it will use the Find and Replace functionality to change the name of the recordset within the page. Use the resulting Find and Replace dialog to find and replace all instances of the recordset (**Figure 4.8**). Choose Replace All to change each reference to the recordset.

When the simple recordset builder dialog is closed, Dreamweaver updates the query on the page and in the Bindings panel.

### ✔ Tip

■ When selecting a recordset to modify it, be sure to double-click directly on the name of the query. Clicking on the icon to the left of the query does not select it.

**Figure 4.7** When you change the name of an existing query, Dreamweaver lets you know that you will be given a chance to use Find and Replace to change all queries in your page that refer to the recordset.

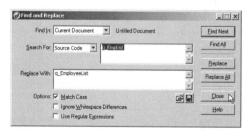

**Figure 4.8** Use Find and Replace to update all queries on your page.

# Copying a Recordset

Creating an entire application using a database usually means you find yourself creating the same recordset over and over again, on different pages. When you create a new page in Dreamweaver, it does not display any recordsets you've created previously. It displays only those that are defined on the current page.

To speed up development, you can copy a recordset from one page to another. To do so, copy the recordset on the Bindings panel of the existing recordset and paste it into the Bindings panel of the new page.

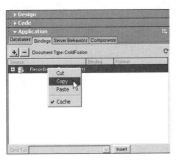

**Figure 4.9**
Use the context menu to copy the query to the Clipboard.

## To reuse a recordset on another page:

1. In the Bindings panel, select the recordset that you wish to put onto another page.

   On Windows, right-click on the recordset and, from the context menu that pops up, choose Copy (**Figure 4.9**).

   On Macintosh, use Control-click on the recordset and choose Copy.

2. Create a new page.

   You will not see any recordsets in the Bindings panel.

3. Paste the recordset into the Bindings panel.

   ▲ On Windows, right-click in the Bindings panel and choose Paste.

   ▲ On Macintosh, use Control-click and choose Paste.

   Dreamweaver places the recordset in the open page as well as in the Bindings panel (**Figure 4.10**).

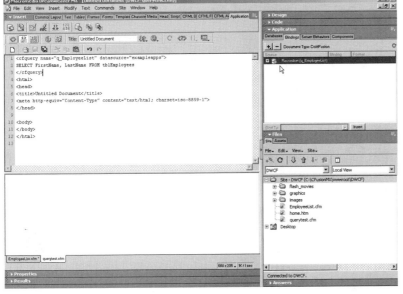

**Figure 4.10** Once the recordset is pasted in, it displays in the Bindings panel and is inserted into the open document.

# Filtering Data in a Simple Query

The simple query that you created in the previous section did not restrict the rows that were returned by the query. You learned only how to restrict the columns that were returned. In order to restrict the rows that get returned in a recordset, add one or more filters to a SQL statement.

A filter is a statement that causes the database to look through the data and find only matching rows to return. Filters in SQL are put into the WHERE clause, and you can have as many of them as you'd like. In the following example, the query returns only those employees with the last name of Camden:

```
SELECT FirstName, LastName
FROM tblEmployees
WHERE LastName = 'Camden'
```

The simple recordset builder can help you build basic WHERE clauses.

## To filter a recordset:

1. Create a new recordset or open an existing one for modification. Here, we're opening the existing q_EmployeeList recordset created in EmployeeList.cfm.

2. Open the filter drop-down list and select the column on which you would like to filter (**Figure 4.11**).

   Here the LastName column is used as a filter.

3. Choose Entered Value in the drop-down list below the filtering column.

4. In the textbox to the right of Entered Value, manually type the value to use as a filter (**Figure 4.12**).

   Here Camden is the filter value.

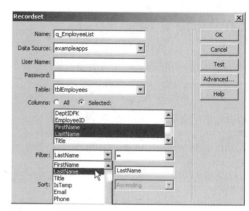

**Figure 4.11** Select a column to filter on.

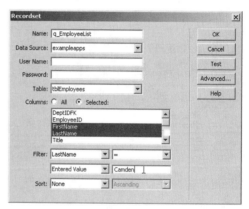

**Figure 4.12** Enter a filter value.

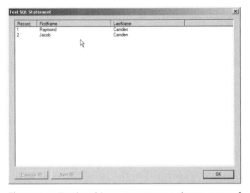

Figure 4.13 Testing this query returns only two rows of data matching Camden.

5. Test the query (**Figure 4.13**).

6. Click OK to close the recordset builder when you are satisfied.

   The recordset builder closes, and Dreamweaver updates the query in the Bindings panel and the open page (**Figure 4.14**).

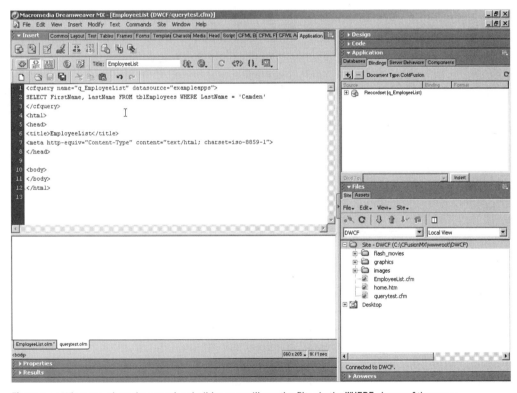

Figure 4.14 When you close the recordset builder, you will see the filter in the WHERE clause of the query.

# Sorting Data in a Simple Query

The ORDER BY clause of a SELECT statement can be used to change the order in which Dreamweaver returns data. Data returned by a SELECT statement can be sorted by one or more columns. The following SQL statement returns all rows in the tblEmployees table in the alphabetical order of last name.

```
SELECT FirstName, LastName
FROM tblEmployees
ORDER BY LastName
```

The simple recordset builder can help you sort on one column.

## To sort data in a recordset:

1. Create a new query or open an existing one from the Bindings panel.

2. Test the query to see how the data will be returned (**Figure 4.15**).

3. In the Sort drop-down list, select the column you would like to sort on and the order—ascending or descending—in which you want the data returned (**Figure 4.16**). Here we're sorting on the LastName column.

4. Test the query to ensure Dreamweaver returns it in the correct order (**Figure 4.17**).

5. Click OK to close the recordset builder when you are satisfied with the sort order.

   The query in the Bindings panel and in the open page are updated.

## ✔ Tip

■ When you organize data in a recordset, it does not physically change the data in the database. So don't worry—reorganize the data as you select it all you like without worrying that it's somehow affecting the database.

**Figure 4.15** The default sort order of the data can't be relied upon unless you explicitly sort it.

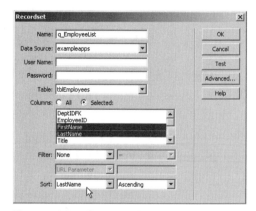

**Figure 4.16** Specify a sort order column and whether it should be ascending or descending.

**Figure 4.17** By sorting on the LastName column, the data is sorted alphabetically.

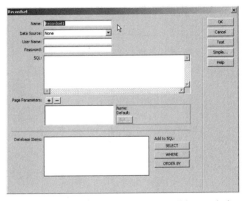

**Figure 4.18** The Advanced Recordset Builder can help you create more sophisticated queries.

# Building an Advanced Recordset

In the recordsets you have created thus far, you can filter using only one column and one value, and you can sort on only one column. SQL allows you to filter on any column in the tables specified and sort on a series of columns, but the simple recordset builder does not have the functionality to handle these more advanced SELECT statements. In order to create more advanced statements, you can use the advanced recordset builder.

You can have as many filters as you need by putting each filter in the WHERE clause within an AND or an OR condition. If you want to return all employees with the last name of Camden or Smith, you use an OR clause as follows:

```
SELECT FirstName, LastName
FROM tblEmployees
WHERE LastName = 'Camden'
OR     LastName = 'Smith'
```

The advanced recordset builder enables you to either manually type the SQL statement, or click and select database objects to help you create the query.

### To create multiple filters:

1. Open the Bindings panel, click the plus sign (+) icon, and create a new query by choosing Recordset (Query).

2. Click the Advanced button to switch from the simple to the advanced record-set builder.

   The dialog changes to a more complex recordset builder (**Figure 4.18**).

   *continues on next page*

**3.** Assign a meaningful name for the query, such as **q_EmpDepartment**, select the data source, and assign an optional user name and password as you did for the simple recordset builder.

**4.** Within the Database Items section of the dialog, expand Tables and expand the table you wish to obtain information from, here tblEmployees (**Figure 4.19**).

**5.** Highlight each column you'd like to see in the result list and click the SELECT button after each one.

The SQL statement that Dreamweaver generates is displayed in the SQL portion of the dialog (**Figure 4.20**).

**6.** Test the query and click OK when you're satisfied.

The recordset builder closes, and Dreamweaver adds the query to the Bindings panel and the open page.

## ✔ Tip

■ When you change the mode of the recordset builder, it continues to open it in that mode whenever you open the recordset builder until you change it again.

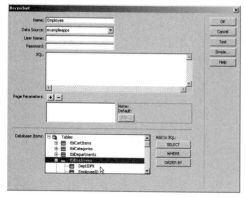

**Figure 4.19** Expand the tables and then expand a table to retrieve information from.

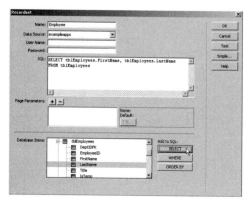

**Figure 4.20** Select columns one at a time to add to the result list.

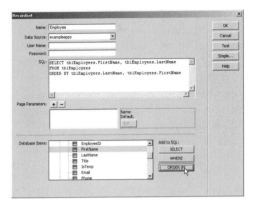

**Figure 4.21** Select columns to sort the data by.

# Sorting on Multiple Columns

A previous section showed you how to sort the data returned from a database using one column, in either ascending or descending order. The advanced recordset builder enables you to sort on many columns. For example, you may want to sort by last name and then, within duplicate last names, by the first name.

## To sort using multiple columns:

1. Create a new query or open an existing one.

2. In Database Items, expand the Tables list, if necessary, and then expand the actual table you'd like to get information from.

3. Locate the column you'd like to sort on and select it; then click the ORDER BY button.

4. Repeat this for each column you'd like in your sort order (**Figure 4.21**).

5. Test the query and click OK to close the dialog. Click OK when you're satisfied with the recordset results.

   The recordset builder closes, and Dreamweaver adds the query to the Bindings panel and the open page.

## ✔ Tip

- The default sort order is ascending. The advanced recordset builder does not allow you to change the sort order to descending. If you wish to do so, you can manually type the keyword **desc** followed by a space next to the column within the SQL section of the dialog.

# Joining Tables in Recordsets

One other limitation of the simple recordset builder is that you can select information from only one table at a time. If you want to join multiple tables together to return a result set, you need to use the advanced recordset builder.

Thus far you have returned information from only one table. In order to return a result set by combining two or more tables, you need to create one or more join conditions.

A *join* is a term that describes an advanced kind of query. In it, two or more tables are combined or "joined" into one for purposes of executing your query. Tables in a database sometimes hold related pieces of information that you want to store separately but want to use in a combined fashion. In a company database, for example, you can store the name of employee departments in a separate table just for departments. This way, if the department name changes, you can make the change in only one place rather than having to search through all employee records.

Databases can keep the right employees related to the right department names by the use of keys. Keys provide a shorthand identifying method for databases to use when storing and joining records; keys give each record a unique identifier. This way, the database can say that Joe Smith is in department 9 and, in a different place, store the fact that department 9 is called Marketing.

A join condition specifies the columns in each table that are equal to each other and thus yield a related data set. In most cases, you create the join condition by specifying the primary key column in one table equal to the foreign key column of the related table.

The exampleapps database has an employee table (tblEmployees) and a department table (tblDepartments). The database was designed with a business rule that an employee has to work in a department (one at a time) and a department contains many employees. In this case, Dreamweaver copies the primary key of the one table (tblDepartments.DepartmentID) into each employee row as a foreign key (tblEmployees.DeptIDFK) (**Figure 4.22**). In order to select information from both of these tables as they are related to one another, you specify a SELECT statement with the following join condition:

```
SELECT tblDepartments.DepartmentName,
       tblEmployees.LastName,
       tblEmployees.FirstName
FROM tblDepartments, tblEmployees
WHERE tblDepartments.DepartmentID =
       tblEmployees.DepartmentID
```

The advanced recordset builder can help you to create the join condition when selecting from multiple tables.

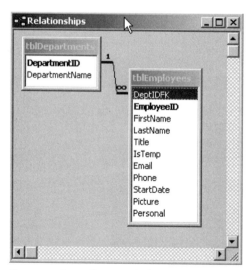

**Figure 4.22** An employee works in one department, and a department can have many employees.

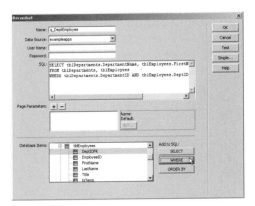

**Figure 4.23** Select each column in the join and then choose the WHERE button to create the join.

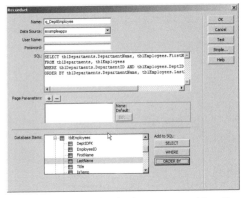

**Figure 4.24** Sort the data by department and then the employee's last name.

**Figure 4.25** The query returns a list of each department and all employees within it.

## To join tables in a recordset:

1. From the Bindings panel, create a new query using the advanced recordset builder.

2. Give the query a meaningful name (such as **q_DeptEmployee**), select the data source (here exampleapps), and assign a user name and password (here it is unnecessary).

3. Expand the Tables selection of the Database Items section so that you can view all the tables.

4. Select the DepartmentName column of the tblDepartments table, and the Lastname and Firstname columns of the tblEmployees table.

5. Expand the tblDepartments table and select the primary key (DepartmentName).

6. Click the WHERE button.
   It will add a WHERE clause and the beginning of the join condition.

7. After the WHERE tblEmployees.DeptIDFK statement in the SQL portion of the dialog, type an equal sign (=).

8. Expand the tblEmployees table and select the foreign key (DeptIDFK).

9. Click the WHERE button.
   Dreamweaver adds the remainder of the join condition to the WHERE clause (**Figure 4.23**).

10. Select DepartmentID and then click the ORDER BY button to sort the data. Next add the LastName column to the ORDER BY (**Figure 4.24**).

11. Test the query (**Figure 4.25**), and when satisfied with the results, click OK twice to close the test query dialog and the recordset builder.

JOINING TABLES IN RECORDSETS

**51**

# DISPLAYING DATABASE DATA

5

In the last chapter, you learned how to query a database table and return the information to ColdFusion MX—yielding a recordset. Each column returned in the recordset is called a recordset field. The next step is to display the recordset fields to the Web page. You can display recordset fields to a Web page using several methods in Dreamweaver MX. In this chapter, you:

◆ Bind recordset fields to a page so that dynamic data is displayed in the first row of data.

◆ Modify the bind data in the page and add a Repeat Region server behavior to display all rows in the recordset.

◆ Use the Dynamic Table application object to display all rows in the recordset as well as format the data into an HTML table.

◆ Use the Live Data view to tweak the layout and design of a dynamically generated page.

◆ Enable viewing of groups of recordset rows in separate pages while adding a navigation bar and navigation status message that identifies the group of rows in view.

◆ Enable ColdFusion MX debugging to view error messages in your ColdFusion pages, and use the Server Debug panel to identify and fix those errors within Dreamweaver MX.

# Using Data Binding

In the previous chapters, we saw how to define data sources on our ColdFusion server and how to pull data from them. In order to use this data on our Web pages, we have to create bindings between the data and the location on the page where the information should go.

You use the Bindings panel of the Application panel group to display the dynamic content elements of a recordset on a page. In Design view, you see placeholders for dynamic content, and in Code view you see the CFML (ColdFusion Markup Language) code that was generated to dynamically display database data. When you finish these tasks, you will be able to display only the first row of a recordset. You learn how to display all or many rows later in this chapter.

**Figure 5.1** The Bindings panel can help you display recordset information on a page.

### To display recordset fields:

1. In Design view, position the cursor in the Document window where you would like the recordset information to display.

2. In the Application panel, click the Bindings panel (**Figure 5.1**).

3. In the Bindings panel, expand a recordset, here the q_EmployeeList recordset.

   Expanding the recordset enables you to view the recordset fields (**Figure 5.2**).

**Figure 5.2** Expand the recordset to view the recordset fields available for display.

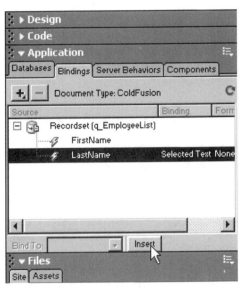

**Figure 5.3** Select the recordset field to display on your Web page and click Insert.

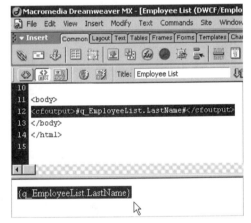

**Figure 5.4** Viewing the results in Code view, you will see a placeholder for any dynamic elements.

4. Select the LastName recordset field and click Insert at the bottom of the panel (**Figure 5.3**).

   Alternately, you can click and drag the elements from the panel and drop them on your page.

5. On the Document toolbar, click Show Code and Design Views to inspect the code (**Figure 5.4**).

*continues on next page*

## Displaying Data in CFML

As can be seen from Code view, binding a page to a recordset field creates the CFML tag <cfoutput> in the code.

```
<cfoutput>#q_EmployeeList.LastName#
</cfoutput>
```

This tag, which always ends with </cfoutput> tag, surrounds any values that you'd like ColdFusion MX to evaluate for you, such as recordset fields. Each recordset field is also to be surrounded by hash marks (#) as well, to indicate to ColdFusion that the variable has to be evaluated and displayed.

USING DATA BINDING

**55**

**6.** Select FirstName and drag it from the recordset list on to the page next to LastName (**Figure 5.5**).

**7.** Choose File > Save to save the file.

**8.** Choose Select File > Preview in Browser > iexplore to browse the file (**Figure 5.6**).

Notice that it displays only the value of the first table row's column in the output instead of all LastName values. You learn how to loop over the recordset and display all column values in a later section.

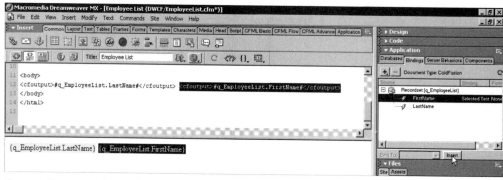

**Figure 5.5** You can continue to drag in any and all recordset fields into Design view.

**Figure 5.6** Binding a recordset field to a Web page enables it to display dynamic data when the page is requested.

## Design View Placeholders

In Design view of the Document window, placeholders such as the following represent dynamic content:

{ q_EmployeeList.LastName}

This placeholder indicates that the data is from the LastName column in the q_EmployeeList recordset and will be inserted at this location on the page when the page runs.

# Using Live Data View

By default, Design view gives you a visual representation of the page without dynamic content. The default view is not ideal if you're designing a dynamic page because the dynamic content fundamentally can change the layout of the page.

To see how dynamic content can affect the layout of a page, Dreamweaver allows you to preview and edit dynamic content using the Live Data window.

While dynamic content is displayed, you can adjust the page's layout and add, edit, or delete dynamic content.

## To turn on Live Data view:

1. Open a page in Design view that contains dynamic content, such as recordset fields.

2. Choose View > Live Data.

   The Document window switches from Design view to Live Data view (**Figure 5.7**). You can also change to the Live Data view by clicking the Live Data View icon on the Document toolbar (**Figure 5.8**).

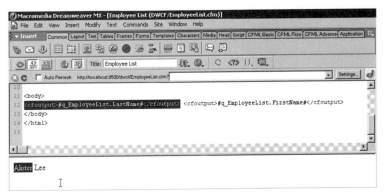

**Figure 5.7** When you're designing a Web page, use the Live Data view so that you can see the dynamically generated contents of the page.

**Figure 5.8** You can alternately use the Live Data View icon on the Document toolbar to toggle between Design and Live Data views.

## Links and Live Data

Links don't work in the Live Data window. To test your links, use the Preview in Browser feature.

**3.** To refresh the page after making a change affecting dynamic content, do one of the following:

▲ With Live Data turned on, click the Document toolbar's Refresh button (**Figure 5.9**).

▲ Click the Document toolbar's Auto Refresh option (**Figure 5.10**).

With Auto Refresh turned on, the page refreshes whenever you make a change affecting dynamic content.

## ✔ Tips

■ If you have a slow database connection, you might want to leave the Auto Refresh option off when working in the Live Data window.

■ When you save your page, Dreamweaver automatically changes from Live Data view back to Design view. You must put it back in Live Data view to continue.

**Figure 5.9** Click the refresh button on the document toolbar to display any changes made during Live Data view.

**Figure 5.10** Turn on the Auto Refresh option if you wish all changes made during Live Data view to be displayed immediately.

## Temporary Files

Dreamweaver runs the dynamic page on your server before displaying it in the Live Data window. Whenever you switch to the Live Data window, a temporary copy of the open document is sent to your application server for processing. The resulting page is returned and displayed in the Live Data window, and the temporary copy on the server is deleted.

# Displaying Multiple Rows

Thus far you have created a recordset of rows from a database table, and yet your page can display only the first row of data. In order to display all rows returned by the recordset, use the Repeat Regions server behavior.

*Server behavior* is a generic term for reusable chunks of code—in this case CFML—that you can apply to your Web pages. Dreamweaver MX comes with a variety of built-in server behaviors for things such as:

◆ Displaying multiple database records on a Web page.

◆ Showing a specific region on a page based on whether a returned recordset is empty.

◆ Inserting, updating, or deleting rows for a database table from a Web interface.

The Repeat Region server behavior lets you loop over the recordset rows and display either a specific number of records or all the records in the recordset. Before you add the Repeat Region server behavior to your page, you must already have a database connection and a recordset defined.

## To use the Repeat Region server behavior:

1. Open the page in which you already have created bindings to recordset fields, here: EmployeeList.cfm.

2. In Design view, select the region on your page that contains the dynamic content to be repeated.

   This region can be a table, table row, or a paragraph. Here, we are selecting the placeholders for the last and first names from the recordset.

3. Choose Insert > Text Object > Paragraph to place the first and last name values in a paragraph so that each employee displays on its own line, (**Figure 5.11**).

   *continues on next page*

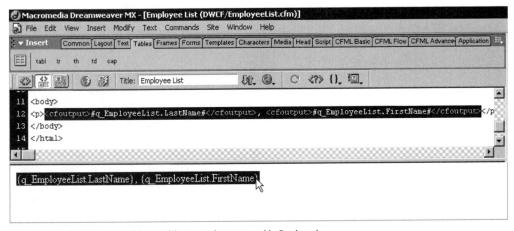

**Figure 5.11** Select the text, table or table row to be repeated in Design view.

**4.** Open the Server Behaviors panel, click the plus (+) button, and choose Repeat Region (**Figure 5.12**).

The Repeat Region dialog opens (**Figure 5.13**). Use this dialog to select the recordset name and number of records to be displayed per page. Here we are choosing to display all rows.

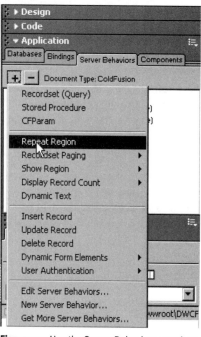

**Figure 5.13** Add a Repeat Region server behavior to display all rows.

**Figure 5.12** Use the Server Behaviors panel on the Application panel group to create a Repeat Region behavior.

## Dreamweaver MX Exchange

You also can write your own server behaviors or install behaviors written by other developers. The Macromedia Dreamweaver MX Exchange, an online repository for shared Dreamweaver information, provides server behaviors that you can download, install, and use in your development. For more information, see Dreamweaver's help for the Extension Manager. You also can choose Commands > Get More Commands to launch the Macromedia Exchange.

**5.** Click OK.

In Design view, a gray outline appears around the repeated region. In the Server Behaviors panel, the Repeat Region behavior is listed (**Figure 5.14**).

**6.** Change to the Live Data view to see all rows being displayed on the page.

All dynamic values will be highlighted in yellow (**Figure 5.15**).

## ✔ Tip

■ Choose Window > Server Behaviors to display the Server Behaviors panel if it is not already displayed.

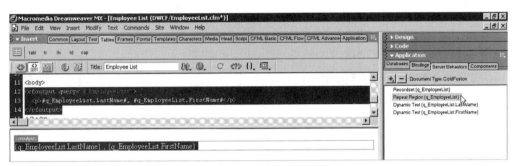

**Figure 5.14** Repeated regions are highlighted with a gray box and are listed in the Server Behaviors panel.

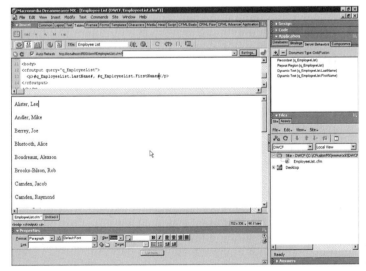

**Figure 5.15** Viewing the result in Live Data view shows that all rows are now displayed.

# Formatting Output in Tables

The output that you have created thus far is created using only paragraph (<p>) tags, and the data does not line up. You may want to format your output using HTML tables to have each column line up neatly. You could use bindings and the Repeat Region server behavior, but Dreamweaver MX has a special application object called a Dynamic Table you could use more easily. This feature enables you to display recordset information in tabular format through a simple dialog.

### To use the dynamic table application object:

1. Open a new page, save it as **EmpList_Table.cfm**, and create a recordset you'd like to display.

2. To display the Dynamic Table dialog, do one of the following:

   ▲ On the Insert bar's Application toolbar, click the Dynamic Table icon (**Figure 5.16**).

   ▲ Choose Insert > Application Object > Dynamic Table.

3. Choose the recordset that you'd like to display in tabular format, set the number of rows to display (here All Records), and set other desired table-formatting properties (**Figure 5.17**).

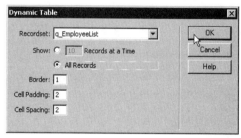

**Figure 5.16** Use the Dynamic Table icon to display a recordset in tabular format.

**Figure 5.17** Set the Dynamic Table dialog properties.

**4.** Click OK.

Dreamweaver MX automatically creates a table with a column for each recordset field, creates a header row from the names of the recordset field names, and sets it up to display all rows returned (**Figure 5.18**).

**5.** Change to the Live Data view to see all rows being displayed in tabular format (**Figure 5.19**).

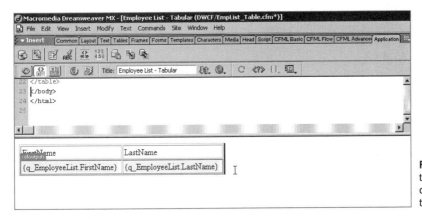

**Figure 5.18** An HTML table is created to display each field in the recordset.

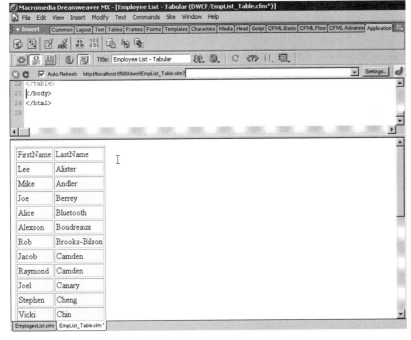

**Figure 5.19** Viewing the result in Live Data view shows that all rows are now displayed in an HTML table.

# Navigating Through Recordsets

Thus far you have displayed all results of a recordset in one page. It is a better design practice to keep the user from having to scroll through long pages of data.

If you recall, both the Dynamic Table application object dialog and the Repeat Region server behavior dialog enable you to restrict the number of rows displayed from all to some number you specify. Using this restricted number of rows, you can break up recordsets into pages so that users can move forward and backward through a set of pages that contain shorter lists of the data. You can accomplish this using one of the following methods:

◆ A Repeat Region server behavior that restricts the number of rows displayed.
  *or*
  A Dynamic Table application object, also restricting the number of rows displayed.

◆ A recordset navigation bar server behavior.

Instead of displaying all records in a recordset, you can choose to display only a certain number of records at a time. You can make this choice when you use either the Repeat Region server behavior or the Dynamic Table application object. Both dialogs enable you to choose to display either all rows, or only a specific number of rows.

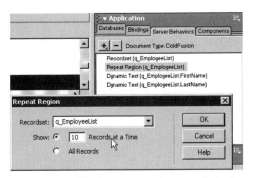

**Figure 5.20** Modify the Repeat Region server behavior to only display 10 rows.

## To restrict the display of records on an existing page:

1. Open a page that has been created using a Repeat Region server behavior or a Dynamic Table application object.

2. Choose the Application panel group's Server Behaviors panel.

   If you used either a Repeat Region or the Dynamic Table server behavior, a Repeat Region server behavior was created.

3. Double-click the Repeat Region server behavior to obtain the dialog.

4. Change the dialog to display only a certain number of records at a time, here 10 (**Figure 5.20**).

5. Click OK.

6. Change to the Live Data view to see all rows being displayed in tabular format (**Figure 5.21**).

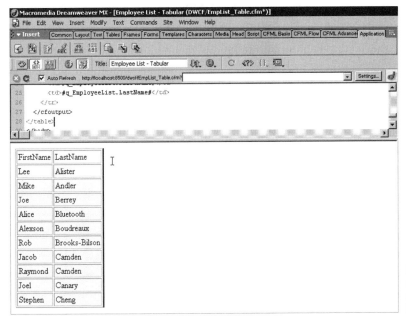

**Figure 5.21** Only the specified number of rows are displayed, here the first 10 rows.

**NAVIGATING THROUGH RECORDSETS**

# Creating a Recordset Navigation Bar

You can create a recordset navigation bar in a single operation using the Recordset Navigation Bar server behavior. The server object adds the following building blocks to the page:

◆ An HTML table with either text or image links

◆ A set of Move to server behaviors

◆ A set of Show Region server behaviors

After placing the navigation bar on the page, you can use Dreamweaver's design tools to customize the bar to your liking. You even can use an object to keep track of which records are being displayed. The Recordset Navigation Status application object creates a text entry on the page to display the current record status. This message displays the current set of rows, as in Records 1 to 5 of 10.

## To create the recordset navigation bar:

**1.** In Design view, place the insertion point at the location on the page where you want the navigation bar to appear.

**2.** To obtain the Recordset Navigation Bar dialog, do one of the following (**Figure 5.22**):

▲ Choose Insert > Application Objects > Recordset Navigation Bar.

▲ On the Insert bar's Application tab, click the Recordset Navigation Bar button.

**3.** Select the recordset you want to navigate from the Recordset pop-up menu.

**4.** From the Display Using section, select the format to display the navigation links on the page.

The Text option places text links on the page.

The Images option lets you use graphical images as links.

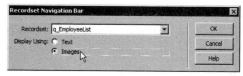

**Figure 5.22** Use the Recordset Navigation Bar dialog to adjust the display of the navigation bar.

## Customizing Navigation

You can create your own navigation bar to have a more complex layout and customized formatting. To do this, you must first create the necessary navigation links in either text or images, place them within the page in Design view, and assign individual server behaviors to each navigation link.

**5.** Click OK.

Dreamweaver creates a table containing text or image links the user can click to navigate through the selected recordset (**Figure 5.23**).

The individual server behaviors that you can assign to navigation links are

◆ Move to first page

◆ Move to last page

◆ Move to next page

◆ Move to previous page

**6.** Change to the Live Data view to see a subset of rows being displayed along with the navigation bar (**Figure 5.24**).

When the first record in the recordset is displayed, the First and Previous links or images are hidden. When the last record in the recordset is displayed, the Next and Last links or images are hidden.

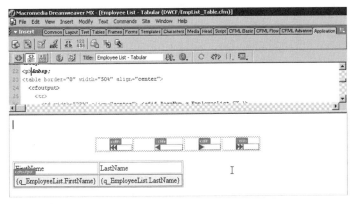

**Figure 5.23** A placeholder for the navigation bar is displayed after you close the Recordset Navigation Bar dialog.

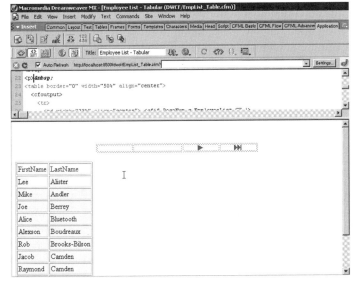

**Figure 5.24** A paged set of data is created with a navigation bar.

**To use the Recordset Navigation Status application object:**

1. Place the cursor at the point where you want to insert the record counter.

2. To display the Insert Recordset Navigation Status dialog, do one of the following:

   Choose Insert > Application Objects > Recordset Navigation Status.

   On the Insert bar's Application tab, click the Recordset Navigation Status button.

   The dialog is displayed (**Figure 5.25**).

3. Select the recordset you want to use from the Recordset pop-up menu.

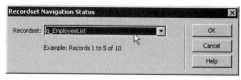

**Figure 5.25** The Insert Recordset Navigation Status dialog requires you to select a query for navigation.

**4.** Click OK.

The Recordset Navigation Status server object inserts a text record counter (**Figure 5.26**).You can use Dreamweaver's page-design tools to customize the record counter.

**5.** Change to the Live Data view to see a subset of rows being displayed along with the navigation bar (**Figure 5.27**).

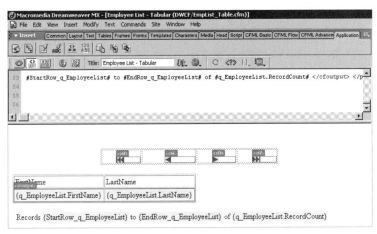

**Figure 5.26** The Recordset Navigation Status inputs the CFML code necessary to display record status information.

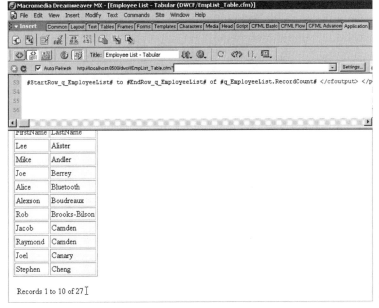

**Figure 5.27** The Recordset Navigation Status displays the status of the currently viewed set of rows.

# Using the Server Debug View

When you are accessing a database to retrieve data to display, errors can occur. For instance, perhaps the database is currently unavailable, or the SQL statement you created contains errors. ColdFusion can display possible causes for the error at the bottom of the page when you open the page in the browser.

However, the Dreamweaver MX Server Debug panel enables you to use and view ColdFusion MX debugging information directly from within the development environment. This panel provides a large amount of useful information, including the following:

◆ All pages the server processed to render the page.

◆ All the SQL queries executed on the page.

◆ A summary of execution times.

In order to use this feature, you must ensure that debugging is enabled in the ColdFusion Administrator.

## To enable ColdFusion MX debugging:

1. Be sure that you are on the testing server that has ColdFusion MX running.

2. To open the Administrator, do one of the following:

   Choose Start > Programs > Macromedia ColdFusion MX > Administrator.

   Browse directly to the Administrator at `http://localhost:8500/cfide/ administrator/index.cfm`.

3. If you assigned a password during installation, you will be prompted for this password to gain access to the Administrator.

4. In the menu to the left, find the Debugging and Logging option and choose Debugging Settings (**Figure 5.28**).

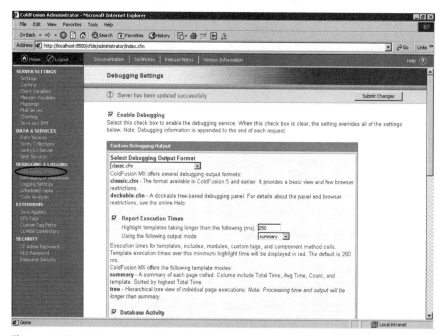

**Figure 5.28** The ColdFusion Administrator enables you to configure debugging settings.

**Figure 5.29** Debugging information can now be displayed at the end of every browsed ColdFusion page.

**Figure 5.30** The Server Debug icon is on the Document toolbar.

**5.** Check the Enable Debugging checkbox.

**6.** Click Submit Changes.

**7.** Browse any ColdFusion page.

Debugging information appears at the bottom of the page (**Figure 5.29**).

## To debug a ColdFusion page within Dreamweaver MX:

**1.** Open the ColdFusion page in Dreamweaver.

**2.** To change to the Server Debug view, do one of the following:

▲ On the Document toolbar, click the Server Debug icon (**Figure 5.30**),

▲ Choose View > Server Debug.

Dreamweaver requests the file from the ColdFusion MX server and displays it in an internal Internet Explorer browser window. If the page contains errors, debugging information is displayed at the bottom of the page (**Figure 5.31**). At the same time, a Server Debug panel opens.

*continues on next page*

**Figure 5.31** The page is browsed, and the Server Debug panel is opened in the Results panel group.

**USING THE SERVER DEBUG VIEW**

**3.** If an Exceptions category appears in the Server Debug panel, click the plus (+) icon to expand the category.

The Exceptions category appears when the server encountered a problem or problems with the page. Expanding the category enables you to find out more about the problem.

**4.** Fix the error, save the file, and click Browse.

Dreamweaver renders the page in the internal browser again and updates the Server Debug panel. If there are no more problems with the page, the Exceptions category does not reappear in the panel.

**5.** Choose View > Design to switch to Design view, leaving the Debug mode.

### ✔ Tip

■ To ensure the debugging information is refreshed every time a page is displayed in the internal browser, make sure Internet Explorer checks for newer versions of the file every time the file is requested. In Internet Explorer, choose Tools > Internet Options, click the General tab, and click the Settings button in the Temporary Internet Files area. In the Settings dialog, select the Every visit to page option.

### Macintosh Support

This feature is not supported on the Macintosh. Macintosh developers can use Preview in Browser (F12) to open a ColdFusion page in a separate browser. If the page contains errors, information about the possible causes for the error appears at the bottom of the page.

### Live Data View Versus Server Debug View

Live Data view is primarily a design-time feature, allowing you to see how the page will be displayed and to use the design tools to tweak the layout. It does not allow you to test any links in your pages.

Server Debug view is a run-time feature, enabling you to view the application as an end user would, with fully functioning links. It also displays any page errors and allows you to go directly to the page that encountered the error to fix it.

# CUSTOMIZING DATA DISPLAY

In the last chapter, you learned how to display all rows in a recordset and how to create navigation that enabled others to page through several rows of data at a time. However, the individual columns that you displayed were only text columns. What if you had a date value or a number that you wanted to format with decimal points? In this chapter, you learn how to use the Bindings panel to display column information formatted in several special ways.

You also learn how to design a data interface so that users can get just what they need without all the clutter of too much information. Why? Users quickly can become overwhelmed if you put too much information on a Web page. Therefore, as a Web developer you need to be creative and give your users only as much information as they need and then allow them to drill down and find more details as they have need of it. One way to do this is to create a master/detail interface, which Dreamweaver MX enables you to quickly create by using the Master/Detail Page Set application object.

# Formatting Date and Time Data

Date and Time formatting enables you to format date and time information in several different ways. **Table 6.1** shows a sample of the formatting available.

### To format date and time data:

1. Open a document with dynamic content in Design view.

2. Choose the Application panel group's Bindings panel.

3. Select the dynamic content in the Document window that you'd like to apply formatting.

   Here, we have selected to format the StartDate recordset column, which contains the employee's start date of employment (**Figure 6.1**).

**Table 6.1**

## Date and Time Formatting Options

| GENERAL DATE FORMATS | GENERAL TIME FORMATS |
|---|---|
| Monday, January 17, 2000 | 2:35:18 PM |
| 17 January 2000 | 14:35:18 |
| 17-01-00 | 02:35:18 P |
| 00-1-17 | 14:35 |
| 00-01-17 | |
| 17-01-2000 | |
| 1/17/00 | |

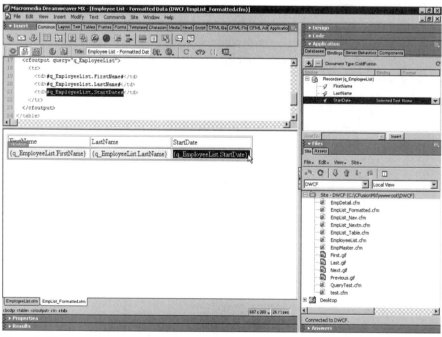

**Figure 6.1** When you select a piece of dynamic content in the Document window, that column will be selected in the Bindings panel.

Dreamweaver highlights the columns in the Bindings panel. Two columns display to the right of the selected dynamic element—Binding and Format.

4. In the Format column, click the down arrow button. If the down arrow is not visible, expand the panel.

5. From the Format pop-up menu, choose Date/Time > General Date Format (**Figure 6.2**).

6. To verify that the format was applied correctly, preview the page by doing one of the following:

   ▲ Change to Live Data view.

   ▲ Preview the page in a browser.

## ✔ Tips

■ Ensure that the data format is appropriate for the type of data you are formatting. For example, the date/time formats work only if the dynamic data consists of date/time data.

■ Note that you cannot apply more than one format to the same dynamic data.

■ You also can select dynamic content elements in Live Data view and apply formatting in the Bindings panel.

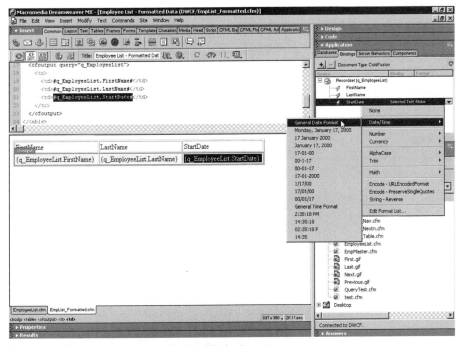

**Figure 6.2** All formatting options are displayed in the Format pop-up menu.

Chapter 6

# Formatting Numeric Data

You can use numeric data formatting to
format either an integer or decimal value
in one of the ways listed in **Table 6.2**.

### To format numeric data:

1. Open a document with dynamic content
   in Design view.

2. Choose the Application panel group's
   Bindings panel.

3. Select the dynamic content in the
   Document window that you'd like to
   apply formatting.

   Here, we have selected to format the
   ItemCost recordset column, which
   contains the cost of each item in the
   tblItems table (**Figure 6.3**).

   Dreamweaver highlights the column
   in the Bindings panel.

**Table 6.2**

## Numeric Formatting Options

| FORMAT TYPE | DESCRIPTION |
| --- | --- |
| Default | Displays a number in a locale-specific format. |
| 2 decimal places | Displays the number with two decimal places. |
| Rounded to integer | Rounds a decimal value to a whole integer. |
| () If negative | Surrounds the number with parentheses if it is a negative number. |
| Minus if negative | Prefix a minus sign (–) in front of negative numbers. |
| Do not group digits | If the number is greater than 999, do not use groupings with commas (or another locale-specific separator). |

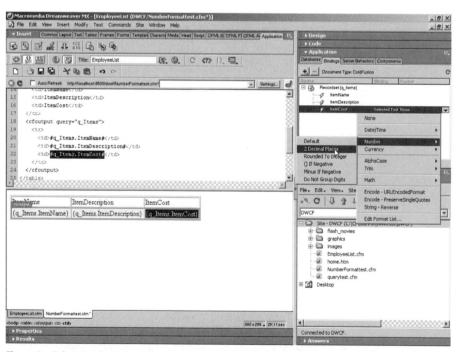

**Figure 6.3** Select the dynamic content you want to format in the Document window and apply formatting in the Bindings panel.

76

**4.** From the Format pop-up menu, choose Number > 2 Decimal Places.

**5.** Preview the page to verify that the format was applied correctly (**Figure 6.4**).

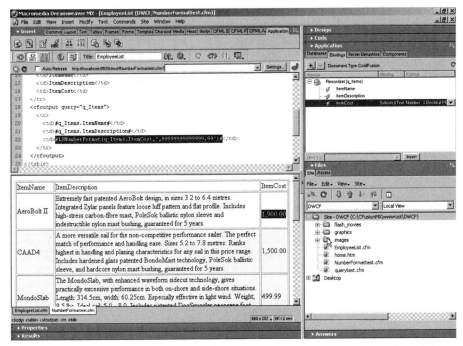

**Figure 6.4** Using Live Data view, you can see that Dreamweaver formats the number with two decimal places.

FORMATTING NUMERIC DATA

## What Is a Locale?

A locale identifies the exact language and cultural settings to use for a user. The locale controls the formats of dates and currencies and the display of time and numeric data.

In ColdFusion, a locale is identified by one or more of the following elements:

◆ Language, such as English, identified by an ISO 639 two-letter language code.

◆ Regional variation, which is identified by an ISO 3166 two-letter country code, for example, the (US) in English (US).

◆ Variant, which create special locales with additional requirements. A common variant example is the euro variant used by European countries that have adopted the Euro as their currency.

# Formatting Currency Data

There are four different formatting options for currency values, shown in **Table 6.3**.

When formatting US currency values that have General or Dollar formatting, Dreamweaver ensures the following:

◆ If the number has more than two decimal places, the data format rounds the number to the closest decimal.

◆ If the number has no decimal places, the data format adds a decimal point and two zeros.

## ✔ Tip

■ ColdFusion data formatting uses Java standard locale formatting rules on all platforms. Please see the ColdFusion documentation for more information on locales.

**Table 6.3**

| Currency Formatting Options | |
|---|---|
| FORMAT TYPE | DESCRIPTION |
| General | The currency format used in the locale; no currency symbol |
| Dollar | The currency format for US dollars with a dollar sign prefix |
| Local | The currency format and currency symbol used in the locale |
| International | The currency format used in the current locale's international standard format |

## To format currency data:

1. Open a document with dynamic content in Design view.

2. Choose the Application panel group's Bindings panel.

3. Select the dynamic content in the Document window that you'd like to apply formatting.

Here, we have selected to format the ItemCost recordset column, which contains the cost of each item in the tblItems table (**Figure 6.5**). Dreamweaver highlights the column in the Bindings panel.

*continues on next page*

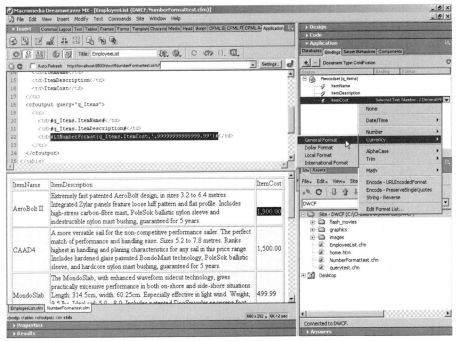

**Figure 6.5** Select the dynamic content you want to format in the Document window and apply formatting in the Bindings panel.

**4.** From the Format pop-up menu, choose Currency > Dollar Format.

**5.** Preview the page to verify that the format was applied correctly (**Figure 6.6**).

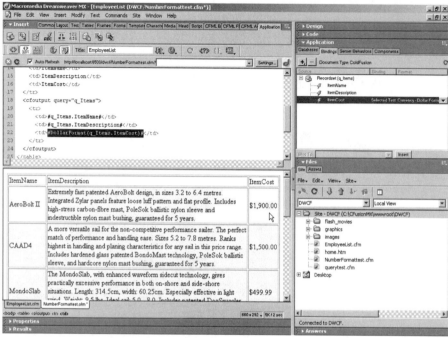

**Figure 6.6** Using Live Data view, you can see that Dreamweaver formats the number with two decimal places and a preceding dollar sign.

**Table 6.4**

### String Formatting Options

| FORMAT TYPE | DESCRIPTION |
|---|---|
| AlphaCase | Makes the string either upper- or lowercase. |
| Trim | Omits any preceding spaces, ending spaces, or both. Can strip the carriage return (CR) character. |
| Reverse | Reverses the order of the characters in an alphanumeric string. |

# Formatting String Data

If the dynamic data being displayed is alphanumeric, you have several options for formatting, as described in **Table 6.4**.

## To format string data:

1. Open a document with dynamic content in Design view.

2. Choose the Application panel group's Bindings panel.

3. Select the dynamic content in the Document window that you'd like to apply formatting.

   Here, we have selected to format the Last-Name recordset column, which contains the employee's last name (**Figure 6.7**). Dreamweaver highlights the column in the Bindings panel.

*continues on next page*

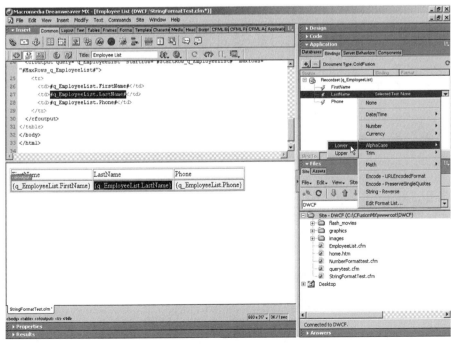

**Figure 6.7** Select the LastName recordset column and apply string formatting to it.

**4.** From the Format pop-up menu, choose AlphaCase > lower.

**5.** Preview the page to verify that the format was applied correctly (**Figure 6.8**).

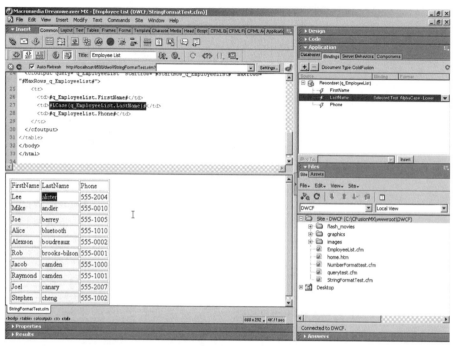

**Figure 6.8** Using Live Data view, you can see that Dreamweaver displays the employee's last name in all lowercase.

## Using Trim

The main reason for using the Trim formatting has to do with how databases store character information. If the column in the database is a fixed-length field, then it might return a fixed length of characters to ColdFusion—including spaces to pad it to the required length.

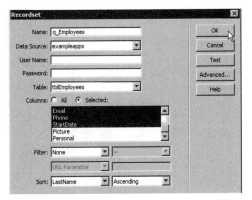

**Figure 6.9** The recordset on the master page should be created to contain all the data for both the master page and the detail page display.

# Creating a Master/Detail Interface

A master/detail interface is one in which Dreamweaver displays a small amount of information (on the master page) and enables a user to click on a hyperlink to get more information on an individual record of data (in a detail page). This common format helps users quickly find information pertinent to them without looking through too much detail until they want to get it. Dreamweaver MX makes the process for creating a master/detail interface simple:

1. Create a blank master page, and create a recordset that contains both the master and the detail page data.

2. Use the Master/Detail Page Set application object, which will display the master page information and create the detail page for you.

The recordset on the master page displays only a few columns from a database table while the same recordset on the detail page displays more columns to provide the extra detail about a specific record.

### To create the master page:

1. Create a blank master page and add a recordset to it.

   Make sure the recordset contains not only all the columns you'll need for the master page, but also all the columns you'll need for the detail page.

   Here, most of the information about an employee is selected. It represents the data needed for both the master and the detail pages (**Figure 6.9**).

2. Save the page. We save the page as **EmpMaster.cfm**.

## To create the detail page:

**1.** Be sure you are in Design view, and choose Insert > Application Objects > Master Detail Page Set.

The Master Detail Page Set dialog appears. **Figure 6.10** shows you an example of how to use this dialog.

**2.** In the Recordset pop-up menu, ensure that the recordset you just created is selected.

In the Master Page Fields area, you can identify the columns to display on the master page. All columns are selected by default.

**3.** Click the minus (–) button to remove any columns that you do not want to see on the master page.

Here three columns will show up on the master page. Next, you choose the order in which you want to display the columns on the master page. The recordset columns will be arranged horizontally in a table.

**4.** Select each column in the list and click the up or down arrow to change the order in which the columns appear.

**5.** In the Link To Detail From pop-up menu, choose the column in the recordset that will display a value that also serves as a link to the detail page.

For example, if you want each employee last name on your master page to have a link to the detail page, choose the recordset column containing last names.

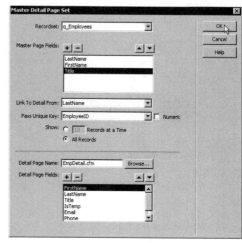

**Figure 6.10** The Master Detail Page Set dialog allows you to set the necessary information to create the detail page and display the master page information.

**6.** In the Pass Unique Key pop-up menu, choose the column in the recordset containing values identifying the records.

Usually, the column chosen is the primary key. This value is passed to the detail page so that it can identify the record chosen by the user. Here the primary key of the tblEmployees table—EmployeeID—is selected.

**7.** Deselect the Numeric checkbox if the unique key column is not numeric. If you do not specify the correct data type of the column here, you will receive an error message on the detail page when you run it.

In this example, the EmployeeID is not numeric, so the checkbox is deselected.

**8.** Specify the number of records to display on the master page.

Here, we elect to see all records.

**9.** In the Detail Page Name textbox, click Browse and enter a name and location for the detail page with a .cfm extension.

The application object will create the detail page for you if it doesn't exist. Here we are choosing to name the detail page EmpDetail.cfm and to store it in the root folder of the DWCF site.

**10.** In the Detail Page Fields area, select the columns to be displayed on the detail page.

By default, Dreamweaver selects all the columns in the master page's recordset. On the detail page, the recordset columns are vertical in a table.

**11.** Select a column in the list and click the up or down arrow to change the order in which the columns appear on the detail page.

*continues on next page*

## Hyperlinks and Passing Values

When you select the Link To Detail column, Dreamweaver creates a hyperlink on that column. This hyperlink takes the user to the detail page, as you specify in the Detail Page Name text field. Because the detail page will display information about only that one record, it needs to uniquely identify that record. This is where the Pass Unique Key value comes into play.

The Pass Unique Key value will be sent to the hyperlink page (here the detail page) on the URL. When the detail page is created for you, Dreamweaver looks for this value and uses it to create a recordset that returns only the one record you chose from the master page.

After you create the master/detail page set application object and when you have the master page open in Dreamweaver, check the Bindings panel to view the URL parameter that was created for you.

For more information about passing values on the URL, see Chapter 15: "Building Customized Master-Detail Interfaces."

CREATING A MASTER/DETAIL INTERFACE

**12.** Click OK.

The application object creates a detail page and adds dynamic content and server behaviors to both the master and detail pages.

The master page is altered to display the recordset in a tabular format (**Figure 6.11**).

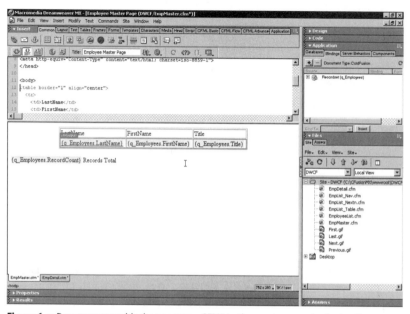

**Figure 6.11** Dreamweaver adds the necessary CFML to the master page to display the master recordset.

Dreamweaver creates the detail page and a new recordset within the page, and then displays the information about the selected row in a vertical table (**Figure 6.12**).

**13.** Save both pages.

*continues on next page*

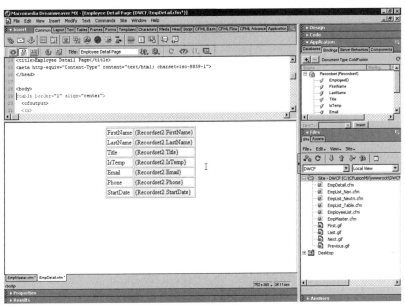

**Figure 6.12** Dreamweaver creates the detail page containing the detail recordset and the display logic.

CREATING A MASTER/DETAIL INTERFACE

**14.** Browse the master page using the preview browser (**Figure 6.13**).

**15.** Click on the last name hyperlink to choose a record.

Dreamweaver directs you to the detail page for more information (**Figure 6.14**).

### ✔ Tips

■ Remember that hyperlinks cannot be tested by using Live Data View—you must browse the page to see the results.

■ When you attempt to use the Master Detail Page Set on a new, unsaved page, Dreamweaver prompts you to first save your master page before continuing.

■ Primary key values usually do not contain information that is pertinent to users. However, this information uniquely identifies the detail record. Even if you don't display it, be sure to include it in the master recordset and set it as the Pass Unique Key value.

**Figure 6.13** The master page contains a listing of the data in tabular format with a hyperlink on the last name.

**Figure 6.14** The detail page contains a vertical table of the selected employee's detail.

# INSERTING
# DATA

In the preceding chapters, you learned how to extract data from a database to display on Web pages in various ways. In this chapter, you learn how to accept input from a user to insert into a database table.

The vehicle for accepting information from a user is by creating a form. A form contains a set of controls that accept user input in a variety of ways—from freely input text to selected radio buttons and checkboxes. Users can submit forms to the server by clicking buttons, which send the data to the Web server and then on to ColdFusion for processing. In this chapter, you process the data by inserting it into a database table.

There are two ways you can create insert forms within Dreamweaver MX:

◆ By using the Record Insertion Form Application Object.

◆ By creating a form with form objects for each database column and by creating an Insert Record server behavior.

# Using the Record Insertion Application Object

You can use a Record Insertion Form application object to create a form that contains form objects that link to columns of a database table. The application object lets you select which columns to include in the form, label each column, and select the type of form objects to insert. When a user enters data in the form fields and clicks the Submit button, Dreamweaver creates the code to insert a new row in a database. You also can set a page to open after a row has successfully been submitted to display a message to the user.

Dreamweaver adds both an HTML form and an Insert Record server behavior to your page, laying out the form objects in a basic table. You can freely customize the forms by using the page design tools.

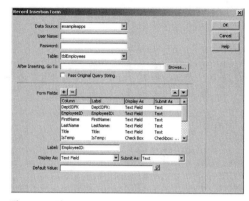

**Figure 7.1** The Record Insertion Form dialog enables you to create an insert form and insert processing.

## To use the Record Insertion application object:

1. Create a new page and position your cursor in the Document window in Design View.

2. In the Insert bar's Application tab, click the Record Insertion Form button.

   Alternately you can choose Insert > Application Objects > Record Insertion Form.

   The Record Insertion Form dialog appears (**Figure 7.1**).

3. Choose the Data Source, type the User Name and type the Password information, if applicable.

4. Select the table to receive a row of data.

   Here we are inserting a row into the tblEmployee table.

**5.** In the After Inserting, Go To textbox, click Browse to choose an HTML page with a success message to display to the user. If you do not have a page to display, leave this value blank.

Leaving the value blank means, however, that Dreamweaver inserts the record without a message to the user—they will be sent to the blank form again.

In the Form Fields section of the Record Insertion Form dialog, you define the form a visitor uses to enter data.

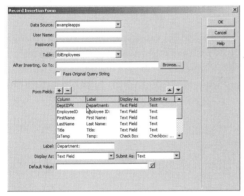

**Figure 7.2** Reword the labels to be meaningful to the user.

**6.** Click the minus sign button (–) to remove the fields you don't want included in the form.

**7.** Select each column in the Form Fields section and change the wording of the label to something meaningful because it will be displayed on the form (**Figure 7.2**).

Depending on the type of data that is stored in the column, Dreamweaver attempts to create each column as an appropriate form object. Notice the `IsTemp` column is detected as a yes/no value and therefore is created as a checkbox.

**8.** For each column in the Default Value textbox, type the initial text you want to appear in the field when it is displayed in the form.

**9.** Click OK to close the dialog.

The form is created, and all processing is included (**Figure 7.3**).

*continues on next page*

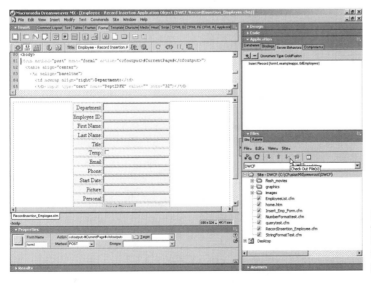

**Figure 7.3** When you close the Record Insertion dialog, Dreamweaver creates the form and includes all processing for an insert.

THE RECORD INSERTION APPLICATION OBJECT

**91**

**10.** Save the page, preview it in a browser, and then insert a new record to test the page (**Figure 7.4**).

If the insert is successful in this example, you will see the blank form reappear after insert.

Note that if you are following this example, you will either have to find a valid department ID value to input or you will have to leave that text field blank to avoid errors.

### ✔ Tip

■ In order to confirm that Dreamweaver successfully inserted the row, you can choose the Databases panel of the Application panel group, drill down into the data source and table, right-click on the table and choose View Data. Another method to confirm the insertion of the row is to write a page that displays all rows of the target table and use that page in the After Inserting, Go To box of the Record Insertion Form dialog.

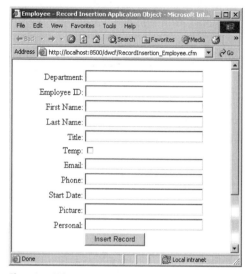

**Figure 7.4** When you preview the page, you see the employee insertion form and can submit a new employee.

# Using Dynamic Form Objects

In the example of creating an insert form to insert employee records, one column is a foreign key to the `tblDepartments` table (`DeptIDFK`). This column must contain the ID of a valid Department from the `tblDepartments` table. By keeping the default of a text field for this column in the Record Insertion dialog, you require the user to know a valid ID in order to insert the row.

Instead, you can use a recordset of rows from the `tblDepartments` table within a menu form object to display a valid list of departments. In order to do so, you must first create a recordset object of the `tblDepartments` table, and then use the Recordset Insertion application object and the new recordset to populate the menu.

## To use dynamic data in form objects:

1. Create a recordset to return all rows and columns from the `tblDepartments` table. Sort the rows by the `DepartmentName` column (**Figure 7.5**).

2. Position your cursor inside the Design view window and choose the Application toolbar's Record Insertion Form button.

3. Choose the Data Source, type the User Name, and type the Password information, if applicable.

4. Select the table to receive a row of data. Here we are inserting a row into the `tblEmployees` table.

5. Modify any label information and the order of the form fields, if desired.

*continues on next page*

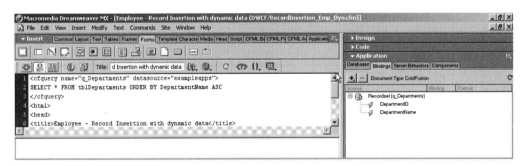

**Figure 7.5** Create a recordset that contains all rows and columns in the tblDepartments table.

**6.** For the `DeptIDFK` column, change the Display As value to Menu.

The dialog changes and now includes a Menu Properties button (**Figure 7.6**).

**7.** Click the Menu Properties button to open the Menu Properties dialog (**Figure 7.7**).

**8.** Change the Populate Menu Items option from Manually to From Database.

**9.** Select the recordset that you created for the departments.

**10.** Select DepartmentName as the Get Labels From value the user will see in the menu.

**11.** Select the Get Values From to the primary key column, in this case `DepartmentID`.

**12.** In the Set Value Equal To textbox, assign the value insert into the database as a foreign key, in this case the `DepartmentID` column.

**13.** Click OK to close the dialog and return to the Record Insertion Form dialog.

**14.** Click OK to close the Record Insertion Form dialog.

**15.** Save the file and preview it in the browser.

Dreamweaver creates the form in which the Department form field is a menu with a valid list of departments (**Figure 7.8**).

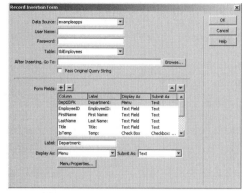

**Figure 7.6** Change the Display As value for the DeptIDFK column to menu.

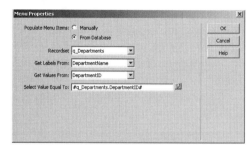

**Figure 7.7** Choose the recordset to be used to dynamically populate the Dept menu.

**Figure 7.8** Create the Employee insertion form with the Department ID field as a menu of valid departments.

# Setting Up Form Input Validation

It is always best to enforce data validation rules in the form whenever possible. When you attempt to enter data that does not match the data type required by the database table, the database returns an error to the user. Also, if the database requires a value in a column and the form does not supply it, an error occurs.

You can validate the contents of a form object by using the Validate Form behavior. The Validate Form behavior checks the contents of the specified text field or fields to ensure that the user has entered the correct type of data, or entered data if it is required.

Attach this behavior to individual text fields to validate the fields as the user is filling out the form, or attach it to the form to evaluate several text fields at once when the user clicks the Submit button. Attaching this behavior to a form tells the browser not to submit the form to the server if any of the specified text fields contains invalid data.

## To use the Validate Form behavior:

1. Choose Window > Behaviors to display the Behaviors panel, a member of the Design panel group (**Figure 7.9**).

   To validate individual fields as the user fills out the form, you must tell Dreamweaver which fields require validation.

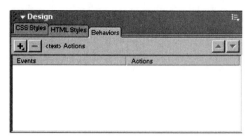

**Figure 7.9** If the Behaviors panel is not already displayed, choose Window > Behaviors to display it.

2. To specify which field or fields require validation, do one of the following:

   ▲ Select a text field to require the validation of just that field.

   ▲ In the lower-left corner of the Document window click the `<form>` tag in the tag selector, click the plus (+) icon and then, in the drop-down list, choose Validate Form to require the validation of multiple fields.

   The Validate Form dialog displays (**Figure 7.10**).

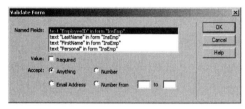

**Figure 7.10** The Validate Form dialog displays to set validation on one or more form fields.

3. In the Named Fields list, select the field or fields to be validated by doing one of the following:

   ▲ If you are validating individual fields, select the same field that you have selected in the Document window from the Named Fields list.

   ▲ If you are validating multiple fields, select a text field from the Named Fields list.

4. Select the Required option if the field must contain some data.

5. To select the validation type of either Anything, E-mail, Number or Number From, do one of the following:

   ▲ If you are validating one field, select it and apply its validation type.

   ▲ If you are validating multiple fields, select each one and apply its validation type.

   Here we want to require that both the EmployeeID and LastName values are supplied, so we choose each of these and check the Required checkbox.

### Validation Types

The Anything option requires that the field is required but need not contain any particular kind of data.

The E-mail address option requires that the field contains an @ symbol.

The Number option requires that the field contains only numerals.

The Number From option requires that the field contains a number in a specific range.

**Figure 7.11** The browser displays validation error messages when the user attempts to submit the form without data.

6. Click OK.

   If you are validating multiple fields when the user submits the form, the onSubmit event automatically appears in the Events pop-up menu.

   If you are validating individual fields, check that the default event is onBlur or onChange.

7. Save the file and preview it in the browser.

   When you attempt to submit an empty form, the browser displays a JavaScript alert with an error message (**Figure 7.11**).

## ✔ Tip

■ When applying behaviors, you need to make sure that every form object in your document (and every other object) has a unique name. If you use the same name for two different objects, behaviors may not work properly—even if the objects are in different forms.

---

### On What?

User actions on the form trigger the onSubmit, onChange, and onBlur events.

The onSubmit event fires when the user clicks the Submit button for the form.

The onChange event occurs when the user moves away from a form field and has typed something into that field.

The onBlur event occurs when the user moves away from a form field, whether or not the user has typed a value in that field.

The onBlur event is preferred when you have specified that the field is required.

# Creating a Form

The Record Insertion Form application object created both the form and the processing logic for the form for you. However, you can create the form page and processing page manually if you want greater control and customization.

Each form has two logical parts:

◆ The form that contains the user interface elements, known as form objects, collects information from users.

◆ The action handles the processing of the form page data. This value is a ColdFusion page. In these examples, the action page refers to the form page itself, although it could be an entirely different CFML page.

When a user submits a form, the Web server stores the values the user entered in the form in variables and then sends them to the action page for processing (**Figure 7.12**).

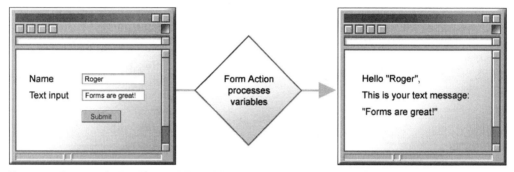

**Figure 7.12** The user submits a form, and the Web browser passes its data to the Web server for processing.

CREATING A FORM

**Figure 7.13** Insert bar's Form tab contains the form button.

You can use Dreamweaver MX to create forms and add form objects to them.

## To create a form:

1. On the Insert bar's Form tab, click the Form button (**Figure 7.13**).

   Dreamweaver MX inserts an empty form in the Document window. In Design view, a dotted red outline represents a form (**Figure 7.14**).

2. In the Property Inspector, provide a unique name to identify the form.

3. Provide the name of the action page to which the data will be sent.

4. Select POST as the method of passing data (**Figure 7.15**).

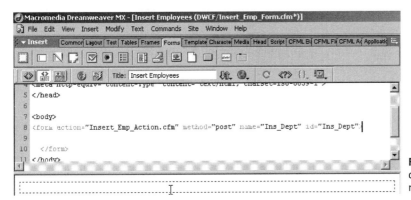

**Figure 7.14** Forms are displayed with a dotted red line in Design view.

**Figure 7.15** In the Property Inspector, set the required options of name, action, and method.

# Creating Form Objects

After you insert a form on your page, you can start adding form objects. A form object captures user input through visual elements such as a textbox or a checkbox. For each form object you define, the Web server creates a variable to hold the value entered by the user. After form submission, the Web server passes this variable to the action page. You can use the Forms tab on the Insert bar to create form objects.

**Table 7.1** reviews the most common types of objects that you can add to a form.

## Planning an Insert Form

Before creating an insert form, examine the data that you'd like to capture. Ensure that you have a database table to store the information, and decide which columns you want to fill with data. Also, ensure that you create a form object for each column that requires a value by the database rules.

Next, determine which form objects would best suit the type of data you are trying to capture. For instance, if you had a column that stored a yes/no value, you would want to use a check box instead of having them directly type in the values. Using the correct form object can help get more clean data from the users and into the database.

**Table 7.1**

### Form Objects

| FORM OBJECT | DESCRIPTION | CAPACITY | EXAMPLES |
|---|---|---|---|
| Text | Uses types alphanumeric characters | Single line | Name |
| | | | Email address |
| | | | Passwords (asterisks replace typed characters) |
| | | Multiple lines | Comments |
| Checkbox | User selects or deselects a checkbox | One option | On or Off |
| | | Multiple options | |
| Radio button | User selects one option within a group, automatically deselecting all the others | Multiple options | |
| List/Menu | User selects option(s) | One option | Pop-up menu |
| | | Multiple options | Scrolling list |
| Button | User clicks a button | An action occurs | Submit Form |
| | | | Reset Fields |

## To create text field form objects:

1. In Design view, position the cursor in the Document window within the red dotted line that represents the form.

2. Type a text label that will precede the text field to identify the information users must supply.

3. In the Insert bar, click the Forms tab.

4. On the Forms tab, click the Text Field button (**Figure 7.16**).

5. Use the Property Inspector to name the form object, preferably the same name as the database column if you plan to insert this data into a database column (**Figure 7.17**).

6. Set the Char Width to the visual size of the text object you'd like to see.

7. Set the Max Chars value to the number of characters that can be accepted into the target database column.

8. Save the page and preview the results in a browser to see the form (**Figure 7.18**).

### ✔ Tip

■ As you did with the form created by using the Record Insertion Form application object, you can now add form validation using the Behaviors panel, as well as dynamic values using the Server Behaviors panel.

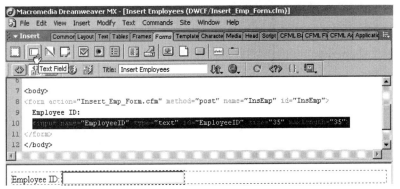

**Figure 7.16** Use the Form tab's Text Field button to create a text object.

**Figure 7.17** Set the form object's properties in the Property inspector.

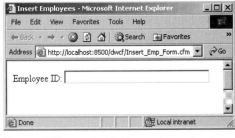

**Figure 7.18** The new text field accepts user input.

### Designing a Form

For simplicity's sake this example form does not use formatting. However, it's best to line up form labels and form objects by using tables.

**101**

## To create checkbox form objects:

1. To insert a checkbox control, create a text label and then choose the Checkbox button on the Forms tab of the Insert bar (**Figure 7.19**). Use this type of form object for database columns that accept yes or no values.

2. In the Property Inspector, name the checkbox, preferably the same name as that of the target database column.

3. Assign a checked value to send to the action page if the user checks the checkbox, usually a value of 1 (**Figure 7.20**).

4. Save the page and preview it in a browser to see the form (**Figure 7.21**).

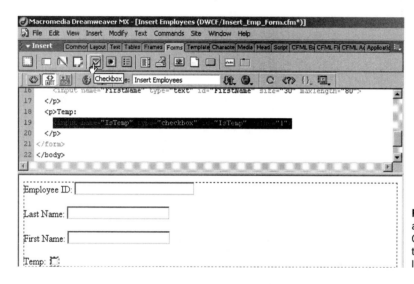

**Figure 7.19** To create a checkbox, use the Checkbox button on the Forms tab of the Insert bar.

**Figure 7.20** Assign a unique name and a checked value in the Property Inspector.

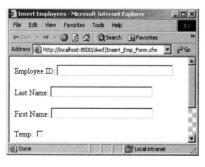

**Figure 7.21** Dreamweaver adds a checkbox to the form to collect information about temporary employees.

## To create long text form objects:

1. To insert a long text field, create a text label for the form object and then, in the Insert bar's Forms tab, click the Textarea icon (**Figure 7.22**).

2. In the Property Inspector, name the text area, preferably the same name as the target database column.

3. In the Char Width textbox, assign the viewable width of the object.

4. In the Num Lines textbox, assign the viewable number of lines that users can see onscreen.

5. In the Wrap drop-down list, assign the text wrapping property of Default, Off, Virtual, or Physical.

   Here, we are using Virtual (**Figure 7.23**).

*continues on next page*

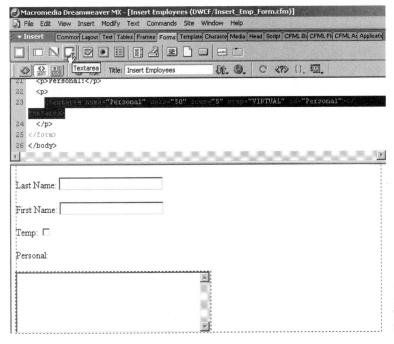

**Figure 7.22** To create a long text field, use the Textarea icon on the Forms tab of the Insert bar.

**Figure 7.23** Assign a unique name, the Char Width, Num Lines and Wrap settings in the Property Inspector.

CREATING FORM OBJECTS

**103**

**6.** Save the page and preview it in a browser to see the form (**Figure 7.24**).

### ✔ Tips

- To enable the user to type a return character that is then stored in the database, you will need to use a textarea form object. You cannot store return characters in a text form object.

- You cannot limit the number of characters that a person types within a textarea control unless you code some JavaScript to do so.

### To create button form objects:

**1.** On the Forms toolbar, click the Button icon to insert a button at the bottom of the page (**Figure 7.25**).

Every form must have a button to submit the form data to the server.

**Figure 7.24** A textarea form object stores long textual information.

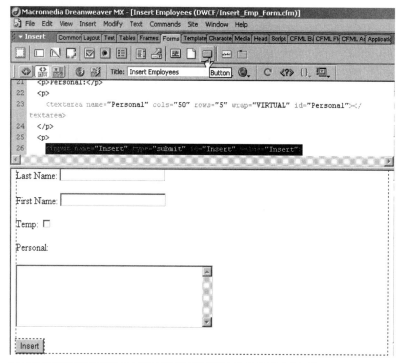

**Figure 7.25** Create a button on the form to submit the data to the server.

CREATING FORM OBJECTS

**2.** In the Property Inspector, name the button and put in a label that will show on the button in the form.

**3.** Leave the action set to Submit form (**Figure 7.26**).

**4.** Save the page and preview the page in a browser to see the form (**Figure 7.27**).

**Figure 7.26** Change the button's label for display.

**Figure 7.27** By previewing the page in a browser, you can see the form you created.

## Wrap Settings

Use the Wrap setting in the Property Inspector to set how multiple lines in long text fields are both viewed and stored.

◆ Off or Default prevents text from wrapping to the next line. When the user's input exceeds the right boundary of the text area, text scrolls toward the left. Users must press Return to move the insertion point to the next line in the text area.

◆ Virtual sets Word Wrap in the text area. When the user's input exceeds the right boundary of the text area, text wraps to the next line. When data is submitted for processing, Word Wrap isn't applied to the data. It is submitted as one string of data.

◆ Physical both wraps text to the next line visually within the long text field as well as inserts a character for the line break into the value when it is submitted for processing.

# Inserting Database Records

After you create a form on the insert page, you are ready to process the insert. To insert a row from a form submission, you use the Insert Record server behavior. The Insert Record server behavior generates the server-side code that is necessary to add information captured by the form to the database.

## To use the Insert Form Page server behavior:

1. Position your cursor anywhere inside the Document window of the insert form.

2. In the Application panel, click the Server Behaviors panel. Click the plus sign and select Insert Record (**Figure 7.28**).

   The Insert Record dialog displays (**Figure 7.29**).

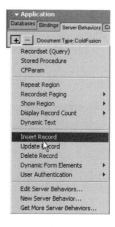

**Figure 7.28** Use the Server Behaviors panel to add an Insert Record server behavior to the action page.

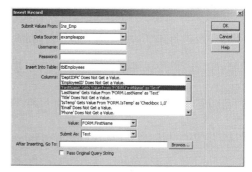

**Figure 7.29** Use the Insert Record dialog to insert the form's row into the database table.

## Columns and Form Objects

The column section of the dialog attempts to match up any form fields with columns in the database. It does this by matching the name of the form field with the name of the database column. This is why it is recommended to name each form object the same as the target database column.

If the form fields and database columns do not match correctly, or if you chose form fields names that are different from the column names, you will have to select each column and change the Value drop-down list to the correct form field.

3. In the Submit Values drop-down list, ensure that the name of the form that you created is selected.

4. Select the Data Source and specify any login information required.

5. In the Insert Into Table drop-down list, select the table to receive the data.

6. In the Columns list, ensure that each column is matched up with the appropriate form object.

7. In the Submit As drop-down list, ensure that the Web server submits each form object with the correct datatype, checking your database table for the correct datatypes, if necessary.

8. In the After Inserting, Go To textbox, specify the page to send to a user, either a page that gives them a message after a successful insert or another page entirely.

9. Click OK.

10. Save the file and preview the file in the browser.

## SQL INSERT Statement

The Insert Record server behavior creates a SQL INSERT statement using the form data. The SQL INSERT statement creates a new data entry in a database table. This statement is in the <cfquery> tag, as shown in this example:

```
<cfquery datasource="Test">
 INSERT INTO Employee (LastName,Phone)
 VALUES ('#FORM.LastName#',
→ #FORM.Phone#')
</cfquery>
```

The INSERT INTO statement is followed by the name of the table and the list of columns into which you insert data.

Then VALUES is followed by the values being inserted into the database. In this case, form data are the variables.

# UPDATING DATA

In the last chapter, you learned how to display a blank form and enable the user to fill in a new row and submit it for saving in the database.

Updating a row of data involves the following two parts:

1. A List page, which displays a set or all the rows so users can select one to update.

2. A Form page, which displays the row in a form, allows the user to update information and then processes the update in the database.

In this chapter, you learn how to pass data on the URL from one page to another, display data in a form, and update a row of data in the database. You learn to do so by first using the Record Update Form application object, and then by manually creating the update form and use the Update Record server behavior.

# Creating a List Page

A List page is created to enable the user to choose a row to update. This page contains the following:

◆ A recordset to display the rows.

◆ A hyperlink on some data in the row so the user can click on that hyperlink and get sent to the update form.

◆ A URL parameter to pass the primary key of the chosen row.

### To create the listing page:

1. Create a new page with a recordset of the table data you'd like to update, here called qEmployeeList.

   In this example, we are updating several columns in a row in the tblEmployees table.

2. Use the Dynamic Table application object to display all rows in the table (**Figure 8.1**).

3. Create a new page, title it, and save it without further coding.

   Here we are saving the page as Emp_Upd_Form.cfm. You will build this page in the next task. This will be the update form page we want the hyperlink to go to.

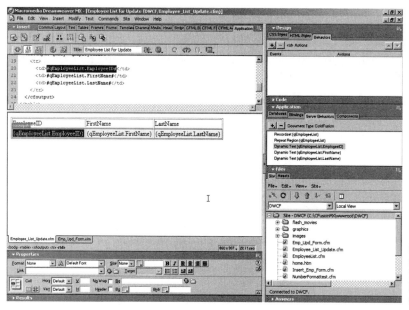

**Figure 8.1** Create a recordset and display the data using the Dynamic Table application object.

**4.** Return to the listing page and highlight the data you would like to make a hyperlink.

Here we are using the `EmployeeID` column.

**5.** In the Property Inspector, click the Browse for File icon to select the new page in which to create the hyperlink.

Dreamweaver underlines the column to denote the hyperlink (**Figure 8.2**).

*continues on next page*

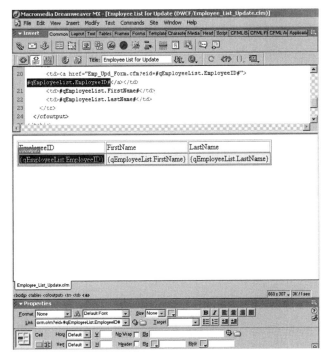

**Figure 8.2** Create a hyperlink from the EmployeeID column to the newly created update form page.

## What Is a Query String?

A *query string* is a term used to describe the data that can be passed between two pages on the URL. The parts of the query string given in the task "To create a listing page" are

◆ The question mark (?) tells the browser that anything to the right of the question mark is not part of the address but instead data that needs to be sent to the page in the address.

◆ `EID=#qEmployeeList.EmployeeID#` creates a variable called `EID` and sets it to the value of the `qEmployeeList` query's `EmployeeID` column value. The hash marks (#) make ColdFusion inspect this variable and convert it to the value of the `EmployeeID` of the selected row.

◆ The ampersand (&) separates the URL variables if more than one of them is set in the query string.

CREATING A LIST PAGE

**6.** Save the file and preview in a browser.

The Employee ID column of data has been turned into hyperlinks for each row (**Figure 8.3**). When you test a hyperlink, it takes you to the blank form page.

**7.** Return to the Employee Listing page, and, in the Property Inspector's Link textbox, type the following query string after the page name:

`?EID=#qEmployeeList.EmployeeID#`

**8.** Save the page, preview it in the browser, and click the hyperlink.

The browser opens the blank form page. Notice in the URL that the EID variable has been sent (**Figure 8.4**).

## ✔ Tips

■ Refer to Chapter 4, "Retrieving Database Data," for more details on creating a recordset.

■ Refer to Chapter 5, "Displaying Database Data," for more details on using the Dynamic Table application object.

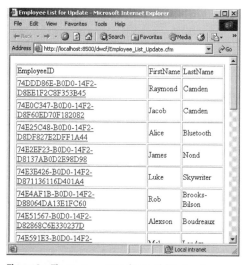

**Figure 8.3** The EmployeeID column of data has been created as a set of hyperlinks.

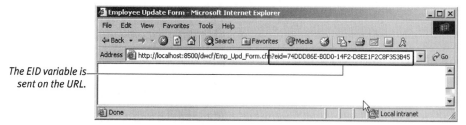

*The EID variable is sent on the URL.*

**Figure 8.4** Click the hyperlink and notice that the browser displays the EmployeeID for the selected row in the URL.

CREATING A LIST PAGE

URL.EID

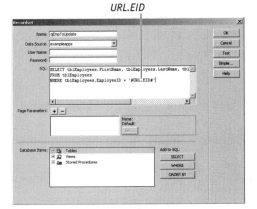

**Figure 8.5** Create a recordset to return the row to update by using the URL.EID variable's value.

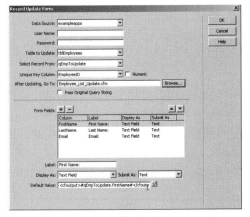

**Figure 8.6** Use the Record Update Form to create the update form and processing.

## Updating Primary Key Values?

You assign primary keys to uniquely identify a row of data. Primary keys also are used as foreign key values in other tables to associate one table to another. Therefore, it is recommended that you do not modify primary key values, or you will have extra work to do to update any existing foreign key values as well.

# Using the Record Update Form Application Object

To update a row of data in the database, you can use the Record Update Form application object. This application object provides a dialog that builds the update form, displays the row to be updated, and also builds in the update logic.

The components of an update form page are

◆ A recordset with a filter that uses the URL parameter to return only the row identified.

◆ A form and update processing that was created using the Record Update Form application object.

### To create the update form:

1. Open the page you created in the last task, here called Emp_Upd_Form.cfm.

2. Create a recordset to retrieve the columns that you allow your users to update in the table you desire.

   Here we are selecting only a few columns to be updated in the tblEmployees table.

3. In the recordset, create a filter using the URL parameter that was passed into the page, here called EID (**Figure 8.5**).

   You must manually type the EID variable in the WHERE clause and surround it with hash marks (#). Because this is a character value, ensure it is enclosed in single quotes.

4. From the Insert menu, select Application Objects > Record Update Form.

   The Record Update Form dialog displays (**Figure 8.6**).

5. Select the Data Source, provide any required login information, and select the Table to Update.

*continues on next page*

**6.** In the Select Record From drop-down list, select the recordset that you created in steps 2 and 3.

**7.** In the Unique Key Column drop-down list, select the primary key of the table, here EmployeeID.

**8.** In the After Updating, Go To textbox, click the Browse button and choose the employee listing page that you created in the last task.

After the users update the data, Cold-Fusion takes them back to the listing page.

**9.** In the Form Fields area, select the columns that you have selected in the recordset to create a form object for each one. Do not include the primary key column in the list because you do not want to display and/or update that value.

**10.** For each column that remains, set the Label, Display As and Submit As value appropriately. Be sure that all the types of data match those in the database columns.

**11.** Also for each column, set the Default Value textbox to the matching query column value.

**12.** Click OK.

Dreamweaver creates the form and update processing logic for you.

**13.** Save the page.

**14.** Return to the listing page to preview in the browser and select a hyperlink of a row to update.

The Web server sends you to the update form page (**Figure 8.7**).

**Figure 8.7** Choose a hyperlink and receive that row in a pre-filled form. Update a value and click Update Record.

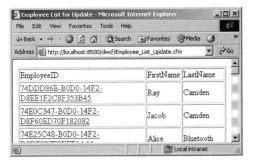

**Figure 8.8** When you make changes and submit the form, ColdFusion sends you to the listing page, where you can see the change made.

**15.** Update a value and click Update Record.

Here, we are updating the first name from Raymond to Ray. ColdFusion updates the row and sends you back to the listing page. If you updated any data on the listing page, you should see that change (**Figure 8.8**).

## ✔ Tip

■ While you are developing the update form page, it is easy to mistakenly try to execute that page on its own. However, since this page requires the URL parameter of EID to be passed in, ColdFusion gives you an error message. See Chapter 11, "Hand Coding CFML," for information on testing for existence of variables to ensure errors can't occur if the user mistakenly tries to browse directly to the form page.

# Manually Creating an Update Form

The Record Update Form application object created both the form and the processing logic for the form for you. An alternative is to create the update form and update logic yourself, just as you did with inserts in the last chapter. The process for updating a row of data is as follows:

1. Display the rows to the user in a list.

2. Allow the user to click on a hyperlink of a desired row to update. Pass the unique identifier (the primary key) of the row to the update form.

3. Display the selected row in a pre-filled form by retrieving it using the unique identifier (primary key) that was passed in to the page.

4. Allow the user to make any changes to the row.

5. When the user clicks the Submit button, make any changes to the row in the database by using the Update Record server behavior.

## To create an update form:

1. Create a blank ColdFusion page, which will be used to create the manual update form. Save the page.

   Here we are saving the page as Emp_Upd_Form_Manual.cfm.

2. Create a new page to list all the rows in the table using a recordset and the Dynamic Table application object. Point the hyperlinked column to the blank form page (Emp_Upd_Form_Manual.cfm) and pass the primary key value in the URL.

   Alternately, you can save the listing page you created in a previous section as a new page and change the hyperlink page name to point to this new form.

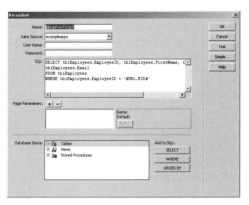

**Figure 8.9** Retrieve the row the user has selected to display in the form for update.

3. Return to the update form (`Emp_Upd_Form_Manual.cfm`) and create a recordset that returns all desired columns from the table, using the URL variable in the filter (**Figure 8.9**).

4. Create a form and populate it with form objects for each column value you want to update.

   Here we are creating a form to update some columns of the tblEmployees table (**Figure 8.10**).

5. Select the form object for the LastName.

*continues on next page*

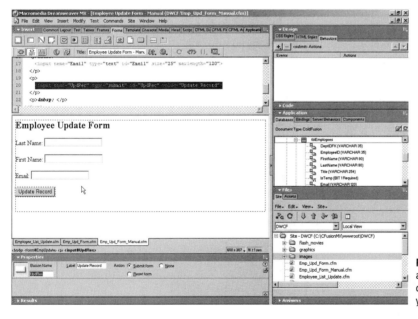

**Figure 8.10** Create a form based on a database table just as you did in Chapter 7.

MANUALLY CREATING AN UPDATE FORM

**6.** In the Property Inspector, to the right of the Init Val textbox, click the Bind to Dynamic Source (lightening bolt) icon (**Figure 8.11**).

Dreamweaver displays the Dynamic Data dialog (**Figure 8.12**).

**7.** Find the recordset that retrieves the row to update and expand it. Choose the LastName column of the recordset.

**8.** Click OK.

You will see the dynamic text for the recordset's LastName column in the form object.

**9.** Repeat these steps for the FirstName and Email form objects (**Figure 8.13**).

To uniquely identify the row to update, you must supply the primary key in the form. However, you do not want to allow the user to view and/or change it. Therefore, you use a hidden form object to pass the `EmployeeID` in the form.

**Figure 8.11** Use the Property Inspector to bind the dynamic source to the last name form object.

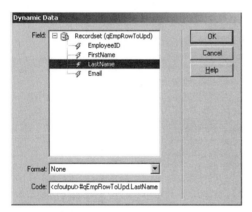

**Figure 8.12** The Dynamic Data dialog enables you to set the form object to the value of a recordset column value.

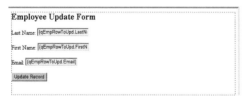

**Figure 8.13** Set each form object's default value to the matching recordset columns.

**10.** On the Insert bar's Forms toolbar, insert a hidden form object (**Figure 8.14**) anywhere within the form.

You should see a yellow indicator of the hidden field on the form (Figure 8.14).

**11.** In the Property Inspector, set the name of the form object to EmployeeID.

**12.** In the Property inspector, to the right of the Init Val textbox, click the Bind to Dynamic Source lightening bolt.

The Dynamic Data dialog will display.

**13.** Set the dynamic value to the `EmployeeID` column of the recordset.

**14.** Click OK.

Now you are ready to drop in the update processing using the Update Record server behavior, as described in the following section.

## ✔ Tips

■ Refer to the task in "Creating a List Page" section for more detail on working with primary keys by sending them on the URL.

■ Refer to Chapter 7, "Inserting Data," for details about creating a form based on a database table.

Hidden form object

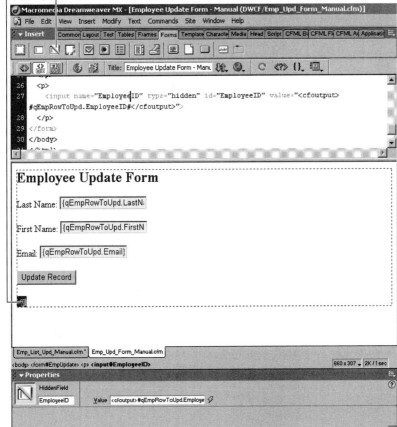

**Figure 8.14** The Forms tab on the Insert bar contains a hidden form object button. The hidden form object is displayed as a yellow icon in Design view.

# Using the Update Record Server Behavior

If you have manually created an update form, you can use the Update Record server behavior to drop in the update processing logic.

## To use the Update Record server behavior:

1. Open the form that was created for the update.

2. In the Application panel group's Server Behaviors panel, select the plus (+) icon and choose Update Record (**Figure 8.15**).

   The Update Record dialog displays (**Figure 8.16**).

3. Set the Submit Values From drop-down list to the name of the update form.

4. Set the Data Source and login information appropriately.

5. In the Update Table drop-down list, select the table, here tblEmployees.

6. In the Columns area, ensure that each form object matches up with the appropriate database table column. Also ensure that each Submit As column matches the form data to the database table column data type.

   Be sure to always include the primary key in the list, or you will receive an error message.

7. For the primary key column, select the Primary Key checkbox.

8. In the After Updating, Go To textbox, browse to the listing page to route the user to the list page when the update is complete.

9. Click OK.

10. Save the page.

11. Return to the list page and preview it in the browser. Select a row to update. You should see the pre-filled form.

12. Submit any changes.

    ColdFusion routes you back to the list page.

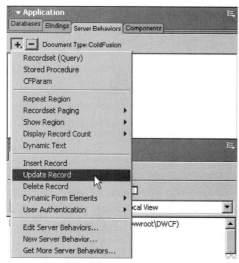

**Figure 8.15** Add the Update Record server behavior from the Server Behaviors panel.

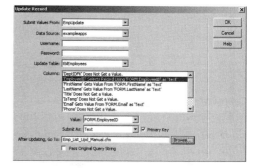

**Figure 8.16** Fill out the Update Record dialog to create the update processing logic.

USING THE UPDATE RECORD SERVER BEHAVIOR

# BUILDING A SIMPLE SEARCH INTERFACE

Thus far you have displayed all rows in the recordset, either in one page or in a set of pages. You may find this to be an ineffective way to work with data, especially when you're working with a large volume of data that is increasing. (Consider a page that displays all the data and the data is increasing rapidly over time.) The answer to volumes of ever-increasing data is to create search pages.

You've already created forms to both accept and insert data, as well as display and update data. Using a form, you also can allow your Web site users to search for specific data in a database. You create a search form and a results page to implement a search interface.

If you have only one search parameter, Dreamweaver lets you add search capabilities to your Web application by simply designing your pages and by completing a few dialogs. If you have more than one search parameter, you need to write more code by hand. The more advanced search is covered in Chapter 16, "Building an Advanced Search Interface."

# Creating a Search Form

The search page contains a form in which the user enters search parameters. When the user clicks the form's Submit button, the browser sends the search parameters to the results page on the server.

## To create a search form:

1. Create a new page in Dreamweaver MX.

2. On the Insert bar, use the Forms toolbar to insert a form (**Figure 9.1**).

3. In the Property Inspector, change the name of the form.

   Here we are setting the form to EmpSearch. The Action property value should match the name of the results page, which you create in the next task. Here we are designating the page EmpSearchAction.cfm.

4. Inside the form, create a text label for the form object, here labeled Last Name.

5. Next to the text label, use the Forms toolbar to insert a text form object.

6. In the Property Inspector, name the form object.

   Here we are creating a search parameter for looking up employees by last name in the tblEmployees table, so we are naming the text object LastName to match the database column. The size is 20, and the char width setting is set to 80, the max length in the database column.

7. On a new line, create a Submit button that has the text Search on the button.

8. Save the file.

   Here we are saving the file as EmpSearchForm.cfm.

## ✔ Tip

■ If you are having a hard time creating the form, refer to Chapter 7, "Inserting Data," for a refresher on creating forms.

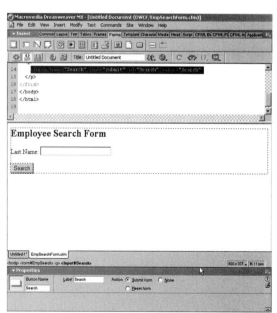

**Figure 9.1** Create a form with a form control on the column you'd like to search in the database.

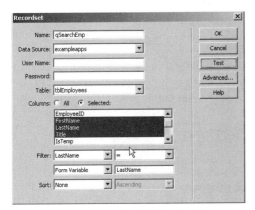

**Figure 9.2** Create a recordset binding that filters on the entered form value.

# Creating a Results Page

The results page is responsible for retrieving records from the database that meet the search criteria. To process a search request, the results page:

◆ Uses the data submitted by the user to search the database for matching rows

◆ Builds a recordset from the records found

◆ Displays the contents of the recordset

To search a database, you build a dynamic recordset. A dynamic recordset is one in which parts of the query statement change based on user input.

On the results page, you can create a dynamic recordset using the simple Recordset dialog with a filter to exclude records that don't meet the search parameters sent by the search page.

### To create the results page:

**1.** Create a new page and save it with the name that you specified as the Action attribute of the search form.

Here we are saving it as EmpSearchAction.cfm.

**2.** Open the Bindings panel, click the plus (+) button, and, from the drop-down list, select Recordset to create a new recordset, making sure the simple Recordset dialog appears (**Figure 9.2**).

**3.** Type a name for the recordset and set the connection information.

**4.** In the Table drop-down list, select the table to be searched in the database.

*continues on next page*

CREATING A RESULTS PAGE

**5.** To select the columns you wish to display on the results page, do one of the following:

▲ Control-click (Windows) each column name in the list

▲ Command-click (Macintosh) each column name in the list.

**6.** From the Filter area's first drop-down list, select a column in the table to compare against the search parameter sent by the search page.

The search form prompts for the last name, so we chose the `LastName` column.

**7.** From the drop-down list beside the column you just selected, select the equal sign (it should be the default).

This choice states that the user wants only those employee records in which the `LastName` column is exactly the same as the one specified on the search page.

**8.** From the third drop-down list, select Form Variable.

This list specifies where the value sent by the search page is currently stored on the server.

**9.** In the fourth drop-down list, enter the name of the form object that accepts the search parameter on the search page.

The text object on the form also is called `LastName`, so that name is given.

**10.** Click Test to test the recordset.

Dreamweaver prompts you for the missing value (since the form was not submitted).

**11.** Enter a last name (**Figure 9.3**), here Camden, and click OK to return the results (**Figure 9.4**).

**Figure 9.3** When you test a recordset with a form value filter, you will be prompted for a value.

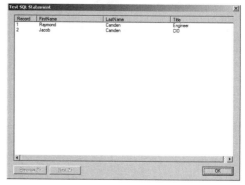

**Figure 9.4** Entering a filter of 'Camden' as test data returns two rows.

**Figure 9.5** Test the search form by searching for "Camden" and you should see two rows returned.

**12.** Click OK to insert the query into the action page.

**13.** Use the Dynamic Table application object to display the results of the query.

**14.** Save the page.

**15.** Return to the form page (`EmpSearchForm.cfm`) and preview the form in the browser. Enter a last name to search for and submit the form.

You should see the filtered results in the results page (**Figure 9.5**).

**16.** Click the Back button in the browser to return to the form and search for Smith.

You will see two different rows of data.

## ✔ Tips

■ Refer to Chapter 5, "Displaying Database Data," for a refresher on using the Dynamic Table application object.

■ Ensure that the form's Property Inspector value for Method stays at POST, or you will receive errors when you submit the form. Using POST send the information as form data, where using GET sends the data on the URL.

# Handling Empty Results Pages

When you try to search for employee records and do not specify a last name (in other words, you submit a blank form), Dreamweaver does not return any rows. Also, when you submit a last name that doesn't exist or an incomplete last name value, you will not receive any rows in the recordset on the results page. Only the table heading will display.

In the cases in which the results page returns no data, you may want to display a more user-friendly message, such as No records returned from your search.

You can use the following two other Show Region server behaviors to display the data if there was some returned, or a message if there was no data returned:

♦ Show If Recordset Is Empty—If a recordset is empty, you can display a message informing the user that no records were returned.

♦ Show If Recordset Is Not Empty—If a recordset is not empty, the results are displayed.

## To handle no rows returned:

1. Open the results page.

2. Below the table, type a message
   No records match your search criteria.

3. Select the table that displays the records returned from the search.

4. In the Application panel, click the Server Behaviors panel. Click the plus sign and select Show Region > Show If Recordset Is Not Empty (**Figure 9.6**).

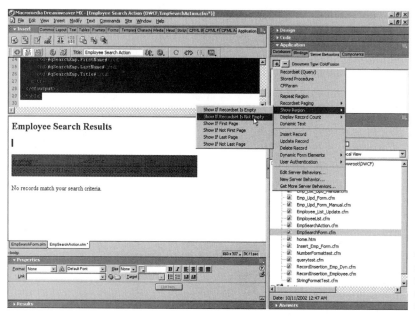

**Figure 9.6** Use the Show Region server behaviors to perform an action based on a condition.

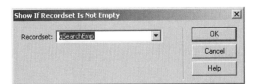

**Figure 9.7** Use the Show If Recordset Is Not Empty server behavior to display results.

**Figure 9.8** When a blank form is submitted, a message is displayed that no rows were returned.

**5.** From the dialog's Recordset drop-down list, select the search recordset (**Figure 9.7**).

**6.** Click OK.

**7.** Highlight the empty recordset text you added. In the Server Behaviors panel, click the plus sign and select Show Region > Show If Recordset Is Empty. From the dialog's Recordset drop-down list, select the search recordset.

**8.** Click OK.

**9.** Save the file.

**10.** Return to the search form and preview it in a browser. Submit a search form without specifying a search value.

You should see the message that no rows were returned (**Figure 9.8**).

## ✔ Tip

- If you attempted to add the Show If Recordset Not Empty server behavior to the table, and then add the message, Dreamweaver considers the text message to be part of that server behavior section. If you then attempt to add the Show If Recordset Is Empty server behavior to the message, Dreamweaver displays an error message stating that you cannot overlap server behaviors. This is why you must put in the message first, select each section, and then add the server behavior to it.

# PASSWORD PROTECTION AND SECURITY

Security of Web applications is a major concern, especially those Web applications that allow manipulation and access to sensitive data in a database. In a secure Web application, you want to know who uses the system and what they do, so you must set up user authentication. *User authentication* is a term that refers to accepting the users who are allowed on the system, and approving them for any secure actions.

In Dreamweaver MX, you can generate a moderate degree of security to your Web application. You can enable security by using the following methods:

◆ Enabling password protection, so users must log in to the Website or secure parts of it.

◆ Tracking a user's session by saving information between each page request.

◆ Allow a user to log out of the system when they are done.

In this chapter, you learn how to set up password protection, enable session management, and restrict access to pages in your site by using server behaviors.

# Creating a User Session

When you create a Web application, you are creating a set of pages that are related only by hyperlinks in which you pass information on the URL, or by submitting form data from one page to another. To this point in this book, this is the only way that you have learned to pass information from one page to another. We refer to such a Web application as a *stateless application*; the state of the current user is unknown from page to page.

To create a ColdFusion application that can track a user from page to page, you need to create a user session. A session usually is defined in one of the following ways:

◆ In a site without user authentication, a session starts from the time the user enters any page on the site until he does not access that site for a specified period of time (usually a session expires after 20 minutes of inactivity).

◆ In a site with user authentication, a session starts from the time the user logs in and is authenticated until he explicitly logs out, or the session expires with no activity.

An application also can be a combination of both of the above; ColdFusion can track a user when he requests a page in the site, and then track additional information after he logs in.

To use the built-in security generation features of Dreamweaver MX, you need to enable a session by using the Application Framework. The Application Framework is actually a file, always named `Application.cfm`. This page, when present in the path, automatically will be included at the top of every ColdFusion page that is requested. To be in the path of a ColdFusion page, the `Application.cfm` file must be stored in the same directory, or any directory above it. In this way, an entire directory structure, which represents a ColdFusion application, can share a common `Application.cfm` file. One way you can use an Application Framework is in setting variables shared by all pages.

## To create the application framework:

1. Create a new ColdFusion page.

2. Save the page in the top-level directory of your ColdFusion application as `Application.cfm`.

   Since the `Application.cfm` file should not contain any HTML code, you will need to remove all code in Code view.

---

### OnRequestEnd.cfm

Upon finding and including an `Application.cfm` at the beginning of each page, ColdFusion also appends another file to the end of every ColdFusion page. This file, named `OnRequestEnd.cfm`, must reside in the same directory as the `Application.cfm` file. ColdFusion often uses this file for clean-up operations.

---

### Session Administration

The ColdFusion Administrator has default settings for using sessions. These settings can establish the default and maximum session timeout values, or they can override the use of session variables altogether. If you are working in a hosted environment, check with your Site Administrator as to the session settings.

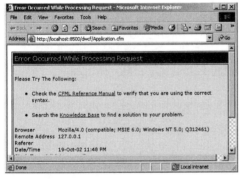

Figure 10.1 To remove all HTML code, change to Show Code and Design View.

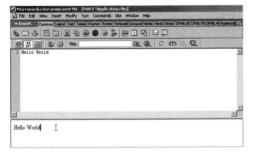

Figure 10.2 To test the Application.cfm file, insert a test message.

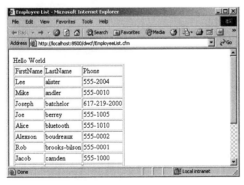

Figure 10.3 You cannot directly browse an Application.cfm file without receiving an error.

Figure 10.4 ColdFusion includes the Application.cfm file at the top of every page within the page's path.

3. Use the button on the Document toolbar (**Figure 10.1**) to change the view to Show Code and Design View.

4. Select all code in the Code view window and delete it.

5. In the Design view pane, insert a Hello World message in this file to test inclusion (**Figure 10.2**).

   If you attempt to browse an Application.cfm file directly, you will receive an error message (**Figure 10.3**).

6. Open any other ColdFusion page in the same directory or in a subdirectory and preview it in a browser.

   You should see the Hello World text at the top of that page (**Figure 10.4**).

## ✔ Tips

- Since ColdFusion is not a case-sensitive language, naming the Application.cfm file with or without the capital letter **A** makes no difference on the Windows or Macintosh platforms. However, if you are creating ColdFusion applications to run on the Unix platform, the filename must have a capital **A** since Unix is case sensitive.

- ColdFusion will search directories for an Application.cfm file all the way up to the drive root. If you are experiencing anomalies with inclusion of additional code that you had not expected, check to see if an Application.cfm file exists on the path all the way up to the drive root.

- ColdFusion will include only one Application.cfm file, and you cannot prevent ColdFusion from including it if it is found. If you wish to have different processing for each site section, you can create a subdirectory under the root folder for each section and then have a different copy of the Application.cfm file in each subdirectory for inclusion.

CREATING A USER SESSION

**131**

# Enabling Session Management

Creating the Application Framework is the first step in enabling your ColdFusion applications to share information about a user's session between page requests. The next step is to enable session management. You enable session management in the `Application.cfm` file.

Once a user requests a page and the session begins, ColdFusion will write two cookies on the user's browser in order to keep track of that user from page to page. Therefore, cookies must be enabled in the browser in order for session management to work.

## To enable session management:

1. Open the `Application.cfm` file. If you are using the file created in the last task, remove the `Hello World` text so the file is now blank.

2. On the Insert bar, choose the CFML Advanced toolbar to make it the current toolbar.

3. On the CFML Advanced toolbar, choose the cfapplication toolbar item (**Figure 10.5**).

   The Tag Editor for the `<cfapplication>` tag displays (**Figure 10.6**).

**Figure 10.5** Choose the cfapplication toolbar item to enable session management.

## What Is a Cookie?

A *cookie* is a small piece of information stored on the user's machine in a file or a set of files, depending on the browser. Typically, a cookie records your preferences or a unique identifier for the browser when using a particular site. Only the Website domain that wrote the cookie can read that cookie on subsequent requests.

You can view the cookies that have been stored on your hard disk. The location of the cookies depends on the browser.

◆ Internet Explorer stores each cookie as a separate file in a Windows subdirectory.

◆ Netscape stores all cookies in a single cookies.txt file.

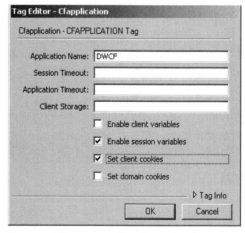

**Figure 10.6** Use the tag editor for creating the `<cfapplication>` code needed to enable session management.

4. Enter a unique name in the Application Name text field of the dialog, here DWCF.

5. Select the Enable Session Management and the Set Client Cookies checkboxes.

6. Leave all other options blank.

7. Click OK to close the dialog and write the tag onto the page.

   If you browse any page within the directory of the Application.cfm file, or in a subdirectory, ColdFusion now detects a first time user and writes two cookies to start tracking sessions. You will not see any other visual effect in the page.

### ✔ Tips

- By default, ColdFusion sessions require the use and acceptance of cookies on the user's browser. There are ways, however, for you to manually code the session information between page requests by appending this session information at the end of the URL. While this approach is possible, it is outside the scope of this book.

- You will learn more about sessions and the <cfapplication> tag in Chapter 14: "Session Management."

## Tag Editors

This is the first time that you've seen a tag editor in this book. A tag editor is more commonly seen for hand-coding CFML tags. Each CFML tag in the language has a tag editor that helps you write the tag without remembering its full syntax. You will be using these tag editors more as you start hand-coding your pages.

## Refreshing the Property Inspector

Because you are using a tag editor to write a ColdFusion tag for the first time, you may notice that the Property Inspector changes to have a Refresh button (**Figure 10.7**). When you start hand-coding CFML code, you may have to refresh the Property Inspector for Dreamweaver to resynchronize with the code that you have entered. The reason for this is that you have in essence put code into the Code view, and the Design view will need to be refreshed.

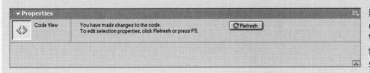

**Figure 10.7** If you make any changes to code in the Code View, you need to refresh the Design View in order to synchronize the two views.

# Creating a Login Procedure

Now that you have enabled session management, you can begin the process of authenticating the user. In order to enable authentication, you will need a database table of users to validate against. A table and its columns for a simple user authentication are described in **Table 10.1**.

Other columns can store the user's full name, address, email address, or any other useful information. In this example, we are using the `tblStoreCustomers` table in the `exampleapps` database so that you can recreate these steps without having to create your own database.

In order to authenticate a user with a username and password, you must first create a form to prompt for that information, and then use the Log In User server behavior to determine eligibility for entrance into the site.

**Table 10.1**

| User Authentication Table | |
|---|---|
| COLUMN | DESCRIPTION |
| Username | Identifying name of the user, without spaces or special characters. |
| Password | Secure password of the authenticating user. |
| Group | Type of user, grouped into well-defined roles based on what they are able to do in the system. |

## To create a login form:

1. Create a new ColdFusion page.

2. Create a form (**Figure 10.8**).

3. Insert a text field into the form to capture the username information. Remember to name this form field the same as the target database column, whenever possible.

4. Insert a password field into the form to capture the password information.

5. Add a Submit button to the form.

6. Save the page.
   Here we are saving the page as login.cfm.

7. Set the form action to the name of the current page—here login.cfm.

8. Save the page.

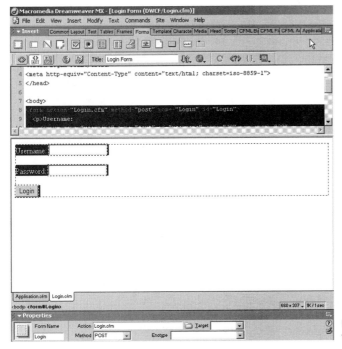

**Figure 10.8** Set the form action to the current page for processing.

CREATING A LOGIN PROCEDURE

## To create a home page:

1. Create a new ColdFusion page.

2. Insert a test message to indicate that a user has entered the system.

   In this case, we are displaying the name of the book as a heading 2 (**Figure 10.9**).

3. Save the page as home.cfm.

## To authenticate the user:

1. Return to the login form page.

2. Choose the Server Behaviors panel from the Applications panel group.

3. Click the plus icon and choose User Authentication > Log In User.

   The Log In User dialog appears (**Figure 10.10**).

4. Set the Get Input From Form drop-down list to the name of the form on the login page—here login.

5. Select the Username Field and Password Field to reflect those fields from the form.

6. Set the Validate Using Data Source option to the data source that contains the user table, here exampleapps.

   Set any username and password information to access that data source if necessary.

7. Set the Table drop-down list to the table in the database that will be used, here tblStoreCustomers.

8. Set the Username Column value to the column in the table that contains the user name.

9. Set the Password Column value to the column that contains the user's password.

Macromedia ColdFusion MX Development with Dreamweaver MX: Visual QuickPro Guide

**Figure 10.9** Create a home page to test the login procedure.

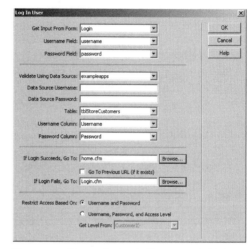

**Figure 10.10** Choose the Log In User server behavior to generate the security code.

**10.** Set the If Login Succeeds, Go To value to the starting page of the application.

Most ColdFusion applications have a designated home page of either index.cfm or home.cfm. Here, we are specifying the home.cfm page that you created in a previous task.

**11.** Set the If Login Fails, Go To value to either an error page or to the login page again.

In all cases you will want to give the user an indication of success or failure. Here, we are simply redirecting the user back to the login.cfm page.

**12.** Set the Restrict Access Based On value to Username and Password for this example.

We will be authenticating using user groups in a later example.

**13.** Click OK.

**14.** Save the login form page.

**15.** Preview the login form page in the browser.

If you use a valid username and password combination, you should be redirected to the home page.

If you type in an erroneous username or password, you should be redirected back to the login form.

## ✔ Tip

■ The exampleapps database does not come with data in the tblStoreCustomers table. You either can manually enter in user information using Microsoft Access, or you can create an insert form and insert users prior to testing authentication.

## To personalize the home page:

1. Return to the home page, here `home.cfm`.

2. After the book title heading in Design view, insert a new line.

3. On a new line, insert the text 'Hello.

4. Choose the Bindings panel of the Applications panel group.

5. Click the plus icon and choose Session Variable (**Figure 10.11**).

   A Session Variable dialog displays.

6. Type the following variable name: `MM_username`, the name of a variable created by the login process to identify the logged in user.

7. Click OK.

   The session variable displays in the Bindings panel.

8. In Design view, at the end of the Hello text, drag in the `MM_username` variable from the Bindings panel.

   You will see the dynamic text field represented in Design view (**Figure 10.12**).

9. Save the page.

You cannot test this page without first going through the login form to create the session variable.

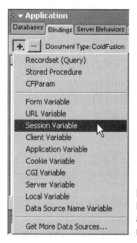

**Figure 10.11** Use the Bindings panel to create a session variable to reference on the page.

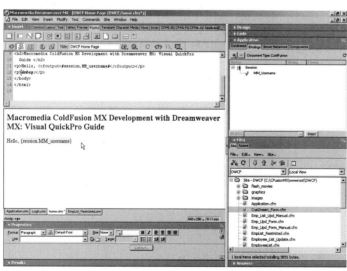

**Figure 10.12** Display the contents of the session.MM_username variable.

**Figure 10.13** Preview the login form.

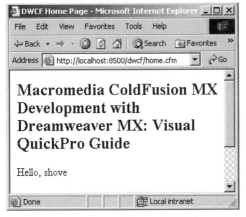

**Figure 10.14** Upon successful login, ColdFusion routes you to the personalized home page.

## To test the login procedure:

1. Open the login form.

2. Preview the login form in a browser (**Figure 10.13**).

3. Insert a nonexistent user.
   ColdFusion routes you back to a blank login form.

4. Insert a valid user and password.
   ColdFusion routes you to the home page where you see the customized Hello message (**Figure 10.14**).

CREATING A LOGIN PROCEDURE

# Logging Out Users

When a user logs in at this point, she can be considered logged out only if the session expires after a certain period of inactivity. In order to better secure your application, you should allow your users to voluntarily log out of the system. You can add logout functionality by using the Log Out User server behavior.

## To enable user logout:

1. Open a page where you would like to enable the user to log out.

   In this case, we are choosing the home page.

2. Choose the Server Behaviors panel of the Applications panel group.

3. Click the plus icon and choose User Authentication > Log Out User.

   The Log Out User dialog appears (**Figure 10.15**).

   Dreamweaver offers two options for logging out a user: when a link is clicked or when the page loads.

4. Choose the Link Clicked option to allow Dreamweaver to create the link for you.

5. In the When Done, Go To text field, specify the login.cfm page.

6. Click OK.

   ColdFusion adds a Log Out hyperlink to your page, which enables the logout procedure (**Figure 10.16**).

7. Save the page, log in if the session has since expired, and preview the page in a browser.

8. Click the Log Out hyperlink.

   ColdFusion routes you back to the login page.

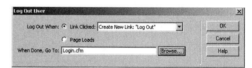

**Figure 10.15** Use the Log Out User server behavior to enable users to kill sessions.

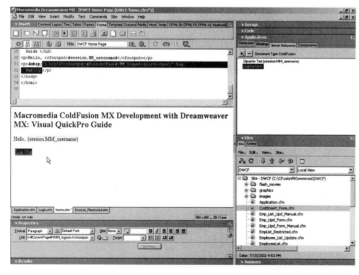

**Figure 10.16** ColdFusion creates the Log Out hyperlink that kills the session when clicked.

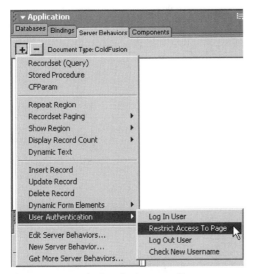

Figure 10.17 Use the Restrict Access to Page server behavior to ensure the user first logs in before viewing the page.

Figure 10.18 Restrict the page to only valid users and route unauthorized users to the login page.

# Restricting Access to Pages

If a user always starts at the login form, the application is secure. However, in a stateless environment like the Web, a user can come into a Website at any angle—from a previously set bookmark or a hyperlink from outside the system.

The next step in securing the application is to restrict access to each individual page. In order to restrict access to pages that may contain data or operations that are sensitive and secure in nature, you can use the Restrict Access To Page server behavior.

## To restrict access to a page:

1. Open the home page.

2. Choose the Server Behaviors panel of the Applications panel group.

3. Click the plus icon and choose User Authentication > Restrict Access To Page (**Figure 10.17**).

4. In the Restrict Access To Page dialog, choose Restrict Based On Username and Password (**Figure 10.18**).

5. In the If Access Denied, Go To field, choose the page to send the unauthorized user to.

   In this case, we are sending the user back to the login page.

6. Click OK.

   ColdFusion adds the Restrict Access to Page server behavior to the Server Behaviors panel and puts code into the page to test for authorization.

7. Browse the page.

   ColdFusion routes you to the login page. After you log in successfully, ColdFusion routes you back to the home page.

# Using User Groups and Roles

Most users are familiar with a login and password, with which they log into many different applications. The group information pertains to the level of permissions within the application, or what they can and cannot do. In a simple Web application, there may be only two levels of authorization:

◆ User, which specifies any Website user with some activities restricted.

◆ Admin, which specifies a site administrator with full privileges.

To use the access levels that are in the user database table, you can alter the Log In User server behavior.

## To use access levels:

1. Open the login form you created in a previous task.

2. Save the file as `login_levels.cfm`.

3. Choose the Server Behaviors panel from the Applications panel group.

4. Double-click the Log In User server behavior.
   The Log In User dialog appears.

5. Change the Validate Using Data Source option to the data source that contains the user table, here dwcf (**Figure 10.19**).

6. Change the Table drop-down list to the table in the database that will be used, here User.

7. Change the Username Column value to the column called Username.

8. Change the Password Column value to the column called Password.

9. Change the If Login Fails, Go To value to `login_levels.cfm`.

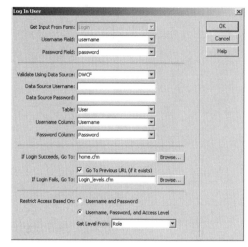

**Figure 10.19** Alter the Log In User server behavior to use a database that has user and role information.

## exampleapps Database

Thus far, you have used the exampleapps database for all tasks. Unfortunately, the tblStoreCustomers table does not contain a role or group column so that we can demonstrate roles-based security. In this case, you may want to create a database with only a Users table with the following columns:

◆ UserID—a system-assigned primary key.

◆ Username—the user's name

◆ Password—the user's password

◆ Role—the role of the user, either admin or user

This task assumes a column of data named Role. The companion Website for this book, as referred to in the "Introduction," contains a copy of a Microsoft Access database table for your use.

10. Change the Restrict Access Based On value to Username, Password and Access Level.

11. Change Get Level From to Role.

12. Click OK.

13. Save the login form page.

## To use the new login form:

1. Open the `home.cfm` page.

2. Choose the Server Behaviors panel of the Applications panel group.

3. Double-click on the Restrict Access to Page server behavior to display the dialog.

4. Change the If Access Denied, Go To value to the new login form, `login_levels.cfm`.

5. Click OK to close the dialog and update the server behavior.

6. Double-click the Log Out User server behavior to display the dialog.

7. Change the When Done, Go To value to the new login form, `login_levels.cfm`.

8. Save the file.

USING USER GROUPS AND ROLES

## To display the user's authorization:

1. Choose the Bindings panel of the Applications panel group.

2. Click the plus icon and choose Session Variable.

   A Session Variable dialog displays.

3. Type the following variable name: MM_userauthorization, the name of a variable created by the login process to identify the access level of the logged in user.

4. Click OK.

   The session variable displays in the Bindings panel (**Figure 10.20**).

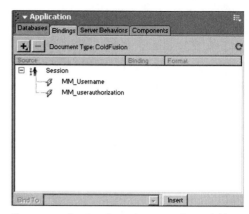

**Figure 10.20** Create a dynamic text session variable called MM_userauthorization.

**5.** At the end of the `Hello` text message in Design view, type a period and then the message `Your access level is` and then drag in the `MM_userauthorization` variable from the Bindings panel.

You will see the dynamic text field represented in Design View (**Figure 10.21**).

**6.** Save the file.

**7.** Preview the home page in the browser.

If it does not route you to the `login_level.cfm` page, choose Log Out to clear the session.

When you log in with bad username information, ColdFusion redirects you back to the `login_levels.cfm` page.

When you log in successfully, ColdFusion routes you to the home page, which displays your access level (**Figure 10.22**). To use the database found on this book's Website, you can log in as shove with a password of 2many to test authentication.

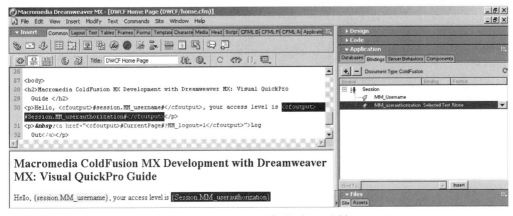

**Figure 10.21** Display the contents of the session.MM_userauthorization variable.

**Figure 10.22** Now that you've used the access level to log in a user, you can display and use that level in your application pages.

# Routing the User After Login

Now when a user requests a page other than the home page, ColdFusion routes him to the login form. After he successfully logs in, Cold-Fusion routes him to the home page. This routing system is due to the fact that we set up the Log In User server behavior to always send successful logins to the home page.

To send the user to the originally requested page after login, you need only to change an option in the Log In User server behavior.

### To route to the requested page:

1. Return to the `login_levels.cfm` form page.

2. Choose the Server Behaviors panel of the Applications panel group.

3. Double-click the Log In User server behavior.

   Dreamweaver opens the behavior in a dialog.

4. Select the Go To Previous URL (if it exists) checkbox (**Figure 10.23**).

5. Save the page.

6. Return to another restricted page (besides the home page) and browse the page.

   ColdFusion routes you to the login page.

7. Log in with a valid username/password combination.

   ColdFusion routes you back to the original requested page.

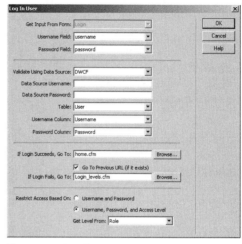

**Figure 10.23** Use the Go To Previous URL option to route the user to the original page request.

# Restricting Access to Pages Based on Levels

Thus far, you have allowed a user to log in using a username and password combination. You also have displayed the user's role in the system. In order to use that user's role in determining if they can access a page, you can alter the Restrict Access To Page server behavior.

### To create a authorization error page:

1. Create a new ColdFusion page.

2. In Design view, type the text You are not authorized to access the requested resource.

3. Save the page as AuthDenied.cfm.

### To restrict page display by authorization level:

1. Create a new ColdFusion page to which you'd like to restrict access based on user level.

   Here, we are creating a dummy admin page with only the text Welcome to the administrator's page on it (**Figure 10.24**).

2. Insert a Restrict Access To Page server behavior.

*continues on next page*

**Figure 10.24** Create a dummy administrator's page to restrict to only admin users.

RESTRICTING ACCESS TO PAGES

**147**

**3.** Select the Restrict Based On the Username, Password and Access Level radio button (**Figure 10.25**).

**4.** Set the If Access Denied, Go To value to the login_level.cfm page.

**5.** Next to Select Level(s), click Define.

The Define Access Levels dialog appears (**Figure 10.26**).

**6.** Click the plus icon and add admin as a level.

**7.** Click OK to close the define levels dialog.

**8.** Click OK to close the server behavior dialog and write the code to the page.

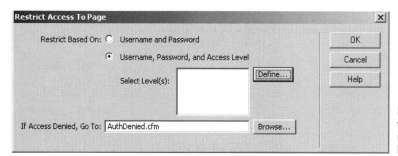

**Figure 10.25** Select to restrict not only on username and password, but also Access Level.

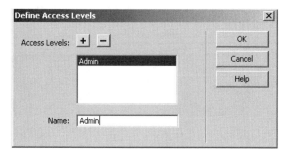

**Figure 10.26** Define the access levels to test for on this page in order to give access.

## To test login using access levels:

1. Open the home.cfm page.

2. Add a hyperlink with the text Admin Page that points to the administrator's page you created (here AdminPage_Restricted.cfm) (**Figure 10.27**).

3. Browse the home page.

   ColdFusion routes you to the login page. (If ColdFusion doesn't route you to the page, your session has not expired and you need to click the Log Out hyperlink.)

4. Log in as a real user who does *not* have admin privileges.

   ColdFusion routes you to the home page. You can use a login of joe and a password of 82many as a valid user without admin privileges.

5. Click the Admin Page hyperlink.

   ColdFusion routes you to the authentication error page.

6. Return to browsing the home page and click the Log Out hyperlink to clear the session.

7. Log in as a user who *does* have admin privileges. You can use a login of above and a password of 2many for a valid user with admin privileges.

   ColdFusion grants you access to the admin page.

**Figure 10.27** To test the login, add a hyperlink on the home page to the admin page.

# INTRODUCING HAND CODING CFML

As you've seen in the first section of this book, Dreamweaver MX helps you accomplish an amazing number of tasks without having to write a single line of ColdFusion code on your own. It may be tempting to rely exclusively on Dreamweaver's visual tools, but you eventually will encounter a problem that built-in code generation simply cannot solve.

In this chapter, you learn how to optimize your development environment for writing code. Next, you learn to insert and edit ColdFusion tags by hand. You also learn how to set, manipulate, and output variables, functions, and expressions. Finally, you learn how to process conditional logic.

Making the move from designer to developer can be daunting. You're going to cover a lot of ground in this chapter, and the new information might seem a bit overwhelming. But not to worry: Remember that ColdFusion is a tag-based language, which means that if you're familiar with HTML (Hypertext Markup Language) you'll find CFML (ColdFusion Markup Language) easy in no time. Also, the rest of the book builds on the knowledge you gain from this chapter, so if you don't understand a concept the first time, you'll have the opportunity to put it into practice later.

# Working with CFML

CFML, of course, is the markup language that powers ColdFusion. CFML uses a set of tags to generate HTML or issue commands to the server. As you've already seen, CFML looks very much like HTML. Just like HTML tags, CFML tags contain both optional and required attributes that let you modify the properties of the tag.

Dreamweaver reflects this similarity: You can use the Dreamweaver Tag Editor to insert or modify ColdFusion tags just like you would HTML tags.

Dreamweaver offers a dizzying array of ways to insert ColdFusion code into your page. You can choose one of the following:

◆ Choose Insert > ColdFusion Basic Objects (**Figure 11.1**).

◆ Insert behaviors via the Server Behaviors Panel (**Figure 11.2**).

**Figure 11.1** You can insert CFML from a menu...

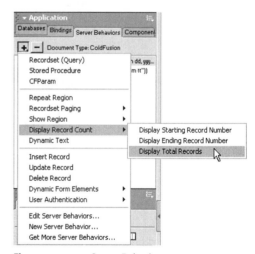

**Figure 11.2** ... or a Server Behavior...

◆ Click an icon on any of the CFML Insert menu bars (**Figure 11.3**).

◆ Type the code by hand in the Code window (**Figure 11.4**).

To help you become accustomed to working with CFML, the remainder of this book relies primarily on hand coding and Auto Tag Completion. You should experiment with the different methods introduced in this section to find the one that's best for you. The primary point you should take away from this section is this: Your Dreamweaver HTML skills apply directly to working with CFML.

## To insert a new ColdFusion tag:

1. Create a new ColdFusion page, title it, and save it.

2. If you are not in Code view already, do one of the following:
   ▲ Choose View > Code.
   ▲ Choose View > Code and Design View.
   ▲ Dreamweaver shows the HTML code of your page.

3. Place your cursor in the first line of the Code window, click your mouse, and press Enter to create a blank line above the opening <html> tag.

4. Type this code:
   <cfloc

   Dreamweaver suggests that the tag you want is <cflocation> (**Figure 11.5**).

*continued on next page*

**WORKING WITH CFML**

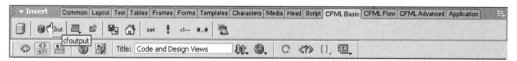

**Figure 11.3** ... or an icon...

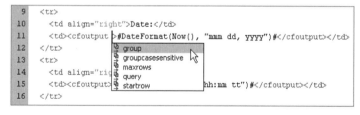

**Figure 11.4** ... or by hand.

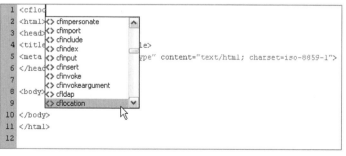

**Figure 11.5** The Dreamweaver Auto Tag Completion feature increases efficiency.

**5.** Press Enter.

Dreamweaver inserts the `<cflocation>` tag on your page. Note that the tag does not include a closing bracket. You will now add attributes to the tag.

**6.** Press the spacebar.

Dreamweaver creates a code hint, showing the attributes `addtoken` and `url`.

**7.** Select `url` and type this URL within the attribute's quotation marks:

`http://macromedia.com/NotAPage.cfm`

**8.** Insert the closing bracket.

Your entire `<cflocation>` page should look like **Figure 11.6**. The `<cflocation>` tag redirects the user's browser to the page specified in the `url` attribute.

**9.** Press F12 to preview the page in a browser.

Assuming that you are connected to the Internet, you should be redirected to an error page. NotAPage.cfm doesn't exist —at least not at the time of this writing.

**10.** Leave the page open because you learn how to correct the problem in the next section.

## ✔ Tips

■ If the Code Hints and Tag Completion do not appear in your Code view, make sure they're turned on in your Preferences by choosing Edit > Preferences, or pressing Ctrl+U. In the Preferences window, select Code Hints. Ensure that the options Enable Auto Tag Completion and Enable Code Hints are selected. You also may want to set the delay to a low number.

■ Knowing where you should insert your CFML code can be tricky. As a very rough rule of thumb, consider inserting application logic and initialization code at the very top of your document and presentation code within your document. That advice might not make much sense yet, but we'll return to the idea toward the end of this chapter.

■ ColdFusion file names are not case-ensitive unless your ColdFusion server is hosted on Unix.

```
1  <cflocation url="http://macromedia.com/NotAPage.cfm">
2  <html>
3  <head>
4  <title>cflocation test</title>
5  <meta http-equiv="Content-Type" content="text/html; charset=iso-8859-1">
6  </head>
7
8  <body>
9
10 </body>
11 </html>
```

**Figure 11.6** This is a complete cflocation listing.

## To edit an existing ColdFusion tag:

1. Ensure that Dreamweaver is set to Code view and that the page you created in the last step is open.

2. In the Code view, select the <cflocation> tag, and do one of the following:

   Right-click (Windows) or Control+click (Macintosh) and choose Edit Tag (**Figure 11.7**).

   Press Ctrl+F5.

   Dreamweaver opens the Tag Editor with the attributes already populated (**Figure 11.8**).

3. Type this URL:

   `http://macromedia.com/`

4. Click OK and test the page.

   Assuming that you are connected to the Internet, you should be taken to the Macromedia home page.

### ✔ Tip

■ Of course, you could have simply retyped the `url` attribute by hand. The point is that Dreamweaver offers you a number of ways to add and edit CFML code.

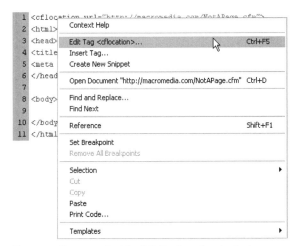

**Figure 11.7** You can select the Edit Tag from the shortcut menu.

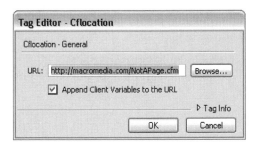

**Figure 11.8** Use the Tag Editor to insert or edit a <cflocation> tag.

WORKING WITH CFML

# Working with Variables

*Variables* are nothing more than containers for information. To use a variable, you create the container and you assign a value to it. For example, the variable myName could contain the value Marc. As the application handles the variable, the information within the container can change.

You create variables and define their values using the tags <cfset> and <cfparam>. You can combine and modify your variables by using *expressions*. You also can alter the value of your variables by using built-in bits of logic called *functions*. Finally, when you are ready to display a variable's value to the user, you print the variable to the screen with the <cfoutput> tag.

As with most of this chapter's content, you've already worked with the concepts of setting variables and outputting their content. In Chapter 5, you learned how to display variable data in the form of a database recordset. In Chapter 6, you learned how to pass one kind of variable, the URL parameter, from one page to another in order to display a recordset detail. In Chapter 7, you worked with another kind of variable, form data, to insert a record into your database. Thus, in this section you simply learn how to write the code that underlies variables and their use.

## Creating and Displaying Variables

You create a variable and set its initial value with the tag <cfset>. The format is this:

```
<CFSET variableName = "variableValue">
```

In other words, to create a variable called myName with the value Marc, you would use this syntax:

```
<CFSET myName = "Marc">
```

### ✔ Tips

- You may be familiar with other programming languages that require you to first *declare* a variable, and then *initialize* it. ColdFusion handles both steps with the <cfset> tag.

- <cfset> does not require a closing tag.

Variables also exist in certain *scopes*. Values in the VARIABLE scope exist only for the life of the page. Values in the URL or FORM scopes can be passed from one page to another, while values in the APPLICATION scope exist throughout the application. Don't be too concerned with scope for the moment; just be aware that it exists. We return to the concept of scope again in later chapters.

You can check for the existence of a variable with the <cfparam> tag. If the variable doesn't already exist, you can create it and assign a default value to it. The <cfparam> tag uses this syntax:

```
<cfparam name="nameOfVariable"
→ default="defaultValue">
```

This code checks whether a variable named myName exists, and if not, assigns a default value of Bubba.

```
<cfparam name="myName" default="Bubba">
```

Use the tag `<cfoutput>` to display the contents of the variable. You must surround the variable's name with hash marks (#). To output the variable we just created, use this syntax:

```
<cfoutput>#myName#</cfoutput>
```

The `<cfoutput>` tag prints to the page anything in between the opening and closing tags, but it processes only the code surrounded by hash marks.

You will find these concepts are much easier to understand once you've worked with the code.

## Understanding Variable Scope

Assume that you have a dinner date at the house of your girlfriend (or boyfriend or spouse). You're running late, so you buy a cheese pizza from a carryout chain and rush over to her house. You ring the bell, and as soon as your girlfriend opens the door she looks at you and says, "Greasy and unsophisticated."

You're taken aback, and say to yourself, "I'm bathing more often these days, and I read Jane Austen when ESPN goes to commercial. Oh, maybe she means the pizza."

You have a *scoping* issue. Since your girlfriend did not specify the scope of her comment, you had to take a moment to guess whether she referred to you or the pizza. And for all you know, you guessed wrong.

ColdFusion treats variable scope in the same way: when you don't specify your variable's scope, ColdFusion tries to guess the scope in the following order:

◆ Query results
◆ Local variables
◆ CGI variables
◆ FILE variables
◆ URL variables
◆ FORM variables
◆ COOKIE variables
◆ CLIENT variables

As you can see, if you create a local variable ColdFusion doesn't have to do much work to guess the proper scope. But if you want to access a form variable without including its scope, you're asking ColdFusion to make a lot of guesses before it gets the right one. Unless you actually want to be ambiguous, it's good practice to scope most variables.

As you write more ColdFusion code, you'll get a better sense of when to explicitly scope your variables.

WORKING WITH VARIABLES

## To set and display a variable:

1. Create a new ColdFusion page, title it, save it, and ensure that you have set Dreamweaver either to Code view or Code and Design view.

2. Place your cursor in the Dreamweaver Code window, and in between the opening and closing <body> tags, insert this code:

   ```
   <cfoutput>myName</cfoutput>
   ```

   Your code should look like the code listed in **Figure 11.9**.

3. Save the page and view it in a browser. ColdFusion, just like a pesky kid brother, takes your words very literally and outputs "myName." Let's try again.

4. Select myName in the Code view.

5. To finish the output line, do one of the following:

   Choose Insert > ColdFusion Basic Objects > Surround with #.

   ▲ Type a hash mark before and after myName in the Code view.

   The effect is the same, and your output line should now look like this:

   ```
   <cfoutput>#myName#</cfoutput>
   ```

6. Save the page and preview in a browser. ColdFusion displays an error message: Variable MYNAME is undefined (**Figure 11.10**). Of course, ColdFusion cannot output a value for a variable until you've created the variable in the first place.

7. Insert your cursor at the very top of the Code view, press Enter to add a new line, and insert this code:

   ```
   <cfparam name="myName"
    → default="Sue Hove">
   ```

```
1  <html>
2  <head>
3  <title>cfset and cfoutput</title>
4  <meta http-equiv="Content-Type" content="text/html; charset=iso-8859-1">
5  </head>
6
7  <body>
8  <cfoutput>myName</cfoutput>
9  </body>
10 </html>
```

**Figure 11.9** This <cfoutput> tag produces very literal results.

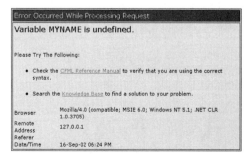

**Figure 11.10** ColdFusion can't output a variable until the variable is defined.

**8.** Save the page and preview in a browser. ColdFusion outputs Sue Hove, the value you assigned via the <cfparam> tag.

**9.** Immediately beneath the <cfparam> line, insert this code to set the value of myName to Marc Garrett:

`<cfset myName = "Marc Garrett">`

Your code should look like the code listed in **Figure 11.11**.

**10.** Save the page and preview in a browser. You'll see that ColdFusion has set the variable's value to Marc Garrett.

## ✔ Tips

- Remember, you don't have to declare a variable in ColdFusion before you set its value. Still, it's a good idea to use <cfparam> to set a default value for a variable and check for its existence. You certainly will end up with fewer errors in your application.

- If you prefer not to type the code in step 2, you can accomplish the same thing by choosing Insert > ColdFusion Basic Objects > CFOUTPUT.

## Using Functions

ColdFusion functions typically take a parameter, perform a task on it, and produce a result. For example, the ColdFusion function reverse() reverses the order of characters in a string, converting you to uoy. While not all functions require a parameter, all functions return a result. Functions follow this format:

`function(argument1, argument2, …)`

You will find ColdFusion functions invaluable when you want to perform tasks such as manipulating strings or getting and displaying the current time.

## ✔ Tips

- The parentheses following function names imply that the function accepts a parameter. This can bit confusing because even functions that don't accept parameters include parentheses with the function name.

- You're not limited to using the functions built into ColdFusion. Although it's beyond the scope of this book, you should be aware that you can write your own functions. If you'd like to learn more, search the ColdFusion MX documentation for "User-defined Functions."

```
1  <cfparam name = "myName" default="Sue Hove">
2  <cfset myName = "Marc Garrett">
3  <html>
4  <head>
5  <title>cfset and cfoutput</title>
6  <meta http-equiv="Content-Type" content="text/html; charset=iso-8859-1">
7  </head>
8
9  <body>
10 <cfoutput>#myName#</cfoutput>
11 </body>
12 </html>
```

**Figure 11.11** This page sets and displays the variable myName.

## To use a ColdFusion function:

1. Create a new ColdFusion page, title it, and save it.

2. Use <cfparam> to define a variable named myString with the default value of ColdFusion.

   See the previous section of this chapter if you've forgotten how to set a variable with <cfparam>.

3. In between the opening and closing <body> tags, create an output block with this code:

   <cfoutput>#UCase(myString)#</cfoutput>

   ColdFusion converts the value of the variable myString into uppercase.

4. Add a line break and output your original variable to see its contents.

   Your output block should look like the code in **Figure 11.12**.

5. Save your page and preview in a browser.

   Note this important distinction: A function changes the output to the page, but it does not actually change the value contained in the variable. The value output by UCase(myString) is COLDFUSION, but the value of myString is still ColdFusion.

6. Add this code anywhere within the body of the page:

   <cfoutput>#Left(myString, 4)#
   → </cfoutput>

   ColdFusion outputs "Cold," the first four letters of the variable myString. You can also combine functions.

7. Add this code anywhere within the body of the page:

   <cfoutput>#Left(Reverse(myString), 4)#
   → </cfoutput>

8. Save the page and preview in a browser. ColdFusion outputs nois.

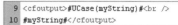

```
9  <cfoutput>#UCase(myString)#<br />
10 #myString#</cfoutput>
```

**Figure 11.12** This code outputs a ColdFusion function.

## ✔ Tips

- Many functions accept more than one parameter.

- ColdFusion processes nested functions in order from the innermost function to the outermost function.

- ColdFusion has over 250 functions. Refer to the documentation for a complete list.

WORKING WITH VARIABLES

## Using Expressions

According to the Macromedia ColdFusion MX documentation, "expressions consist of operands and operators. Operands are comprised of constants and variables. Operators are the verbs that work on the operands."

You may have better luck if you simply use the same test for expressions that Justice Potter Stewart used to define obscenity: You'll know them when you see them.

ColdFusion has four kinds of operators:

- Arithmetic: These operators perform mathematical calculations on their operands. Examples are +, -, *, /, and MOD.

- Boolean: These operators are often called "logical operators" and include NOT, AND, and OR.

- Decision: Also called "comparison" operators, these operators compare one operand to another. Examples include IS, IS NOT, and CONTAINS.

- String: The string operator concatenates strings. The only string operator is &.

You'll see decision operators in action when you work with conditional processing later in this chapter. For the moment, let's look at Arithmetic and String operators.

### XHTML Line Breaks

If you choose Insert > Special Characters > Line Break to add line breaks to your page, you may notice that Dreamweaver inserts <br> into HTML documents. The code listings here, however, use the XHTML style <br /> because the author types the line breaks by hand. If you prefer to insert XHTML line breaks from the Dreamweaver Insert menu, you can do so by changing your page's DOCTYPE. Either way, browsers going all the way back to Internet Explorer 1 and Netscape Navigator 1 support both <br> and <br />.

WORKING WITH VARIABLES

## To build an expression with operators:

1. Create a new ColdFusion page, title it, and save it.

2. At the top of the page, insert this code to create two variables:

   ```
   <cfset theFirstNumber = 4>
   <cfset theSecondNumber = 5>
   ```

   ColdFusion creates two variables, each with a different number value.

3. Use an arithmetic operator to add the two numbers and assign the value to a new variable:

   ```
   <cfset theSum = theFirstNumber +
   → theSecondNumber>
   ```

   ColdFusion adds the values of the two variables. Note that ColdFusion is not concatenating the words theFirstNumber and theSecondNumber.

4. In between the opening and closing <body> tags, output the value to test the addition.

   ```
   <cfoutput>#theSum#</cfoutput>
   ```

   Your page, in its entirety, should look like the code listing in **Figure 11.13**.

5. Save the page and preview in a browser. You will see that theSum is equal to 9.

6. Create two more variables and populate them with text:

   ```
   <cfset theFirstWord = "Cold">
   <cfset theNextWord = "Fusion">
   ```

7. Concatenate the variables with the string operator and insert the resulting value into a new variable:

   ```
   <cfset theNewWord = theFirstWord &
   → theNextWord>
   ```

   ColdFusion concatenates the value of the variables.

```
1  <cfset theFirstNumber = 4>
2  <cfset theSecondNumber = 5>
3  <cfset theSum = theFirstNumber + theSecondNumber>
4
5  <html>
6  <head>
7  <title>Expression Examples</title>
8  <meta http-equiv="Content-Type" content="text/html; charset=iso-8859-1">
9  </head>
10
11 <body>
12
13 <cfoutput>#theSum#</cfoutput>
14 </body>
15 </html>
```

**Figure 11.13** You can build expressions with an arithmetic operator.

**8.** Output the value to test the concatenation:

`<cfoutput>#theNewWord#</cfoutput>`

Your page, in its entirety, should look like the code listed in **Figure 11.14**.

**9.** Save the page and preview in a browser. The variable `theNewWord` outputs as `ColdFusion`.

```
5  <cfset theFirstNumber = 4>
6  <cfset theSecondNumber = 5>
7  <cfset theSum = theFirstNumber + theSecondNumber>
8
9  <cfset theFirstWord = "Cold">
10 <cfset theNextWord = "Fusion">
11 <cfset theNewWord = theFirstWord & theNextWord>
12
13 <html>
14 <head>
15 <title>Expression Examples</title>
16 <meta http-equiv="Content-Type" content="text/html; charset=iso-8859-1">
17 </head>
18
19 <body>
20
21 <cfoutput>#theSum#</cfoutput><br />
22 <cfoutput>#theNewWord#</cfoutput>
23
24 </body>
25 </html>
```

**Figure 11.14** You can add and concatenate within expressions.

# Understanding Conditional Processing

So far, this book has taught you how to take a value or set of values and perform an action with them. For example, in Chapter 9 you learned how to return a recordset filtered with a search term. That's fine as far as it goes, but what if you don't want to perform the search at all unless a certain condition is met? Performing certain tasks based on conditions you assign is known as conditional processing.

## IF-THEN-ELSE

IF-THEN-ELSE statements allow for basic conditional processing. ColdFusion provides three tags for IF-THEN-ELSE processing:

◆ `<cfif>` tests a condition and performs an action only if the condition is TRUE.

◆ `<cfelseif>` tests a second condition only if the preceding `<cfif>` tested FALSE and then performs an action if the condition is TRUE.

◆ `<cfelse>` performs an action if and only if the `<cfif>` and preceding `<cfelseif>` tags test FALSE.

If the bulleted points sound confusing, don't worry about the language. Focus instead on the concept. You already understand intuitively how conditional processing works: In Chapter 10 you protected a page with a username and password. **If** the username and password match a certain set of values, the user gains access to a page, **else** the user does not.

## To use `<cfif>` in a conditional statement:

1. Create a new ColdFusion page, title it, and then save it.

2. Insert this code to set a URL parameter with the default value of Nobody:

   ```
   <cfparam name="url.myName"
   → default="Nobody">
   ```

   ColdFusion will now look for a variable called myName in the URL scope and assign it the value Nobody if it doesn't exist.

3. Insert this code to set a parameter to create a response for the user:

   ```
   <cfparam name="variables.myResponse"
   → default="Just a default response.
   Move along.">
   ```

   ColdFusion will now look for a variable called myResponse in the variables scope and assign it the value Just a default response. Move along if the variable hasn't already been created.

4. Underneath the parameters you just created, insert this code:

   ```
   <cfif Len(url.myName) IS 10>
   <cfset variables.myResponse =
   → "Your name is 10 characters long.">
   </cfif>
   ```

   You have given ColdFusion the following instructions: "Check the myName variable included in the URL. If it's ten characters in length, set a variable called myResponse with the value 'Your name is 10 characters long.'" Your conditional code should look like the code in **Figure 11.15**.

```
4  <cfif Len(url.myName) IS 10>
5      <cfset variables.myResponse = "Your name is 10 characters long.">
6  </cfif>
```

**Figure 11.15** This `<cfif>` block checks the length of a name.

**5.** In between the opening and closing `<body>` tags, insert this code to output the results to the user:

```
<cfoutput>#variables.myResponse#
→ </cfoutput>
```

Your page will output the value contained in the variable `myResponse`.

**6.** Save the page, view it in a browser, and then use this URL to test the page:

```
http://localhost/dwcf/Ch11/
→ conditional.cfm
```

You can see the beauty of the `<cfparam>` tag at work here: Even though you didn't pass the `myName` variable in the URL, ColdFusion didn't display an error message (throw an error). Instead, ColdFusion assigned the default value of `Nobody` to `myName`. Now examine the condition:

```
<cfif Len(url.myName) IS 10>
```

When the page loads, ColdFusion actually processes the conditional line like this:

```
<cfif 6 IS 10>
```

Since `Nobody` is, in fact, not ten characters long, the conditional code is not processed.

**7.** Use this URL to test the page again:

```
http://localhost/dwcf/Ch11/
→ conditional.cfm?myName=AnnJohnson
```

ColdFusion recognizes that the name is ten characters long and thus processes the conditional code.

## ✔ Tips

- You may need to alter the URL depending on your system's ColdFusion setup.

- You can't be reminded of this fact often enough: Users can change URL variables just by typing a new URL into the browser's address window. Be careful with how you handle URL variables. If you need to pass sensitive information, consider using a form with the `POST` method.

- `<cfif>` statements may be nested, but doing so slows down the page processing and makes your code difficult to read. If you need to build complex conditional statements, consider using `<cfswitch>` as shown later in this section.

UNDERSTANDING CONDITIONAL PROCESSING

## To use <CFELSEIF> and <CFELSE> in a conditional statement:

1. Make sure the page that you created in the previous section is open in Dreamweaver.

2. Within the opening and closing `<cfif>` tags, insert this code:

   ```
   <cfelseif Len(url.myName) LT 10>
   <cfset variables.myResponse = "Your
   → name is less than 10 characters long.">
   ```

   Your complete conditional statement should look like that in **Figure 11.16**. You have told ColdFusion that, if the name is not ten characters in length, it should check to see whether the name is less than ten characters in length, and if so, set an appropriate response.

3. Use this URL to test the page:

   ```
   http://localhost/dwcf/Ch11/
   → conditional.cfm?myName=Marc
   ```

   You'll see, unsurprisingly, that the name Marc is less than ten characters in length. But you haven't covered all logical possibilities. So far, you've told ColdFusion to check whether a name is less than ten characters, or whether it is precisely ten characters. Names, of course, can be more than ten characters too. Let's add that last piece of code.

4. Following the `<cfelseif>` block, add this code:

   ```
   <cfelse>
   <cfset variables.myResponse = "Your
   → name is more than 10 characters long.">
   ```

   Your entire conditional block should now look like that in **Figure 11.17**. You have now told ColdFusion to follow these rules: "If the name is not equal to ten characters, and if it is not less than ten characters, it must be greater than ten characters. Assign a response accordingly."

5. Test the page with the name of your choice.

   You will see that no matter which name you enter, all logical options are covered.

### ✔ Tip

- Pay careful attention to the indenting shown in the figures. Although there's no right or wrong way to indent your conditional code, you'll have a much easier time debugging it if it's indented properly.

```
 8  <cfif Len(url.myName) IS 10>
 9      <cfset variables.myResponse = "Your name is 10 characters long.">
10      <cfelseif Len(url.myName) LT 10>
11          <cfset variables.myResponse = "Your name is less than 10 characters long.">
12  </cfif>
```

**Figure 11.16** You have created a conditional statement with `<cfelseif>`.

```
 8  <cfif Len(url.myName) IS 10>
 9      <cfset variables.myResponse = "Your name is 10 characters long.">
10      <cfelseif Len(url.myName) LT 10>
11          <cfset variables.myResponse = "Your name is less than 10 characters long.">
12      <cfelse>
13          <cfset variables.myResponse = "Your name is more than 10 characters long.">
14  </cfif>
```

**Figure 11.17** This conditional statement covers all possibilities for the length of a name.

UNDERSTANDING CONDITIONAL PROCESSING

## Switch-Case

Creating blocks of nested IF-THEN-ELSE logic quickly can get out of hand. Not only will ColdFusion process your page slowly, but you also will have difficulty debugging your code.

Fortunately, ColdFusion provides the `<cfswitch>` and `<cfcase>` tags. `<cfswitch>` lets you assign an expression to evaluate and performs a certain action in case the expression has a specified value. For example, you can tell ColdFusion to check a form variable and perform an action you assign based on that variable's value. Consider using switch-case logic when you have three or more possible values for any expression.

### To evaluate an expression using switch-case:

1. Copy the file **submitString.cfm** from the Web site and save it in your DWCF site.

2. Open the file in Dreamweaver and examine it in Code and Design View.

   You do not need to make any changes to this page. However, you should notice this: The submitString.cfm page includes a simple `cfform` that accepts a word and lets you select a string function to perform on the word. The form submits the text string and the value of the select list to an action page, which you build in the next step.

3. Create a new ColdFusion page, title it, and save it.

   Here we titled the page Switch-case: Action Page and the filename switchCase.cfm.

4. On the first line of the page, insert this code:

   ```
   <cfparam name="form.txtString"
   → default="You did not enter a string">
   <cfparam name="form.selectFunction"
   → default="">
   ```

   ColdFusion sets values for the variables `form.txtString` and `form.selectFunction` if they do not exist. (If you need a quick refresher on `<cfparam>`, see the previous section of this chapter).

5. Below the parameter tags, create a new switch:

   ```
   <cfswitch
   → expression="#form.selectFunction#">
   </cfswitch>
   ```

   Your page will now look for a variable named `selectFunction` in the `form` scope and evaluate the expression. The page is not complete, however. You must tell ColdFusion what to do in case it finds a variable you want to act upon.

   *continues on next page*

**6.** In between the opening and closing
`<cfswitch>` tags, insert this code:

```
<cfcase value="LCase">
<cfset myNewString =
→ LCase(form.txtString)>
</cfcase>
```

In English, you have given the following
set of commands to ColdFusion: "Look
for the variable `form.selectFunction`. If
you find it, check its value. In case the
value is LCase, take the text string passed
from the form page and set it to lowercase." Your code should look like that in
**Figure 11.18**.

**7.** Add two more cases following the first
case, with this code:

```
<cfcase value="UCase">
<cfset myNewString =
→ UCase(form.txtString)>
</cfcase>
<cfcase value="Reverse">
<cfset myNewString =
→ Reverse(form.txtString)>
</cfcase>
```

Your page will now look for three cases,
LCase, UCase, and Reverse, and perform
the requested function on the text string
passed from the form page.

**8.** Insert this code to specify which action
to take by default, thereby covering your
bases:

```
<cfdefaultcase>
<cfset myNewString = "No action
→ was taken">
</cfdefaultcase>
```

The `<cfdefaultcase>` tag tells
ColdFusion which action to take if none
of the cases matches those listed by the
`<cfcase>` tag. Your switch-case code
should look like **Figure 11.19**.

**9.** Within the page's `<body>` tags, insert
this code to output the variables you've
created:

```
<cfoutput>
Your old string:
→ <strong>#form.txtString#</strong><br />
Your new string:
<strong>#myNewString#</strong>
</cfoutput>
```

```
4  <cfswitch expression="#form.selectFunction#">
5      <cfcase value="LCase">
6          <cfset myNewString = LCase(form.txtString)>
7      </cfcase>
8  </cfswitch>
```

**Figure 11.18** An incomplete `<cfswitch>`
code block looks like this.

```
4   <cfswitch expression="#form.selectFunction#">
5       <cfcase value="LCase">
6           <cfset myNewString = LCase(form.txtString)>
7       </cfcase>
8       <cfcase value="UCase">
9           <cfset myNewString = UCase(form.txtString)>
10      </cfcase>
11      <cfcase value="Reverse">
12          <cfset myNewString = Reverse(form.txtString)>
13      </cfcase>
14      <cfdefaultcase>
15          <cfset myNewString = "No action was taken">
16      </cfdefaultcase>
```

**Figure 11.19** A complete `<cfswitch>`
code block looks like this.

**UNDERSTANDING CONDITIONAL PROCESSING**

**10.** Save the page, and then test the form submission page in your browser.

ColdFusion takes the word you enter and transforms it according to the function you specify in the drop-down list.

### ✔ Tips

- Always assign a default case. Doing so can help you cover for errors in your code. For example, you might later return to the form page included in this section in order to add more functions to the drop-down list. If you forgot to add a corresponding case statement on the form action page, the <cfdefaultcase> will keep the page from generating an error.

- As an exercise in futility, you could rewrite this switch-case page as a series of IF-THEN statements, or as a few nested IF-THENs. You would quickly discover, though, that the logic is hard to follow, and the situation only worsens as the number of cases grows.

## Looping

You may not realize it, but you already are familiar with the concept of looping. In Chapter 5, you learned how to display multiple rows of data using the Repeat Region server behavior. In essence, you used <cfoutput> to produce the contents of a query onto your page, line by line. Thus, you looped through each record, printed its contents to the page, and stopped looping when you reached the last record.

The <cfloop> tag works in a similar fashion, allowing you to process code or output data repeatedly until a condition is met. There are five types of loops: index, conditional, query, list, and collection.

- ◆ An *index loop* increments a counter by a specified amount until the counter reaches a value you specify.

- ◆ A *query loop* steps through the rows of each query, much like the <cfoutput> tag.

- ◆ A *list loop* steps through the members of a list.

In this section, you see each of the loops listed above in action. As with other sections of this book, you have the opportunity to enter the code by hand or insert the looping code using Dreamweaver's menus.

### ✔ Tip

- Collection and conditional loops are beyond the scope of this book but are thoroughly described in the ColdFusion MX documentation.

UNDERSTANDING CONDITIONAL PROCESSING

## To create an index loop:

1. Create a new ColdFusion page, title it, and save it.

2. In the View menu, choose Code and Design View.

3. In the Insert menu, choose ColdFusion Flow Objects, and then choose CFLOOP.

   Dreamweaver opens the Cfloop Tag Editor (**Figure 11.20**).

4. Accept the default Loop Type, Index.

5. In the Index textbox, type myCount.

   The Index attribute specifies the parameter that holds the loop's value.

6. In the From textbox, type 1.

   The From attribute specifies the beginning value of the index.

7. In the To textbox, type 10.

   The To attribute specifies the ending value of the index.

8. Leave the Step textbox blank.

   The optional step attribute specifies the step with which you increment or decrement the index value.

9. Click OK.

   Dreamweaver inserts a <cfloop> tag in your Code view and a CFLOOP placeholder in your Design view (**Figure 11.21**).

**Figure 11.20** Dreamweaver's cfloop Tag Editor looks like this.

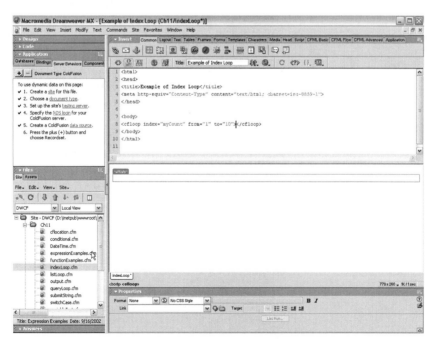

**Figure 11.21** cfloop appears in both Code and Design views.

**10.** Save your page and preview it in a browser.

An empty screen appears in your browser window. CFLOOP may have looped through the index you created, but there's no way to tell because you haven't yet specified any output.

**11.** In the Dreamweaver Code view and in between the opening and closing <cfloop> tags, add this code:

`<cfoutput>#myCount#<br /></cfoutput>`

Your code should look like that in **Figure 11.22**.

**12.** Click anywhere within your Design window.

Two things immediately happen in Dreamweaver: {myCount} is inserted into the Dreamweaver Design view, and the Server Behaviors panel recognizes myCount as dynamic text (**Figure 11.23**).

**13.** Save your page and view it in a browser.

You will see the numbers 1 through 20 displayed on your screen. ColdFusion has looped through each number, and with each pass through the loop stored the value in the variable myCount.

```
1  <html>
2  <head>
3  <title>Example of Index Loop</title>
4  <meta http-equiv="Content-Type" content="text/html; charset=iso-8859-1">
5  </head>
6
7  <body>
8  <cfloop index="myCount" from="1" to="20">
9      <cfoutput>#myCount#<br /></cfoutput>
10 </cfloop>
11 </body>
12 </html>
```

**Figure 11.22** This code listing creates an index loop.

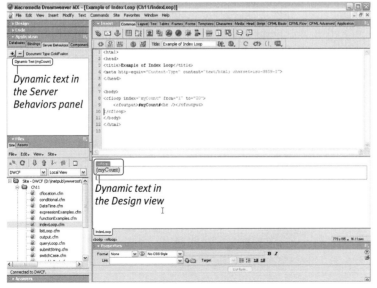

*Dynamic text in the Server Behaviors panel*

*Dynamic text in the Design view*

**Figure 11.23** The loop's index appears in both the Design view and the Server Behaviors panel.

## To create a query loop:

1. Create a new ColdFusion page, title it, and save it.

2. Using the DSN exampleapps, create a new recordset named q_Employees by doing one of the following:

    Manually type it.

    Use the Server Behaviors panel.

3. Add this SQL query to the recordset:

    `SELECT * FROM tblEmployees`

    Dreamweaver lists the new recordset in the Server Behaviors window. (If you have forgotten how to create a recordset, please see Chapter 4, Retrieving Database Data).

4. Place your cursor anywhere within the `<body>` tags and in the Insert menu, choose ColdFusion Flow Objects> CFLOOP.

    Dreamweaver opens the CFLOOP Tag Editor.

5. In the Loop Type select control, choose Query Loop.

    Dreamweaver changes the options to reflect the query loop attributes.

6. In the Query Name textbox, type q_Employees

7. In the Start Row textbox, type 1, and in the End Row textbox, type 5 (**Figure 11.24**).

    In English, you have told ColdFusion, "Loop through the list of employees, starting with row 1 and ending with row 5." The `startrow` and `endrow` attributes are optional but useful when you want to work with a portion of a large recordset. Unlike an index loop, you do not specify an `index` attribute for a query loop.

8. In the Dreamweaver Code view and in between the opening and closing `<cfloop>` tags, add this code:

    ```
    <cfoutput>#FirstName# #LastName#
    → <br /></cfoutput>
    ```

    Your code should look like that in **Figure 11.25**.

9. Save your page and preview it in a browser.

    ColdFusion loops through a list of the first five employees in tblEmployees.

```
11  <cfloop query="q_Employees" startrow="1" endrow="5">
12      <cfoutput>#FirstName# #LastName#<br /></cfoutput>
13  </cfloop>
```

**Figure 11.25** This code listing creates a query loop.

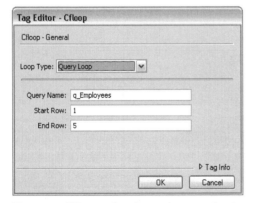

**Figure 11.24** This query loop has a start row and end row specified.

UNDERSTANDING CONDITIONAL PROCESSING

## To create a list loop:

1. Create a new ColdFusion page, title it, and save it.

2. Place your cursor anywhere within the <body> tags, and in the Insert menu, choose ColdFusion Flow Objects > CFLOOP.

   Dreamweaver opens the CFLOOP Tag Editor.

3. In the Loop Type select control, select List Loop.

   Dreamweaver changes the options to reflect the query loop attributes.

4. Type i for the Index Value.

5. For the list, type this code:

   `Ambition, Distraction, Uglification; Derision`

   Note that there's a semi-colon between the third and fourth words.

6. Leave the Delimiters field blank and click OK.

7. In between the opening and closing <cfloop> tags, insert this code:

   `<cfoutput>#i#<br /></cfoutput>`

   Your entire query loop block should look that in like **Figure 11.26**.

*continues on next page*

```
8  <cfloop index="i" list="Ambition, Distraction, Uglification; Derision" delimiters=",;">
9     <cfoutput>#i#<br /></cfoutput>
10 </cfloop>
```

**Figure 11.26** This code listing creates a list loop.

8. Save your page and preview it in a browser.

   A funny thing happens: You may have expected to see four list items, but only three appear (**Figure 11.27**). "Uglification" and "Derision" are both treated as the same list item. Why?

   By default, ColdFusion looks only for commas to delimit list items. Thus, ColdFusion treated our loop list like this:

   ▲ First item: Ambition

   ▲ Second item: Distraction

   ▲ Third item: Uglification; Derision

   You can specify, however, that ColdFusion look for delimiters in addition to the default comma.

9. In Code or Design view, highlight the `<cfloop>` tag, and then, in the Modify menu, choose Edit Tag.

   ColdFusion reopens that CFLOOP Tag Editor with the properties you've already specified.

10. In the Delimiters field, type a comma and a semi-colon, like this:

    `,;`

    ColdFusion now will look for both commas and semi-colons as list delimiters.

11. Save the page and preview it in a browser.

    The list now contains four items (**Figure 11.28**).

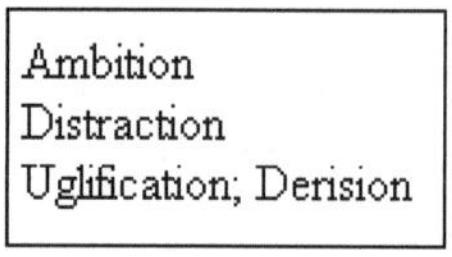

### ✔ Tips

■ You also can use a list loop to loop over the contents of a text file. You must tell ColdFusion to recognize the end of each line of text as the delimiter for your list items, like this:

`delimiters="#chr(10)##chr(13)#"`

■ If you're wondering, Ambition, Distraction, Uglification, and Derision are the Mock Turtle's four branches of Arithmetic.

**Figure 11.27** By default, ColdFusion looks only for commas to delimit a list ...

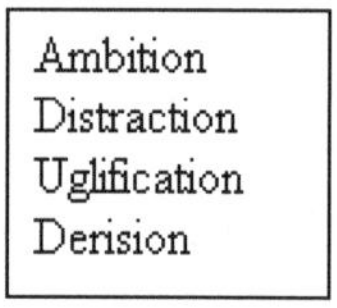

Ambition
Distraction
Uglification; Derision

**Figure 11.28** ... but you can specify additional delimiters.

Ambition
Distraction
Uglification
Derision

## Separating Application Logic from Content

Of all the practices you can adopt right now to make your code easier to update and debug over the long run, separating application logic from content is probably the most effective. (Although commenting your code runs a pretty close second!)

What does that mean? Let's look back at two examples earlier in this chapter.

First, you learned how to check for the existence of a variable with the <cfparam> tag. To review, in order to check for the existence of myName and set its default value to "Marc," you used this code:

```
<cfparam name="myName" default="Marc">
```

It's possible, though, to write this code much less efficiently. In fact, many beginning ColdFusion programmers would solve the problem like this:

```
<cfif NOT isDefined("myName")>
<cfset myName = "Marc">
</cfif>
```

Worse, many beginners would put this code in the body of the page just before the <cfoutput> tag. Try to avoid coding this way at all costs.

For a second example, look at the code from the previous section that used switch-case logic to alter a string using a ColdFusion function of your choice. To recap, in each <cfcase>, you performed the transformation on the original variable and set the new value into the variable myNewString. Only after the entire switch had run its course, you output the new string with a <cfoutput> tag. Why not simply output the new value with a <cfoutput> within each <cfcase>?

First, doing so adds a lot of code to your page. That translates into more typing for you and more processing time for the page. Why output each time you set the variable when you can do so only once at the end of the switch?

Second, outputting the new value with a <cfoutput> within each <cfcase> makes your code hard to maintain. In our case, we simply output the variable myNewString as plain text. But what if the variable was included in a complex table your designer had spent hours creating? A beginning ColdFusion developer (not you) might be tempted to pack the entire switch-case logic into a table cell and output within each <cfcase>. But the experienced ColdFusion developer knows to handle the switch-case logic at the very top of the page, and output the resulting value where necessary in the body of the page.

To their eternal credit, the engineers at Macromedia understand the importance of keeping application logic separated from content presentation. Examine the source code of the pages you've created in earlier chapters using Dreamweaver's code generation tool. Over and over again, you'll see that they tend to fall into two sections: first, a large block of code that defines and initializes variables, executes queries, and generally sets up the values to be used on the page; and second, the HTML body itself, which displays the values created in the code section.

You can't always keep the two strictly separate of course, but adopting this practice right now and keeping it in mind any time you build a dynamic page will make your life as a developer much, much easier. I promise.

SEPARATING APPLICATION LOGIC FROM CONTENT

# EXTENDING DREAMWEAVER MX

In the previous chapter, you took a whirlwind tour of CFML (ColdFusion Markup Language). Let's step back a moment and look at the bigger picture: Every line of code that you've created in this book could have been written in Notepad or any other text editor. Nothing requires that you use Dreamweaver MX to build your ColdFusion Web sites.

Why use a visual tool at all then? The answer, as you read in the Introduction and have seen in each chapter, is that Dreamweaver MX, by automating repetitive processes and generating code, helps you build your sites more quickly and accurately than if you simply typed the code in a text editor.

Dreamweaver MX ships with a large number of server behaviors (for example, Repeat Region and Recordset paging) that accomplish the tasks most developers confront daily. As you build more and more sites, however, you will find yourself writing the same pieces of code over and over. The real beauty of Dreamweaver MX is that you can teach it to create and recognize your code—in other words, you can write your own server behaviors and even share them with other developers. In fact, Macromedia has created the Exchange, a thriving community where Extension Developers build and share server behaviors, commands, panels, and other pieces of reusable code.

In this chapter, you learn how to build your own server behaviors. You also learn how to download, install, and use those third party extensions. However, you can't write an extension unless you have a block of working code to reproduce. Thus, we take a brief detour in the middle of the chapter to introduce you to working with dates in ColdFusion.

# Working with Third Party Extensions

Today several hundred extensions are available that are designed to increase your productivity with Dreamweaver. More and more extension developers post extensions they've created on their own sites. Macromedia also provides the Exchange, where you can download extensions or even upload those you've written on your own. Fortunately, Macromedia has devised a set of rigorous tests to ensure that extensions receiving the Macromedia Approved icon 🔥 behave in a way familiar to Dreamweaver users.

There are many different types of extensions: objects, behaviors, commands, inspectors, floating panels, server behaviors, and more. In this chapter, you learn about floating panels and server behaviors.

A *floating panel* (commonly called a "floater") is a window that floats above the Dream-

weaver application interface and provides information or helps you accomplish a coding task. Built-in floaters include the Code Inspector and the Sitespring panel. In this section, you download a floater and use it to insert ColdFusion functions.

A server behavior adds server-side code to your document. You already know about server behaviors and their power: You've used them throughout this book. Later in this chapter, you build two of your own server behaviors.

To download an extension, go to the Macromedia Web site and navigate to the Dreamweaver Exchange. Many extensions are available for both Macintosh and Windows (**Figure 12.1**). The very best extensions identify a need that's not directly addressed in the Dreamweaver MX interface.

Macintosh and Windows downloads

**Figure 12.1** Many Dreamweaver extensions are available for both Macintosh and Windows.

**Figure 12.2** Locate the Extension Manager under All Programs > Macromedia.

Later in this chapter, you learn about writing ColdFusion date functions. Wouldn't it be nice to have an extension that lists all available date and time functions, and with the click of a mouse inserts the correct function into your document? Luckily, the Flash Expression Panel does exactly what we need.

## To download and install an extension:

1. You can download the Flash Expression Panel in one of two ways:

   ▲ Go to the download section of this book's Web site and download the zipped file that accompanies this chapter. Locate and extract the file MX450887_FlashExpression.mxp.

   ▲ Go to the Macromedia Dreamweaver Exchange and search for Flash Expression Panel. Follow the instructions onscreen to download the file.

   Either way, ensure that you save the extension in a location on your hard drive where you can easily find it. Macromedia has created the .mxp file format for storing, describing, and installing extensions. In order to use an .mxp file, you must have the Extension Manager installed.

2. Locate and run the Macromedia Extension Manager (EM). You can do this one of two ways:

   ▲ In a typical installation, you can find the Extension Manager icon under All Programs > Macromedia (**Figure 12.2**).

   ▲ In the Dreamweaver interface, choose Help > Manage Extensions.

*continues on next page*

### A Moving Target

Software programs change, some more quickly than others. As of this writing, Macromedia is revising the Exchange and the Extension Manager. By the time you read this book, Macromedia may have released new versions of each. The fundamentals of downloading, installing, and using extensions will remain the same. If the instructions in this book seem inconsistent with your experience, be sure to refer to the Help files of the program or Web page you're using.

WORKING WITH THIRD PARTY EXTENSIONS

The EM launches. By default, the EM is included when you install Dreamweaver MX. As of this writing, the most current release is EM 1.5.054. The EM interface shows a list of installed extensions for Dreamweaver MX, Fireworks MX, and Flash MX, assuming you have those programs installed on your system (**Figure 12.3**).

3. Install a new extension by doing one of the following:

▲ Click the Install New Extension icon (**Figure 12.4**).

▲ Type Ctrl+I.

The Select window opens.

4. Navigate to the location where you saved the Flash Expression Panel. Select the file MX450887_FlashExpression.mxp and then click Install.

The EM begins the installation and opens a disclaimer window (**Figure 12.5**).

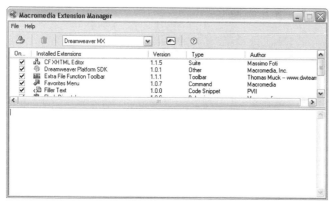

**Figure 12.3** The Extension Manager interface shows a list of installed extensions.

**Figure 12.4** Click the Install New Extension icon to begin the installation process.

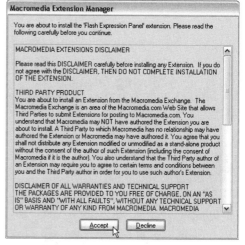

**Figure 12.5** You must agree to the Macromedia disclaimer before you can install an extension.

WORKING WITH THIRD PARTY EXTENSIONS

**Figure 12.6** The Extension Manager notifies you when you have successfully installed and extension.

**5.** Read the disclaimer, and then click Accept if you agree.

The EM installs the extension and prompts you to close and restart Dreamweaver (**Figure 12.6**).

**6.** Click OK.

Your new extension should now be installed.

### ✔ Tip

■ The Flash Expression Panel gets its name from the innovative use of Macromedia Flash as a floater interface.

## Intellectual Property

Writing extensions from scratch is hard work. It's a testament to the generosity of the Dreamweaver community that the vast majority of extensions are free. But just because the extensions are free doesn't mean you can distribute them freely. Most extension developers allow users to download extensions from only a very small number of approved sites. Not only does this help the developer control the distribution of his intellectual property, but it also helps you ensure that you're getting the most current and authentic code.

We asked—and received—permission from Neil Robertson-Ravo, the author of the Flash Expression Panel, to distribute his extension on this book's companion Web site. Please respect his and all other extension developers intellectual property rights and do not redistribute their work without permission.

**WORKING WITH THIRD PARTY EXTENSIONS**

## To use the Flash Expression Panel:

1. Create a new ColdFusion document in Dreamweaver.

2. Choose Window > Others > Expression to open the Flash Expression Panel (**Figure 12.7**). If Expression doesn't appear in your list of other windows, don't forget that you need to close and restart Dreamweaver for the changes to take effect.

   The Flash Expression Panel opens.

3. Click the ColdFusion node to expand the tree (**Figure 12.8**).

   Four nodes open: Functions, Constants, Operators, and Variables. We want to locate the functions for date and time.

4. Click the Functions node.

   The Functions node expands, showing a list of available function groups. Date and Time functions are second on the list (**Figure 12.9**).

**Figure 12.7** Choose Window > Others > Expression to load the Flash Expression Panel.

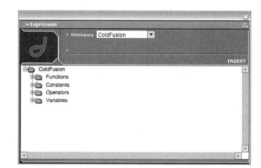

**Figure 12.8** Expand the ColdFusion node to see the available options.

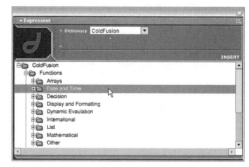

**Figure 12.9** The Flash Expression panels groups ColdFusion functions.

**5.** Click the Date and Time node to view a list of functions.

The Date and Time node expands, listing all ColdFusion Date and Time functions.

**6.** Scroll down the list until you reach the function DayOfWeek. Notice that when you select a function, the Expression Panel lists the functions parameters (**Figure 12.10**).

**7.** Place your cursor anywhere within your document, and in the Expression Panel, click Insert.

The panel inserts the function, with any necessary parameters, into your ColdFusion document (**Figure 12.11**).

For the moment, don't worry about what each function actually accomplishes. To use the Flash Expression Panel successfully, you only need to understand that it allows you to see all ColdFusion functions in grouped lists and to insert the desired function and its parameters with the click of your mouse. In the next section, you learn how to use a few of the date functions and put the Flash Expression Panel to work.

*A function and its parameters*

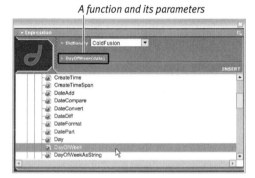

**Figure 12.10** Selecting a function reveals its parameters in the Flash Expression Panel.

*Inserted Code*

*Insert*

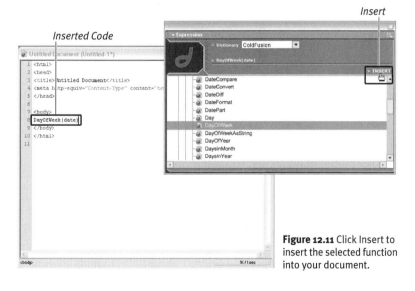

**Figure 12.11** Click Insert to insert the selected function into your document.

# Working with Dates in ColdFusion MX

ColdFusion MX provides you with more than 40 functions to work with dates and times. With a single line of code, you can retrieve the current date or time, calculate differences between dates, compare date values, and much more.

ColdFusion uses the Now() function to return the date and time on the server, accurate to the second. The Now() function, however, does not generate user-friendly results. For example, running the Now() function on October 6, 2002 at 10:39a.m. generates the following output:

```
{ts '2002-10-06 10:39:23'}
```

That's a format only a computer could love.

The DayOfWeek() function retrieves the day of the week in numeric format from the string generated by Now(), and DayOfWeekAsString() creates a human-friendly result such as Sunday when used in conjunction with the DayOfWeek() function. Finally, ColdFusion provides the DateDiff() function to calculate the difference between two dates. We examine each function in detail below.

## ✔ Tips

- If you've forgotten how to work with functions, please see the previous chapter, "Introducing Hand Coding CFML."

- Remember, the Now() function checks the date and time on the server, not on the client. To check the current date on the client, use the JavaScript Date object.

- This section makes use of the Flash Expression Panel extension, installed earlier in this chapter. If you haven't yet installed it or prefer not to use it, you still can type the functions by hand.

## To output the current date:

1. Create a new ColdFusion page in your site folder, title it, and save it. Switch to the Dreamweaver Code view or Code and Design view.

   The page you are creating will tell the user whether she can take the day off or not.

2. Choose Window > Others > Expression to open the Flash Expression Panel. Expand the ColdFusion node to the Date and Time functions.

3. Above the opening <html> tag, type this code:

   ```
   <cfset myDate = >
   ```

   ColdFusion then creates a variable named myDate. You still need to assign a value to the variable.

4. Place your cursor immediately before the closing angle bracket (>) in your variable declaration. In the Flash Expression Panel, select the Now() function and click Insert.

   Dreamweaver assigns the value of the date and time on the server to the myDate variable. Your variable declaration should look like this:

   ```
   <cfset myDate = Now()>
   ```

   You still need to output the value of the variable.

**5.** In between the opening and closing <body> tags, type this code:

`<cfoutput>#myDate#</cfoutput>`

Your entire document should look like the code listed in **Figure 12.12**.

**6.** Press F12 to preview the page in a browser. ColdFusion outputs the value of the variable myDate. As noted in this section's introduction, the output isn't very useful to a person. You need to extract the day of the week from the string generated by the Now() function.

**7.** Add the DayOfWeek() function to your first line of code, like this:

`<cfset myDay = DayOfWeek(Now())>`

You either can type the DayOfWeek() function or insert it from the Flash Expression Panel. If you're unsure of which parameters you need for a given function, don't forget to look at the parameters listed in the Flash Expression Panel.

The DayOfWeek() functions retrieve the day of the week from a date/time string. ColdFusion counts the days of the week beginning with 1 for Sunday, 2 for Monday, 3 for Tuesday, and so on.

Notice how we have nested our functions. ColdFusion always processes functions from the innermost function to the outermost function. Thus, we have told ColdFusion, "First get the date and time from the server and then extract the day of the week from the date and time."

**8.** Press F12 to preview the page in a browser. ColdFusion outputs an integer representing the day of the week, according to the clock on the ColdFusion server. We can still make this code more human-friendly, though.

**9.** Add the DayOfWeekAsString() function to your first line of code, like this:

```
<cfset today =
→ #DayOfWeekAsString
→ (DayOfWeek(Now()))#>
```

ColdFusion sets the value of the variable today to the day of the week, in a human readable form.

The DayOfWeekAsString() function accepts a number from 1 to 7 and returns the day of the week as a string like Sunday or Monday instead of 1 or 2. It's important to understand the difference between DayOfWeek() and DayOfWeekAsString(). You use the former to parse a date/time string and return the day of the week; the latter will take only an integer between 1and 7and return it as a human-friendly string. In other words, this is not a valid function:

`DayOfWeekAsString(Now())`

Now let's process some conditional code based on the date you've generated.

*continues on next page*

```
1  <cfset myDate = Now()>
2  <html>
3  <head>
4  <title>Dates</title>
5  <meta http-equiv="Content-Type" content="text/html; charset=iso-8859-1">
6  </head>
7
8  <body>
9  <cfoutput>#myDate#</cfoutput>
10 </body>
11 </html>
```

**Figure 12.12** This code retrieves the current date and time from the server and outputs the value to the screen.

**10.** Type this code on the second line of the document:

```
<cfset myDayOff = "Sunday">
<cfparam name="myMessage"
→ default="Back to work, you!">
```

ColdFusion creates a variable called myDayOff and assigns it the value Sunday. ColdFusion also checks for the existence of the variable myMessage and, if it doesn't exist, creates it and assigns it a rather brusque value, Back to work, you!

**11.** Following your variable declarations, type this code:

```
<cfif today IS myDayOff>
<cfset myMessage = "Take a break and
→ enjoy yourself."></cfif>
```

ColdFusion compares the value contained in the variable today to the value contained in myDayOff (in other words, Sunday). If the values are equal, ColdFusion sets a cheerful message for the variable myMessage. All that remains is to output the message in the browser.

**12.** In between the document's opening and closing <body> tags, type this code:

```
<cfoutput>#myMessage#</cfoutput>
```

ColdFusion outputs the value contained in myMessage. Your entire document should look like the code listed in **Figure 12.13**.

**13.** Press F12 to preview your page in a browser.

If you run the code on a Sunday, ColdFusion tells you to take a break and enjoy yourself. Actually, that's not bad advice. We'll be waiting here with the next section when you get back.

```
1  <cfset today = #DayOfWeekAsString(DayOfWeek(Now()))#>
2  <cfset myDayOff = "Sunday">
3  <cfparam name="myMessage" default="Back to work, you!">
4  <cfif today IS myDayOff>
5      <cfset myMessage = "Take a break and enjoy yourself.">
6  </cfif>
7  <html>
8  <head>
9  <title>Day off or not?</title>
10 <meta http-equiv="Content-Type" content="text/html; charset=iso-8859-1">
11 </head>
12
13 <body>
14
15 <cfoutput>#myMessage#</cfoutput>
16
17 </body>
18 </html>
```

**Figure 12.13** This code retrieves the current day of the week and processes code depending on the value.

## ✔ Tips

- If you prefer, you can set the variable myDayOff to a day other than Sunday to test the page.

- We could have easily processed the conditional code based on the integer returned by DayOfWeek(). Instead, we took the extra step of making the integer human-friendly with DayOfWeekAsString(). As you'll see later in this chapter, we want to allow users to specify the day off, and it's easier to do so with a value they can recognize.

- Remember that the Flash Expression Panel lists parameters for all ColdFusion functions. For more detailed help with Date and Time functions and an explanation of each parameter, search for "Date and Time functions" in the ColdFusion MX documentation.

### Fun with Counting

If you're coming from another programming language, you might find the ColdFusion method of counting days confusing. Most computer languages start counting from zero, not one. For example, JavaScript counts Sunday as the first day of the week, and begins the count from zero. ColdFusion is unusual in counting the days of the week as one through seven.

## To check the difference between two dates:

1. Create a new ColdFusion page in your site folder, title it, and save it.

   We will use this page to check whether an employee is eligible to receive benefits, and if not, to calculate the number of days remaining before she becomes eligible.

2. On the first line of the page, type this code:

   ```
   <cfparam name="url.id" default=
   → "74E25C48-B0D0-14F2-
   → D8DF827E2DFF1A44">
   ```

   Creating the parameter url.id makes it easier to test this page; this employee id was chosen at random by looking it up in the Access database.

3. Using the Recordset Builder or typing by hand, create a new query using the data source exampleapps:

   ```
   <cfquery name="q_getDate"
   → datasource="exampleapps">
   → SELECT StartDate FROM tblEmployees
   → WHERE EmployeeID = '#url.id#'
   </cfquery>
   ```

   ColdFusion retrieves the field StartDate from the table tblEmployees for the record matching the variable id passed in the URL scope. The field StartDate contains, naturally enough, the date the employee started work.

4. Underneath the query, type this code:

   ```
   <cfparam name="myBenefits" default="You
   → are entitled to benefits.">
   ```

   ColdFusion creates a parameter called myBenefits, if one does not already exist, and assigns it a value.

   *continues on next page*

WORKING WITH DATES IN COLDFUSION MX

**5.** Underneath the parameter declaration, type this code:

```
<cfset theDiff = >
```

ColdFusion creates the variable `theDiff` when you run the page, but you still need to assign a value to it.

**6.** Place your cursor just before the closing angle bracket (>) of the variable declaration. In the Flash Expression Panel, locate the `DateDiff()` function and click Insert. Your line of code should now look like this:

```
<cfset theDiff = DateDiff(datepart,
→ date1, date2)>
```

The `DateDiff()` function accepts three parameters: the `Specifier`, `Date1`, and `Date2`. The `DateDiff()` function calculates the difference between `Date1` and `Date2` in units determined by the `Specifier`. Common specifiers are `d` for day, `m` for month, and `yyyy` for year.

**7.** Type this code to provide values for your parameters:

```
<cfset theDiff = DateDiff("d",
→ q_getDate.StartDate, Now())>
```

In this example, ColdFusion calculates the difference in days between the day the employee started work and today. The value returned is set into a variable named `theDiff`.

**8.** Assuming that an employee must work one year (365 days) before becoming eligible to receive benefits, add this code to check the value contained in `theDiff` and act accordingly:

```
<cfif theDiff LT 365>
<cfset remainingDays = 365 - theDiff>
<cfset myBenefits = "You must work " &
→ remainingDays &
→ " more days to receive benefits.">
</cfif>
```

The code above your `<html>` tag should now look like the code listed in **Figure 12.14**.

ColdFusion compares the number of days worked with the value 365 (in other words, the number of days required to begin receiving benefits). If the value is LT (less than) 365, ColdFusion creates the variable `remainingDays` and subtracts the number of days worked from 365 to determine the number of days left before eligibility. Finally, ColdFusion creates the variable `myBenefits` and populates it with a message to the employee. All that remains is to print the message to the screen.

```
1  <cfparam name="url.id" default="74E25C48-B0D0-14F2-D8DF827E2DFF1A44">
2  <cfquery name="q_getDate" datasource="exampleapps">
3      SELECT StartDate FROM tblEmployees WHERE EmployeeID = '#url.id#'
4  </cfquery>
5  <cfparam name="myBenefits" default="You are entitled to benefits.">
6  <cfset theDiff = DateDiff("d", q_getDate.StartDate, Now())>
7  <cfif theDiff LT 365>
8      <cfset remainingDays = 365 - theDiff>
9      <cfset myBenefits = "You must work " & remainingDays & " more days to receive benefits.">
10 </cfif>
```

**Figure 12.14** This code checks the number of days since an employee's starting date and compares it to the number of days in a year.

```
18  <body>
19
20  <cfoutput>#myBenefits#</cfoutput>
21
22  </body>
```

**Figure 12.15** This body outputs the variable *myBenefits*.

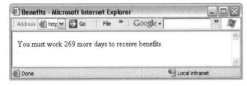

You must work 269 more days to receive benefits.

**Figure 12.16** This employee must work 269 more days before receiving benefits.

**9.** In between the document's opening and closing <body> tags, type this code:

<cfoutput>#myBenefits#</cfoutput>

ColdFusion outputs the value of myBenefits. Your document's body should look like the code listed in **Figure 12.15**.

**10.** Press F12 to preview your page in a browser (**Figure 12.16**).

Your result will vary depending on the start date of the employee you entered, as well as the day you run the page.

**11.** Be sure that you've tested the code from this section, that it works, and that you understand how the functions operate. In the next section, you build server behaviors based on the code you've just written.

## ✔ Tips

- For a complete list of DateDiff() specifiers, see the ColdFusion MX documentation.

- ColdFusion has a wealth of functions to handle times as well as dates. Browse through the function list in the Flash Expression Panel and experiment with the different functions.

WORKING WITH DATES IN COLDFUSION MX

**189**

# Writing Your Own Server Behaviors

So far, this chapter has covered using a third party extension to manipulate date values in ColdFusion. As wonderful as the Flash Expression Panel is, though, it can't help you reuse an entire block of code. If you build human resources applications, you might find yourself writing the same code to manage benefits and days off over and over and over. That's a waste of time better spent at the water cooler or napping.

Server-side code that you find yourself writing more than once is a good candidate for a server behavior. Dreamweaver includes a Server Behavior Builder to help you with this task. You even can build your own sophisticated server behaviors by hand if you have a solid understanding of JavaScript, but that's beyond the scope of this book.

Before you begin writing a server behavior, consider these questions:

◆ Do you have a problem worth automating? Think about the two examples you've built so far in this chapter: a block of code to tell an employee whether to take the day off, and a block of code to determine an employee's eligibility for benefits. The first one is a bit artificial and included mainly to help you build your first simple server behavior. But the second block of code is the sort of function you might find yourself writing many times; it would make a strong candidate for a server behavior in the real world.

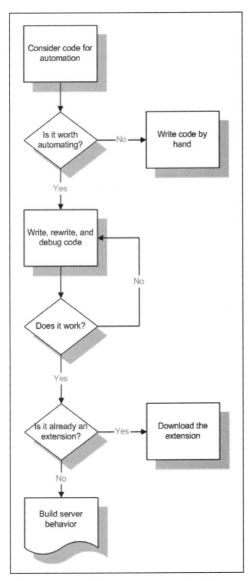

**Figure 12.17** Be certain that you've considered the questions in this flow chart before turning your code into a server behavior.

- Does the code work?

  It's critical that you test and re-test any code you want to include in a server behavior. It's easy to make mistakes when building a server behavior, and when things go wrong, you want to know the problem is with the way the server behavior is built, not with the underlying code.

- Does the extension already exist?

  Someone already may have done your work for you. Before you build a server behavior, search the Dreamweaver Exchange and the popular extension sites for an extension that accomplishes your desired task.

We've distilled this process into the flow chart shown in **Figure 12.17**.

WRITING YOUR OWN SERVER BEHAVIORS

# Building Simple Server Behaviors

The SBB (Server Behavior Builder) creates server behaviors with discrete blocks of code. You can even specify where to insert each code block into your document. Let's start with a simple server behavior that automates the "day off" code you wrote earlier.

### To create a simple server behavior with the SBB:

1. Ensure that the ColdFusion site that you have defined for this book is open in Dreamweaver.

   **This is an important step.**
   Dreamweaver allows you to build server behaviors in several different server models. A server behavior that you build in ASP, for example, will not appear in the Server Behaviors panel of a ColdFusion site.

2. In the Server Behaviors panel, click the plus sign (+) and choose New Server Behavior (**Figure 12.18**).

   Dreamweaver opens the New Server Behavior dialog (**Figure 12.19**).

3. Ensure that you have ColdFusion selected in the Document Type select control, and name your new server behavior Day Off. Click OK.

   ColdFusion opens a Day Off Server Behavior Builder (**Figure 12.20**).

4. Click the plus sign to insert a new code block.

   Dreamweaver opens the Create a New Code Block dialog (**Figure 12.21**) and suggests the name Day Off_block1 for your first code block.

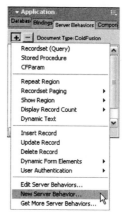

Figure 12.18 To build a server behavior, choose New Server Behavior.

Figure 12.19 The New Server Behavior dialog allows you to specify the document type and name of your server behavior.

Figure 12.20 ColdFusion opens a new dialog with the name of your server behavior.

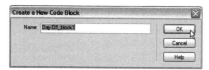

Figure 12.21 Dreamweaver suggests a name for each new code block.

The new code block

The temporary code

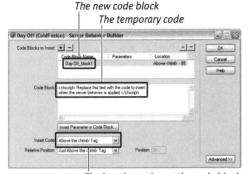

The location to insert the code block

**Figure 12.22** Dreamweaver inserts placeholder code in your new code block.

**Figure 12.23** An incomplete server behavior with one block of code.

**5.** Click OK to accept the code block name.

Dreamweaver creates a new code block with placeholder code (**Figure 12.22**). The program allows you to insert only one set of opening and closing tags in a code block.

**6.** In the code block pane of Day Off_block1, type this code:

```
<cfset today =
→ #DayOfWeekAsString
→ (DayOfWeek(Now()))#>
```

It's so important to get the code right that you may prefer to cut and paste your code instead of typing by hand.

For each new block of code, you must specify where Dreamweaver should insert the code into the document. By default, Dreamweaver inserts the block just above the <html> tag. This position is fine for Day Off_block1. Your Server Behavior Builder should look like **Figure 12.23**.

**7.** Click the plus sign again and click OK to accept the default code block name of Day Off_block2.

**8.** Add this code to Day Off_block2:

```
<cfset myDayOff = "Sunday">
```

**9.** Click the plus sign and click OK to accept the default code block name of Day Off_block3.

**10.** Add this code to Day Off_block3:

```
<cfparam name="myMessage"
→ default="Back to work, you!">
```

*continues on next page*

WRITING YOUR OWN SERVER BEHAVIORS

**11.** Click the plus sign and click OK to accept the default code block name of Day Off_block4.

```
<cfif today IS myDayOff>
<cfset myMessage =
→ "Take a break and enjoy yourself.">
</cfif>
```

You now have four blocks of code, all of which will display above the first <HTML> tag. All that's missing is the code for the body to output your result.

**12.** Click the plus sign and click OK to accept the default code block name of Day Off_block5.

**13.** Add this code to Day Off_block5:

```
<cfoutput>#myMessage#</cfoutput>
```

ColdFusion outputs the variable created and set in your first four blocks of code. But remember, by default Dreamweaver inserts the new block above the <html> tag, where it doesn't do us any good.

**14.** In the Insert Code drop-down list, choose Relative to the Selection. For the relative position, choose Replace the Selection.

Dreamweaver will now replace any code you select in your document with the output from Day Off_block5. Your Server Behavior Builder window should now look like **Figure 12.24**.

**15.** Click OK.

Congratulations! You've just completed your first server behavior. Now you can test it.

**16.** In any ColdFusion document, open the Server Behaviors panel and click the plus sign (+) to view the available server behaviors.

You will see Day Off, the newest server behavior, toward the bottom of the list (**Figure 12.25**).

**Figure 12.24** This window contains a complete server behavior.

**Figure 12.25** The new server behavior appears in the Server Behaviors panel.

**Figure 12.26** Dreamweaver recognizes the new server behavior applied to your page.

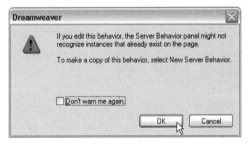

**Figure 12.27** The Edit Server Behaviors allow you to select a server behavior to change.

**Figure 12.28** Dreamweaver warns you to be careful when editing server behaviors.

**17.** Place your cursor anywhere in the body of the page, and apply to the page.

Dreamweaver inserts your variable declarations above the <html> tag, and your output within the page's body. Incredibly, the Server Behaviors panel even recognizes your new extension and the dynamic text it creates (**Figure 12.26**)!

While you've just written a very cool server behavior, its use is limited. After all, not everyone takes Sunday off. Wouldn't it be nice if you could specify the day off when you build the page? You can do so by adding a parameter to the server behavior.

## To add a parameter to a server behavior:

**1.** Create a new ColdFusion page in your Dreamweaver site, title it, and save it.

**2.** In the Server Behaviors panel, click the plus sign (+) and then choose Edit Server Behaviors.

The Edit Server Behaviors dialog opens (**Figure 12.27**). Unless you have written other server behaviors on your own, Day Off is the only server behavior listed.

**3.** Click Edit.

Dreamweaver issues a warning: If you edit this behavior, Dreamweaver may no longer recognize instances of the behavior on your pages (**Figure 12.28**). In our case, that's okay because Day Off is not in production.

**4.** Click OK.

The Server Behavior Builder dialog opens.

*continues on next page*

WRITING YOUR OWN SERVER BEHAVIORS

**5.** Select `Day Off_block2`.

If you built the server behavior following the steps from the previous section, this code appears:

```
<cfset myDayOff = "Sunday">
```

We want to make the extension more flexible by allowing the developer to specify the value of `myDayOff` at design-time.

**6.** With your cursor, select just the letters `Sunday` (not its quotations marks) from the code block. Click the Insert Parameter in Code Block button (**Figure 12.29**).

**7.** Give your parameter a meaningful name like `day` because it will appear later when you apply the server behavior to the page. Do not include spaces in a parameter name. Click OK.

Dreamweaver changes your code block to this code:

```
<cfset myDayOff = "@@day@@">
```

When Dreamweaver applies a server behavior to the page, Dreamweaver looks for the @@ signs to signify a parameter that the user can specify.

**8.** Click Next.

The Generate Behavior dialog opens (**Figure 12.30**). As you can see, your server behavior has only one parameter, `day`, and it will be displayed as a text field when the server behavior is applied to the page.

**9.** Click OK.

Your newly edited server behavior is ready to apply.

**10.** Insert your cursor anywhere in the document's body. Use the Server Behaviors panel to apply `Day Off`.

The Day Off dialog opens (**Figure 12.31**). As you can see, the textbox is labeled `day`, which is the name of your parameter.

**Figure 12.29** The Insert Parameter dialog allows you to create parameters that your users can change.

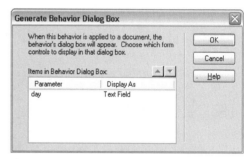

**Figure 12.30** The Generate Behavior Dialog box lets you confirm your behavior's parameters.

**Figure 12.31** When you include a parameter with your server behavior, Dreamweaver automatically creates a dialog box for use in applying and inspecting the server behavior.

WRITING YOUR OWN SERVER BEHAVIORS

**Figure 12.32** Dreamweaver recognizes your parameter in the new server behavior.

## Snippets Versus Server Behaviors

If you've worked for any length of time with Dreamweaver, you've probably discovered snippets. *Snippets* are bits of code stored in Dreamweaver's interface for quick reuse. Dreamweaver includes a Snippets panel in the Code window. Why haven't we focused on snippets in this chapter instead of server behaviors? Because server behaviors have several advantages over snippets.

Snippets are essentially one-way devices for quickly inserting code on your page. Once you've inserted a snippet, Dreamweaver doesn't recognize the code as a snippet and doesn't provide any tools for editing the snippet on the page. By contrast, Dreamweaver recognizes any server behavior on your page and lists the behavior in the Server Behaviors panel of the Application window. What's more, you can inspect your server behavior and use Dreamweaver's visual tools to change the values of any parameters in the server behavior.

Snippets and server behaviors are both essential tools. For more help on snippets, search for "Snippets" in the Dreamweaver MX documentation. For server-side code, however, there's no replacing a good server behavior.

**11.** Type the current day of the week in the Day Off dialog, and then click OK.

We typed **Monday**, but you can pick any day of the week. Dreamweaver applies your server behavior to the page and even recognizes your parameter in the Server Behaviors panel (**Figure 12.32**). You even can inspect your new server behavior, just as you can any of the pre-built server behaviors.

Do you remember which user-friendly feature you included when you first wrote the code? No? Ah, how quickly they forget! You wisely decided to evaluate the current day using DayOfWeekAsString(). This means your users now can specify the desired day as **Monday**, for example, instead of 2.

**12.** Double-click Day Off(Monday) in the Server Behaviors panel.

The Day Off dialog reopens. You can now change the value of **day** to any day you like. When you change the parameter of the server behavior and click OK, the Server Behaviors panel always reflects the current value of the parameter.

# Building Dynamic Server Behaviors

Many of the server behaviors built into Dreamweaver obtain their values dynamically, from database columns. To appreciate why a database-driven server behavior is so much more powerful than a static server behavior, you should understand the difference between design time and run time.

When you specify the value of a variable at the time you write a document, you specify that value at *design time*. The server behavior you wrote in the previous section is one such example; you set the value for the parameter *day* when you wrote the page, but the value remained unchanged each time the page ran.

If you bind your parameter to a database column, however, your server behavior can use a different value for the parameter every time the program runs. In other words, the value of the parameter is determined at *run time*.

In this section, you learn how to bind a parameter to a recordset and column. Thus, you truly can harness the power of dynamic server behaviors.

## To bind server behavior parameters to data:

1. Assemble and test the code you want to use for your server behavior. In this case, use the code that you wrote for the DateDiff() example earlier in this chapter. Refer to **Figure 12.33** for the entire code listing. Note that we have added comments around each code block.

2. Click the plus sign (+) in the Server Behaviors panel and choose New Server Behavior.

   The New Server Behavior dialog opens.

3. Name your server behavior Check Benefits and click OK.

   The Check Benefits Server Behavior Builder opens.

4. Create a new code block and accept the default name Check Benefits_block1. In the code block cell, type this code:

   ```
   <cfparam name="myBenefits"
   → default="You are entitled to
   → benefits.">
   ```

5. Insert the code Above the <html> tag, and set its relative position to Just After the Recordsets.

   Dreamweaver will insert Check Benefits_block1 immediately following any recordsets on the page. This position is necessary because the server behavior retrieves its employee information from a query.

*continues on next page*

```
1  <cfparam name="url.id" default="74E25C48-B0D0-14F2-D8DF827E2DFF1A44">
2  <cfquery name="q_getDate" datasource="exampleapps">
3  SELECT StartDate FROM tblEmployees WHERE EmployeeID = '#url.id#'
4  </cfquery>
5  <!--- begin block1 for SBB --->
6  <cfparam name="myBenefits" default="You are entitled to benefits.">
7  <!--- end block1 for SBB --->
8  <!--- begin block2 for SBB --->
9  <cfset theDiff = DateDiff("d", q_getDate.StartDate, Now())>
10 <!--- end block2 for SBB --->
11 <!--- begin block3 for SBB --->
12 <cfif theDiff LT 365>
13     <cfset remainingDays = 365 - theDiff>
14     <cfset myBenefits = "You must work " & remainingDays & " more days to receive benefits.">
15 </cfif>
16 <!--- end block3 for SBB --->
17
18 <html>
19 <head>
20 <title>DateDiff example</title>
21 <meta http-equiv="Content-Type" content="text/html; charset=iso-8859-1">
22 </head>
23
24 <body>
25 <!--- begin block4 for SBB --->
26 <cfoutput>#myBenefits#</cfoutput>
27 <!--- end block4 for SBB --->
28 </body>
29 </html>
```

**Figure 12.33** This code forms the basis for your new server behavior.

6. Repeat steps 4 and 5 for the second code block, and type this code:

```
<cfset theDiff = DateDiff("d",
→ q_getDate.StartDate, Now())>
```

7. Repeat steps 4 and 5 for the third code block, and type this code:

```
<cfif theDiff LT 365>
<cfset remainingDays = 365 - theDiff>
<cfset myBenefits = "You must work " &
→ remainingDays &
→ " more days to receive benefits.">
</cfif>
```

You now should have three blocks of code, each above the <html> tag and following any recordsets.

8. Create a fourth code block, and then type this code:

```
<cfoutput>#myBenefits#</cfoutput>
```

This time, insert the code Relative to the Selection and set the relative position to Replace the Selection. You now have a complete, if hard-coded, server behavior. Let's add dynamic parameters.

9. Click Check Benefits_block2. Select the code q_getDate, and be careful not to select the period at the end of the query name. Click Insert Parameter in Code Block.

Dreamweaver opens the Insert Parameter dialog.

WRITING YOUR OWN SERVER BEHAVIORS

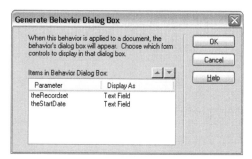

**Figure 12.34** By default the Generate Behavior Dialog Box sets all parameters to display as text fields.

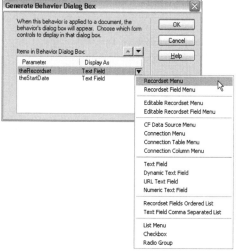

**Figure 12.35** You can change the method of displaying your parameter's input.

**10.** Give your parameter a useful name such as **theRecordset** and click OK.

Dreamweaver inserts the parameter name and placeholders in your code block.

**11.** Select the column name **StartDate**, and click the Insert Parameter in Code Block button to insert a parameter in its place. Name the parameter **theStartDate**.

Your second code block should now look like this:

```
<cfset theDiff = DateDiff("d",
→ @@theRecordset@@.@@theStartDate@@,
→ Now())>
```

**12.** Click Next.

Dreamweaver opens the Generate Behavior dialog. By default, both of your parameters will display as text fields. That's acceptable, but it's not very elegant (**Figure 12.34**).

**13.** Click the text field setting adjacent to **theRecordset** parameter, and from the list that appears, choose Recordset Menu (**Figure 12.35**).

When you add your server behavior to a document, Dreamweaver looks for all recordsets on the page and presents them in a drop-down list.

**14.** Repeat the process for the parameter **theStartDate**, this time choosing **Recordset Field Menu**.

Dreamweaver finds all available columns in the recordset you choose and present them in a drop-down list when you add the server behavior to the document.

**15.** Click OK.

Your dynamic server behavior is complete. Let's test it.

## To test and apply a dynamic server behavior:

1. Create and save a new ColdFusion page.

2. Choose Check Benefits from the Server Behaviors panel.

   Dreamweaver generates an error message (**Figure 12.36**). Dreamweaver looks for a recordset and, when it doesn't find one, asks you to create one before applying this server behavior. This error-handling is one of the primary benefits of specifying Recordset Menu as your display type instead of plain text.

3. Add this code to the very first line of the document:

```
<cfparam name="url.id"
→  default="74E25C48-B0D0-14F2-
→  D8DF827E2DFF1A44">

<cfquery name="q_getDate"
→  datasource="exampleapps">

SELECT StartDate FROM tblEmployees
→  WHERE EmployeeID = '#url.id#'
</cfquery>
```

4. Place your cursor anywhere within the body of the page. Add the Check Benefits server behavior.

   Dreamweaver opens the Check Benefits dialog. Because the page only has one recordset with one field, Dreamweaver correctly guesses the value of the parameters (**Figure 12.37**).

5. Click OK.

   Dreamweaver adds Check Benefits to your page and includes it in the list of server behaviors in the Server Behaviors panel (**Figure 12.38**). As with any dynamic server behavior, you can double-click Check Benefits to inspect its parameters.

**Figure 12.36** Dreamweaver checks the page for a recordset before allowing you to insert the new server behavior.

**Figure 12.37** Dreamweaver automatically populates the server behavior's parameters.

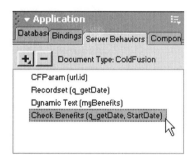

**Figure 12.38** Dreamweaver recognizes your new server behavior.

WRITING YOUR OWN SERVER BEHAVIORS

**6.** Press F12 to preview the page in your browser.

Depending on the employee you entered and the date you run the page, you either receive a message that the employee is entitled to benefits, or the number of days before she becomes eligible.

Why didn't we include the `<cfquery>` code in the server behavior itself? Many different behaviors on a page can use the same recordset. If you make a recordset part of a server behavior and later remove the behavior, it's easy to break other code on your page that relies on the recordset. Also, keeping the query out of the server behavior makes it easy to use the behavior with any query on the page.

## ✔ Tips

■ Refer to the `DateDiff()` section of this chapter if you've forgotten what this code does.

■ For the sake of simplicity, we haven't worried too much about parameter names in server behaviors. If you write many of your own server behaviors and download third party extensions, however, you should consider devising a scheme for making your parameter names unique, such as starting them with your initials or the initials of your company.

## Extending Your Extensions

We've kept our examples simple for purposes of learning how to build server behaviors. But the possibilities are without limit. In the real world, the `cfexamples` database might contain a table listing the work hours for each employee. Instead of a programmer entering these values by hand, a server behavior could retrieve its parameters from the columns of a query, and compare the time as the page loads with the hours that the employee is supposed to be on the job. It's only a few short steps from our server behavior to building an employee time-tracking page. Now that's a useful application!

WRITING YOUR OWN SERVER BEHAVIORS

# GRAPHING YOUR DATA WITH CFCHART

# 13

It turns out a picture isn't just worth a thousands words; it's also worth a few lines of ColdFusion.

By now you've discovered that most of your time writing ColdFusion is spent working with data. So far you've learned to use Dreamweaver's code generation tools to insert, update, and display data in text and in tables. The Web, however, is a visual and dynamic medium. You'll often find that you can communicate more clearly by presenting some of your data graphically instead of textually.

ColdFusion MX introduces a powerful, intuitive graphing engine with the <cfchart> tag. Dreamweaver doesn't include pre-built server behaviors to create ColdFusion graphs for you, so in this chapter you'll need to roll up your sleeves and write the code yourself. True to the CF spirit, you need to learn only three tags—<cfchart>, <cfchartdata>, and <cfchartseries>—to produce elegant, dynamic, charts.

In this chapter, you first learn how to build static charts using data that you provide. You also learn how to manipulate the appearance of charts to tell the story you want to tell. Next, you learn how to populate charts with query data in order to automate their creation. Finally, you learn how to include links within your charts to build graphical, interactive applications.

As with nearly all CF coding, the more SQL you understand, the better your charts will be. If you need a SQL refresher before building your first graph, please read Chapter 4: "Retrieving Database Data." Otherwise, let's get started.

# Building Basic Charts

ColdFusion lets you build charts from data you enter manually, from queries, or from a combination of the two. There are two or three basic steps to building any chart in ColdFusion. First, you must create a container for your chart by using the `<cfchart>` tag. With this tag's attributes, you can specify the size and format of your chart, as well as many features of its appearance.

Second, you must specify which series of data you want to show by using the `<cfchartseries>` tag. This tag also allows you to specify the type of graph you want to build, such as a line graph or a pie graph.

Finally, you can manually assign points of data to track with the `<cfchartdata>` tag.

Keeping in mind the container metaphor, think of `<cfchartseries>` as containing the optional points of data specified with `<cfchartdata>`. Likewise, `<cfchart>` contains the `<cfchartseries>`. If it all sounds a bit confusing, it will become much clearer as soon as you start coding.

## GUI or Hand Coding?

All the steps in this chapter use hand-coding techniques to create graphs and queries. If you're comfortable with the Tag Editor, query builders, and server behaviors, editing code by hand may seem like a nuisance at first. After all, if the tools are available, why not use them?

It's true that Dreamweaver does have an extraordinary GUI (Graphical User Interface), but the more time you spend creating your pages by hand, the better you'll understand the code itself. In addition, many people find typing code by hand faster than relying on the GUI. Ideally, you'll become adept at both methods and learn to use each one when it best serves your needs.

In this section, you build static charts using <cfchart>, <cfchartseries>, and <cfchartdata>. Don't be too concerned at first with the appearance of your charts; just let ColdFusion do the formatting for now.

## To build a container for a static chart:

1. Create a new ColdFusion page, title it, and save it.

2. Choose View > Code.

3. After the opening <body> tag, type this code and press the spacebar:

```
<cfchart
```

As you learned in the last chapter, you can use Dreamweaver's Code Hint and Auto Tag completion features to help you write your code. While working through the following steps, keep in mind that you can either select your tag attributes using Dreamweaver's code completion tools, or you can type the attributes.

4. Insert this code:

```
<cfchart showborder="yes"
chartheight="300" chartwidth="400"
yaxistitle="Projected Population
→ (Millions)" xaxistitle="Year">
</cfchart>
```

You've just specified that you want to create a chart that's 400 pixels wide and 300 pixels high. You've also specified that you want to label the vertical, or y-axis, as "Projected Population (Millions)," and the horizontal, or x-axis, as "Year."

## ✔ Tips

■ Don't forget that <cfchart>, just like most other ColdFusion tags, requires a closing tag.

■ Instead of building the container <cfchart> by hand, you can also choose Insert > ColdFusion Advanced Objects > CFCHART. If you've forgotten how to insert ColdFusion Objects, please refer to Chapter 11: "Introducing Hand Coding CFML."

■ If you're upgrading from ColdFusion 5, you may be familiar with the <cfgraph> tag. This tag has been deprecated in ColdFusion MX and replaced with the much more powerful <cfchart>.

■ It's hard to appreciate ColdFusion graphs in grayscale. You really owe it to yourself to run the code samples included in this chapter to see the graphs in color.

■ If you don't have a large monitor, try switching to Dreamweaver's Code view when you're working with tags that don't have code generation tools.

## To define a chart type with the <cfchartseries> tag:

1. In between the opening and closing <cfchart> tags, type this code:

   ```
   <cfchartseries type="line"
   →  serieslabel="United States">
   </cfchartseries>
   ```

   You've now specified that you want a line chart labeled United States. **Figure 13.1** shows the code you've entered up to this point. You are ready to test what you've built so far.

2. Choose File > Preview in Browser and select your browser of choice.

   Wait for your browser to open and you get ... an empty black border. But something funny is going on here.

3. Move your mouse somewhere within the black border and right-click (Windows) or Control+click (Mac).

   You'll see the Flash Player menu (**Figure 13.2**)! ColdFusion has created an empty graph. In essence, you've built a container for your graph with <cfchart> and told ColdFusion that you want to create a line chart with <cfchartseries>. The next step is to pour some data into the line chart.

### ✔ Tip

- Be careful when typing your <cfchartseries> tag by hand; Dreamweaver does not automatically close this tag for you.

```
9   <cfchart showborder="yes"
10      chartheight="300"
11      chartwidth="400"
12      yaxistitle="Projected Population (Millions)"
13      xaxistitle="Year">
14      <cfchartseries type="line" serieslabel="United States">
15      </cfchartseries>
16  </cfchart>
```

**Figure 13.1** Place the <cfchartseries> tags within the opening and closing <cfchart> tags.

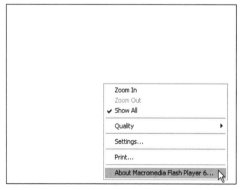

**Figure 13.2** ColdFusion exports only the chart's border if you don't put any data into it.

### Consider the Source

In case you're wondering, the population numbers for the first part of this chapter come from the US Census Bureau. You can download an amazing array of statistics from the American FactFinder Web site (http://factfinder.census.gov). It's even possible to incorporate the stats into your own databases. Sounds like <cfchart> heaven!

Building Basic Charts

## To use <cfchartdata> to manually add data:

**1.** In between the opening and closing <cfchartseries> tags, type this code:

```
<cfchartdata item="2000" value="275">
```

**2.** Press F12 to preview your work in a browser.

There's a lonely square at the top of your chart (**Figure 13.3**). Let's agree that it's a graph, albeit an unimpressive one, and move on.

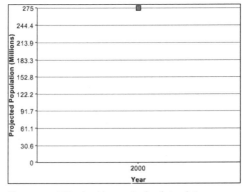

**Figure 13.3** This chart has a single plot point.

**3.** In Dreamweaver's Code view, type this code after the first <cfchartdata> tag:

```
<cfchartdata item="2005" value="290">
<cfchartdata item="2010" value="310">
<cfchartdata item="2015" value="325">
<cfchartdata item="2020" value="350">
<cfchartdata item="2025" value="380">
<cfchartdata item="2030" value="410">
<cfchartdata item="2035" value="450">
<cfchartdata item="2040" value="500">
<cfchartdata item="2045" value="525">
<cfchartdata item="2050" value="550">
```

You've just typed quite a few lines of code. **Figure 13.4** shows the entire code listing for the chart.

*continues on next page*

```
 9  <cfchart showborder="yes"
10      chartheight="300"
11      chartwidth="400"
12      yaxistitle="Projected Population (Millions)"
13      xaxistitle="Year">
14      <cfchartseries type="line" serieslabel="United States">
15          <cfchartdata item="2000" value="275">
16          <cfchartdata item="2005" value="290">
17          <cfchartdata item="2010" value="310">
18          <cfchartdata item="2015" value="325">
19          <cfchartdata item="2020" value="350">
20          <cfchartdata item="2025" value="380">
21          <cfchartdata item="2030" value="410">
22          <cfchartdata item="2035" value="450">
23          <cfchartdata item="2040" value="500">
24          <cfchartdata item="2045" value="525">
25          <cfchartdata item="2050" value="550">
26      </cfchartseries>
27  </cfchart>
```

**Figure 13.4** When you're entering data manually, accuracy is critical.

**BUILDING BASIC CHARTS**

**209**

**4.** Save your file, and then view it in a browser.

You should see a line graph showing the population of the United States increasing from 275 million in 2000 to a projected 550 million in 2050 (**Figure 13.5**). Wow! And you thought space was already tight in the Hamptons.

### ✔ Tips

■ <cfchartdata> doesn't require a closing tag.

■ A graph with too little information just isn't interesting. To give your viewers useful information, you need to show how the data changes over time or how one set of data compares to another.

### To track more than one set of data:

**1.** After the first <cfchartseries> closing tag, type this code:

```
<cfchartseries type="line"
→   serieslabel="Western Europe"
→   markerstyle="triangle">
</cfchartseries>
```

You've just told ColdFusion that you want to add a second line to your existing graph, that you want to label it Western Europe, and that you want to mark the points of data with triangles. Remember, however, that <cfchartseries> is a container tag and does not contain any data until you specify otherwise.

**2.** Press F12 to preview the chart in your browser (**Figure 13.6**).

**3.** In between the opening and closing <cfchartseries> tags you just created, type this code:

```
<cfchartdata item="2000" value="390">
<cfchartdata item="2005" value="395">
<cfchartdata item="2010" value="400">
<cfchartdata item="2015" value="400">
<cfchartdata item="2020" value="400">
<cfchartdata item="2025" value="393">
<cfchartdata item="2030" value="390">
<cfchartdata item="2035" value="380">
<cfchartdata item="2040" value="372">
<cfchartdata item="2045" value="360">
<cfchartdata item="2050" value="355">
```

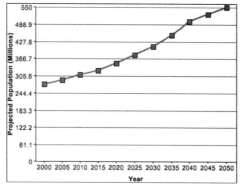

**Figure 13.5** ColdFusion automatically connects your points of data in a line chart.

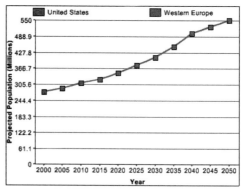

**Figure 13.6** This chart has two series: one populated and one empty.

**Figure 13.7** shows the entire code listing for the chart.

4. Save your work, and then view it in a browser.

The graph shows two series of connected points, one gently descending after leveling off, the other climbing sharply (**Figure 13.8**). Note that even in grayscale, you can distinguish Western Europe's line by the triangle markers.

```
9  <cfchart showborder="yes" chartheight="300" chartwidth="400" yaxistitle="Projected Population
   (Millions)" xaxistitle="Year">
10     <cfchartseries type="line" serieslabel="United States">
11         <cfchartdata item="2000" value="275">
12         <cfchartdata item="2005" value="290">
13         <cfchartdata item="2010" value="310">
14         <cfchartdata item="2015" value="325">
15         <cfchartdata item="2020" value="350">
16         <cfchartdata item="2025" value="380">
17         <cfchartdata item="2030" value="410">
18         <cfchartdata item="2035" value="450">
19         <cfchartdata item="2040" value="500">
20         <cfchartdata item="2045" value="525">
21         <cfchartdata item="2050" value="550">
22     </cfchartseries>
23     <cfchartseries type="line" serieslabel="Western Europe" markerstyle="triangle">
24         <cfchartdata item="2000" value="390">
25         <cfchartdata item="2005" value="395">
26         <cfchartdata item="2010" value="400">
27         <cfchartdata item="2015" value="400">
28         <cfchartdata item="2020" value="400">
29         <cfchartdata item="2025" value="393">
30         <cfchartdata item="2030" value="390">
31         <cfchartdata item="2035" value="380">
32         <cfchartdata item="2040" value="372">
33         <cfchartdata item="2045" value="360">
34         <cfchartdata item="2050" value="355">
35     </cfchartseries>
36 </cfchart>
```

**Figure 13.7** This code listing calls for a chart with two series of data.

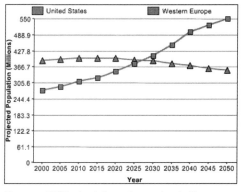

**Figure 13.8** This chart shows two series: both are populated.

# Dressing Up Your Charts

Building a chart and populating it with data is only half the battle. You also need to ensure that your chart tells the story that you want it to tell. ColdFusion's default settings usually get you reasonably close, but you'll find that you often need to make adjustments.

The <cfchartseries> tag offers eleven types of chart: bar, cylinder, horizontal bar, line, area, cone, pyramid, curve, step, and scatter. Your charts can be flat or three-dimensional. As you'll see in this section, selecting the proper chart type is one of the most important factors in determining whether your chart communicates your information clearly.

In addition to the chart's type, you can change almost any feature in your chart's appearance. You can change your chart's colors and fonts to integrate into your Web site's color scheme. You can adjust the grid's numbers to ensure that your chart makes sense.

## To change a graph's grid values:

1. Open the page you created in the last section, and preview the page in a browser.

   Notice that, by default, ColdFusion ends the y-axis with the largest value in the data set (**Figure 13.9**).

2. In the <cfchart> tag, add this attribute and preview the change in your browser:

   scaleto="600"

   Notice that the graph's y-axis now scales to 600, giving the graph a less cluttered appearance (**Figure 13.10**).

   There's another problem with this graph, though: The numbers along the y-axis don't make much sense. Nobody really wants to see a grid line at 133.3 million.

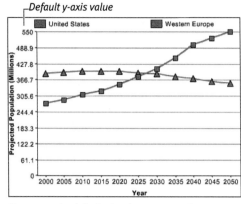

**Figure 13.9** By default, the chart stops at the greatest value in the y-axis.

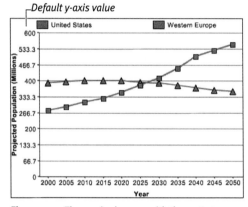

**Figure 13.10** The y-axis changes with the scaleto attribute.

```
9  <cfchart showborder="yes"
10      chartheight="300"
11      chartwidth="400"
12      yaxistitle="Projected Population (Millions)"
13      xaxistitle="Year"
14      scaleto="600"
15      gridlines="7">
```

**Figure 13.11** The code has `scaleto` and `gridlines` attributes.

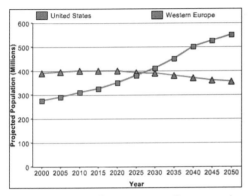

**Figure 13.12** Setting the `gridlines` attribute can make your graph easier to read.

## Telling Stories

What does it mean to "tell a story" with a graph?

Often, graphs are most useful when they communicate a change across some vector. In our Census example, you saw that it wasn't very informative to include a single population figure for one year in the United States. But a remarkable, visual story emerged when you included data for two regions over the next fifty years: By this projection, the population of the United States will overtake Western Europe sometime between 2025 and 2030, and the gap will continue to widen thereafter.

3. In the `<cfchart>` tag, add this attribute and preview the change in your browser:

    `gridlines="7"`

    **Figure 13.11** shows the `<cfchart>` tag with the newly added attributes. Notice that the y-axis numbers have changed to something more user-friendly: 100, 200, 300, etc (**Figure 13.12**). The `gridlines` attribute, naturally enough, specifies the number of lines in your grid. We set the number to 7 in order to get nice intervals up to a maximum value of 600. By setting the `scaleto` and `gridlines` attributes of the `<cfchart>` tag, you can make your graph much easier to read.

4. Save your file with a new name.

    As you work through this section, you'll be able to compare the different charts you've created.

### ✔ Tips

- Don't be confused by the way ColdFusion counts gridlines. The x-axis is included in the gridlines number. Thus, for a value of 600, we want seven gridlines: 0, 100, 200, 300, 400, 500, and 600.

- We cheated a bit with the example in this section because we knew what our maximum value would be. As you'll see in the next section, you also can retrieve data from a query. This means that you won't know ahead of time the best values for your `scaleto` or `gridlines` attributes. By the time you finish this book, you should know enough ColdFusion to be able to set those values programmatically.

**DRESSING UP YOUR CHARTS**

## To change your chart's type:

1. Open the file you created in the previous section if it isn't already open and, in the `<cfchart>` tag, add this attribute and then preview the page in your browser:

   `show3d="yes"`

   You'll see that your chart has taken on a three-dimensional appearance (**Figure 13.13**). Your charts can either be flat or 3-d. It's up to you to decide which appearance provides the most useful information.

2. Add this attribute to the `<cfchart>` tag and preview the change in your browser:

   `format="jpg"`

   You'll see that the chart is considerably less smooth than before.

3. Change the `format` attribute back to Flash and save your file.

4. Change the `type` attribute of both `<cfchartseries>` tags to `bar` and preview your page in a browser (**Figure 13.14**).

   You'll see that the bars for the United States obscure the bars for Western Europe. This problem also occurs when you set your `type` attribute to `area` (**Figure 13.15**).

5. Change Western Europe's `type` attribute to `curve`.

6. Cut your entire Western Europe `<cfchartseries>` and paste it before the United States `<cfchartseries>`.

   **Figure 13.16** shows how the code should appear in Dreamweaver.

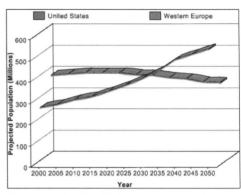

Figure 13.13 You should choose to use a 3-D chart only when that format is best for presenting your data.

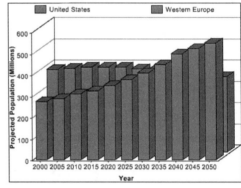

Figure 13.14 A 3-D bar chart can hide your data if you're not careful...

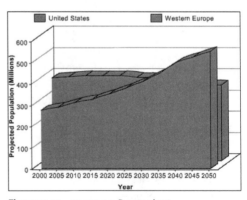

Figure 13.15 ... so can a 3-D area chart.

**7.** Save your page and view it in your browser (**Figure 13.17**).

By using a different chart Type for each series, and by changing the order in which the series appear, you've created a chart that clearly shows the demographic trends of each region. As you've seen, you can change your charts to tell almost any story you like.

*continues on next page*

```
9   <cfchart showborder="yes" chartheight="300" chartwidth="400" yaxistitle="Projected Population
    (Millions)" xaxistitle="Year" scaleto="600" gridlines="7" show3d="yes" format="flash">
10      <cfchartseries type="curve" serieslabel="Western Europe" markerstyle="triangle">
11          <cfchartdata item="2000" value="390">
12          <cfchartdata item="2005" value="395">
13          <cfchartdata item="2010" value="400">
14          <cfchartdata item="2015" value="400">
15          <cfchartdata item="2020" value="400">
16          <cfchartdata item="2025" value="393">
17          <cfchartdata item="2030" value="390">
18          <cfchartdata item="2035" value="380">
19          <cfchartdata item="2040" value="372">
20          <cfchartdata item="2045" value="360">
21          <cfchartdata item="2050" value="355">
22      </cfchartseries>
23      <cfchartseries type="area" serieslabel="United States">
24          <cfchartdata item="2000" value="275">
25          <cfchartdata item="2005" value="290">
26          <cfchartdata item="2010" value="310">
27          <cfchartdata item="2015" value="325">
28          <cfchartdata item="2020" value="350">
29          <cfchartdata item="2025" value="380">
30          <cfchartdata item="2030" value="410">
31          <cfchartdata item="2035" value="450">
32          <cfchartdata item="2040" value="500">
33          <cfchartdata item="2045" value="525">
34          <cfchartdata item="2050" value="550">
35      </cfchartseries>
36  </cfchart>
```

**Figure 13.16** You can rearrange the order of your `<cfchartseries>` tags to change your chart's appearance.

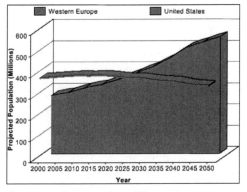

**Figure 13.17** You can assign a different chart type to each chart series.

8. Try experimenting with the different attributes for the <cfchart> and <chartseries> tags to see which effects you can create.

## ✔ Tips

■ Would you prefer to de-emphasize Western Europe's shrinking population relative to the United States? Experiment with the seriesplacement attribute of the <cfchart> tag (**Figure 13.18**).

■ Be careful when changing your chart's colors. ColdFusion will generate an error when reading hexadecimal color values such as #0000FF. You can avoid this error by escaping the hash character; to do so add a second hash: ##0000FF. Note that the Tag Editor escapes the hashes for you.

■ By default, ColdFusion draws its charts using Flash. You can use the format attribute to specify flash, jpg, or png. Flash movies are generally clearer, with smaller file sizes, than jpgs. Your choice of format will depend on your target audience, and the medium in which your use your graph. Your users must have Flash 5 Player or higher installed to view the Flash files generated by <cfchart>.

■ Generating an area chart can consume a lot of your server's resources. If you plan to serve area charts to many site users, consider different strategies to lessen the load on the processor, including caching your charts with the CF Administrator or building your charts ahead of time. See Administering Charts in the ColdFusion MX Documentation.

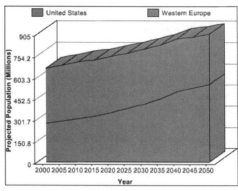

**Figure 13.18** Emphasize different data with the seriesplacement attribute.

## Fun with Chart Junk

Charts can confuse just as easily as they can enlighten. Edward Tufte of Yale University has a name for the gimcracks and doodads that designers use to dress up graphs: "chart junk." Just because you *can* deck out your design with a hundred grid lines and lavender snowflakes doesn't mean you *should*. Instead, concentrate on presenting your data as simply and clearly as possible. If you'd like to learn more about information design, go to your local library and look for Edward Tufte's *The Visual Display of Quantitative Information*, Cheshire, CT: Graphics Press, 1992.

DRESSING UP YOUR CHARTS

## Graphs in the Real World: A Case Study

In this section, you've seen how to build static charts to present more than one series of data. You've also seen how to clarify or obscure the information, depending on the story you want to tell. But how do these skills apply to you, a ColdFusion developer, in the real world?

Assume that you work at a large financial institution. Your boss comes to you Friday afternoon and says the following:

"We're at a crossroads as a lender. Although we operate in the United States and Western Europe, the last few years have been hard on us. We've decided we have the resources to offer new mortgages in only one market, and it's critical that we pick the market that's most likely to grow. This decision is for the long term and will influence the financial health of our institution over the next thirty to fifty years, not to mention your holiday bonus. I think we should focus on United States, but I need to persuade the board in a presentation later today. Put something together for me."

And she didn't even say please!

Mortgages are financial instruments that typically have a life of twenty to thirty years. Other things being equal, as a country's population grows, its demand for mortgages will grow as well. (More people need more houses, and more houses mean more people borrowing to pay for their houses).

After gathering your data, you could type a table that lists the projected population in Western Europe and the United States. In fact, you'd better do so because board members like to throw around numbers in order to sound authoritative. But look at the table on the left (**Figure 13.19**). It's good to have the information at hand, but it requires that you study the data yourself and try to understand what it means.

You quickly decide to build a graph to accompany your table. After experimenting with different graph types, you decide that a graph with one curve series and one area series tells a dramatic and simple story: Demand for mortgages in the United States will grow strongly over the next fifty years, while growth in Western Europe will stagnate and eventually decline (**Figure 13.20**). If you were giving the presentation, would you rather do so with or without the chart?

| Year | United States | Western Europe |
|------|---------------|----------------|
| 2000 | 275 | 390 |
| 2005 | 290 | 395 |
| 2010 | 310 | 400 |
| 2015 | 325 | 400 |
| 2020 | 350 | 400 |
| 2025 | 380 | 393 |
| 2030 | 410 | 390 |
| 2035 | 450 | 380 |
| 2040 | 500 | 372 |
| 2045 | 525 | 360 |
| 2050 | 550 | 355 |

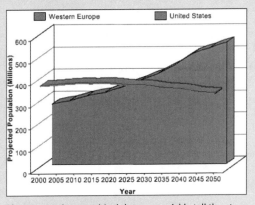

**Figure 13.19** Textual data has its purpose...

**Figure 13.20** but graphical data can quickly tell the story.

# Building Dynamic Charts with CFQUERY

Coders, by and large, are lazy people. (Not you, just those other coders). In the previous section, you learned how to build informative graphs by manually entering plot points with the `<cfchartdata>` tag. While this method gets the job done, it's problematic for a few reasons.

First, building graphs manually probably is not your job. If you work for a large company, someone else may have the responsibility for providing Web content. Even if you're an independent Web developer, your clients probably provide much of their own content. Why spend time entering data when you could be coding new features?

Second, building graphs manually is tedious. You typed only 20 values in the Census example, but what if you wanted to graph 100—or 1,000—points of data?

Third, graphs built manually are not dynamic. Census numbers are relatively static: They change once every ten years. Assume that your company sells widgets, thousands of widgets in different colors, shapes, and sizes. What if your boss tells you to track widget sales daily—by color? You'll quickly find you need to automate the graphing process.

Finally, a static graph provides no opportunity for the user to interact with the graph. Remember, useful interaction is one of the best ways to attract visitors to your Web site and keep them coming back. If you track many pieces of data, you can't assume that your visitors are equally interested in each piece.

Fortunately, you can easily address all these issues by using `<cfquery>` to provide data to your chart.

## Know Your SQL

To become a proficient ColdFusion developer, you need to understand many different technologies: interfaces, application servers, databases, and more. But if you were to pick only one skill to set yourself apart from other developers, choose SQL.

Knowing how to write efficient queries will speed up your application significantly. It also will help you provide better data to your end users. If this book whets your appetite for learning more SQL, check out Ben Forta's *Teach Yourself SQL in 10 Minutes, Second Edition*, Indianapolis: Sams, 2001. It's an easy and affordable introduction to many helpful SQL techniques.

In this section, you learn how to build charts on the fly using data from your database. You also learn how to let users click on your charts to get more information. But first, you briefly go back to SQL school to learn about the GROUP BY clause. Along the way, you're going to learn about a new Cold-Fusion tag charmingly named <cfdump>.

Assume that you have a list of all the National Parks in the United States. Assume also that each park is listed both by region and by state. In other words, Arches National Park is in both Utah state and the Rocky Mountain Region. (Actually, you don't have to make these assumptions. The table tblParks in the exampleapps data source is set up this way). As you look through your list, you may decide you'd like to group Arches National Park with other parks in Utah. You could ask, "How many parks are in Utah versus Alaska?"

Enter the GROUP BY clause. When you group a piece of data with similar pieces of data, you can count those pieces as one unit and compare that unit to other groups. This concept is probably easiest to understand by working through an example. Once you understand how powerful the GROUP BY clause can be, you'll wonder how you ever lived without it.

## Queries by Hand

In this chapter, you can decide whether to type your queries by hand or to use the help of the query builder. It's a good idea to become proficient at both methods. You might find that you like creating queries by hand so much that you do so for most of your recordsets.

Either way, Dreamweaver is so powerful that it will recognize the queries you write by hand and place them in the list of server behaviors.

BUILDING DYNAMIC CHARTS WITH CFQUERY

## To display your data using <cfdump>:

**1.** Create a new ColdFusion file, title it, and save it.

**2.** On the first line of your new page, type this code:

```
<cfquery name="q_ParkList" data
→ source="exampleapps">
SELECT PARKNAME, REGION, STATE
FROM tblParks
ORDER BY PARKNAME
</cfquery>
```

**3.** Inside the document's <body> tags, insert this code:

```
<cfdump var="#q_ParkList#"
→ label="Ungrouped List of US
→ National Parks">
```

**Figure 13.21** shows the complete code listing for the page.

```
1  <CFQUERY name="q_ParkList" datasource="exampleapps">
2  SELECT PARKNAME, REGION, STATE
3  FROM tblParks
4  ORDER BY PARKNAME
5  </CFQUERY>
6
7  <html>
8  <head>
9  <title>US National Parks by State</title>
10 <meta http-equiv="Content-Type" content="text/html; charset=iso-8859-1">
11 </head>
12
13 <body>
14 <CFDUMP var="#q_ParkList#" label="Ungrouped List of US National Parks">
15 </body>
16 </html>
```

**Figure 13.21** Output the contents of a variable with <cfdump>.

**4.** Save the page and preview it in your browser.

You will see a list of over three hundred parks presented in a table (**Figure 13.22**). How did that happen?

<cfdump> outputs the content of any variable in a neatly formatted table. It's very useful for debugging your application.

After you've looked at the data in the list of parks, you can delete the recordset q_ParkList if you like; you won't use it again on this page.

## ✔ Tips

■ Don't <cfdump> on your users. You should use <cfdump> only during application development and debugging.

■ <cfdump> does not require a closing tag.

| | PARKNAME | REGION | STATE |
|---|---|---|---|
| 1 | ABRAHAM LINCOLN BIRTHPLACE NHS | Southeast Region | KY |
| 2 | ACADIA NATIONAL PARK | North Atlantic Region | ME |
| 3 | ADAMS NATIONAL HISTORIC SITE | NORTH ATLANTIC REGION | MA |
| 4 | AGATE FOSSIL BEDS NATIONAL MONUMENT | MIDWEST REGION | NE |
| 5 | ALAGNAK WILD RIVER | Alaska Region | AK |
| 6 | ALASKA PUBLIC LANDS INFO CTR - ANCHORAGE | Alaska Region | AK |
| 7 | ALASKA PUBLIC LANDS INFO CTR - FAIRBANKS | Alaska Region | AK |
| 8 | ALASKA REGIONAL OFFICE | Alaska Region | AK |
| 9 | ALIBATES FLINT QUARRIES NM | SOUTHWEST REGION | TX |
| 10 | ALLEGHENY PORTAGE RAILROAD NHS | MID-ATLANTIC REGION | PA |
| 11 | AMERICAN INDUSTRIAL HERITAGE PROJECT | MID-ATLANTIC REGION | PA |
| 12 | AMERICAN MEMORIAL PARK | Western Region | CM |
| 13 | AMISTAD NATIONAL RECREATION AREA | Southwest Region | TX |
| 14 | ANIAKCHAK NATIONAL MONUMENT | ALASKA REGION | AK |
| 15 | ANTIETAM NATIONAL BATTLEFIELD | National Capital Region | MD |
| 16 | ANTIETAM NATIONAL CEMETERY | National Capital Region | MD |
| 17 | APOSTLE ISLANDS NATIONAL LAKESHORE | MIDWEST REGION | WI |
| 18 | APPALACHIAN NATIONAL SCENIC TRAIL | WASHINGTON OFFICE | WV |
| 19 | APPALACHIAN NATL SCENIC TRAIL | WASHINGTON OFFICE | WV |
| 20 | APPOMATTOX COURT HOUSE NHP | MID-ATLANTIC REGION | VA |
| 21 | ARAHAM LINCOLN BIRTHPLACE NHS | Southeast Region | KY |
| 22 | ARCHES NATIONAL PARK | ROCKY MOUNTAIN REGION | UT |
| 23 | ARLINGTON HOUSE, THE ROBERT E. LEE MEM | National Capital Region | VA |
| 24 | ASSATEAGUE ISLAND NATIONAL SEASHORE | MID-ATLANTIC REGION | MD |
| 25 | BADLANDS NATIONAL PARK | Rocky Mountain Region | SD |
| 26 | BANDELIER NATIONAL MONUMENT | SOUTHWEST REGION | NM |
| 27 | BATTLEGROUND NATIONAL CEMETERY | NATIONAL CAPITAL REGION | MD |
| 28 | BENJAMIN FRANKLIN NATIONAL MEMORIAL | MID-ATLANTIC REGION | PA |
| 29 | BENT'S OLD FORT NATIONAL HISTORIC SITE | ROCKY MOUNTAIN REGION | CO |

Ungrouped List of US National Parks - query

**Figure 13.22** The contents of q_ParkList is displayed via <cfdump>.

**BUILDING DYNAMIC CHARTS WITH CFQUERY**

## To use the GROUP BY clause to group data:

1. To create a new recordset named q_ParksByState with the data source exampleapps, type this code at the top of your document:

```
<cfquery name="q_ParksByState"
datasource="exampleapps">
SELECT STATE, COUNT(*) AS
state_count
FROM tblParks
WHERE STATE IS NOT NULL
GROUP BY STATE
ORDER BY STATE;
</cfquery>
```

2. Replace your old <cfdump> tag with this code:

```
<cfdump var="#q_ParksByState#"
→ label="US Parks Per State">
```

Your code should look like the code in **Figure 13.23**.

3. Save your page and view it in a browser. You will see a list of States, accompanied by the number of parks in each state (**Figure 13.24**).

| US Parks Per State - query | | |
| --- | --- | --- |
| | STATE | STATE_COUNT |
| 1 | AK | 18 |
| 2 | AL | 3 |
| 3 | AR | 5 |
| 4 | AZ | 19 |
| 5 | CA | 21 |
| 6 | CM | 1 |
| 7 | CO | 14 |
| 8 | CT | 1 |
| 9 | DC | 16 |
| 10 | FL | 9 |
| 11 | GA | 12 |
| 12 | GU | 1 |
| 13 | HI | 8 |
| 14 | IA | 2 |
| 15 | ID | 3 |
| 16 | IL | 2 |
| 17 | IN | 3 |
| 18 | KS | 2 |
| 19 | KY | 5 |
| 20 | LA | 1 |
| 21 | MA | 16 |
| 22 | MD | 12 |
| 23 | ME | 3 |
| 24 | MI | 4 |
| 25 | MN | 4 |
| 26 | MO | 6 |
| 27 | MS | 5 |
| 28 | MT | 5 |
| 29 | NC | 6 |

**Figure 13.24** This chart shows the dumped results for q_ParksByState.

```
1  <cfquery name="q_ParksByState" datasource="exampleapps">
2  SELECT STATE, COUNT(*) AS state_count
3  FROM tblParks
4  WHERE STATE IS NOT NULL
5  GROUP BY STATE
6  ORDER BY STATE;
7  </cfquery>
8
9  <html>
10 <head>
11 <title>US National Parks by State</title>
12 <meta http-equiv="Content-Type" content="text/html; charset=iso-8859-1">
13 </head>
14
15 <body>
16 <cfdump var="#q_ParksByState#" label="US Parks Per State">
17 </body>
18 </html>
```

**Figure 13.23** The changed code outputs the results of a grouped query.

Let's examine the SQL line by line to see how you got this result.

```
SELECT STATE, COUNT(*) AS
state_count
```

The SQL function `count()` returns the number of rows in a column. In the line above, you have told the database to give a list of states and a second column with a count called `state_count`.

```
FROM tblParks
WHERE STATE IS NOT NULL
```

You already know about the `FROM` and `WHERE` clauses. You can filter out records that don't have any data using `NOT NULL`. This bit of SQL, in English, means "Don't retrieve records unless they have a value in the state column."

```
GROUP BY STATE
ORDER BY STATE;
```

This phrase tells the query to organize the data by the `STATE` field and then to place the data in alphabetical order based on the state.

While the table produced by `<cfdump>` is informative, it's hard to get a sense of how each region relates to the others. In other words, this table is a good candidate for `<cfchart>`.

## To create a chart using `<cfquery>`:

1. Open the page you created in the last section if it isn't already open. After the query q_ParksByState, type a new query as follows:

```
<cfquery name="q_MyState"
datasource="exampleapps">
SELECT STATE, COUNT(*) AS my_count
FROM tblParks
WHERE STATE = 'AK'
GROUP BY STATE;
</cfquery>
```

This query is almost identical to q_ParksByState. In this case, however, you've limited your results to the state of Alaska.

2. Replace your existing `<cfdump>` tag with the following code and preview the page in your browser.

```
<hr size="1" noshade>
<cfdump var="#q_MyState#"
label="Number of US Parks in
Alaska"><br />
```

This code simply dumps the contents of your new query.

*continues on next page*

BUILDING DYNAMIC CHARTS WITH CFQUERY

3. Just below the q_MyState query, type this code:

```
<cfquery name="q_OtherStates" data-
source="exampleapps">
SELECT COUNT(*) AS other_count
FROM tblParks
WHERE STATE <> 'AK'
</cfquery>
```

This query simply counts the number of parks that are in all states other than Alaska and returns the resulting number as the variable other_count. Your block of queries should look like **Figure 13.25**.

4. Underneath your <cfdump> tag, add another one:

```
<cfdump var="#q_OtherStates#"
→ label="Number of US Parks outside
→ Alaska">
```

The body of your page should look like **Figure 13.26**.

5. Save the page and preview it in a browser. You will see two tables, one showing the number of parks in Alaska, the other showing the number of parks in all states other than Alaska (**Figure 13.27**). You will use this data to build your dynamic chart.

```
1  <cfquery name="q_ParksByState" datasource="exampleapps">
2  SELECT STATE, COUNT(*) AS state_count
3  FROM tblParks
4  WHERE STATE IS NOT NULL
5  GROUP BY STATE
6  ORDER BY STATE;
7  </cfquery>
8
9  <cfquery name="q_MyState" datasource="exampleapps">
10 SELECT STATE, COUNT(*) AS my_count
11 FROM tblParks
12 WHERE STATE = 'AK'
13 GROUP BY STATE;
14 </cfquery>
15
16 <cfquery name="q_OtherStates" datasource="exampleapps">
17 SELECT COUNT(*) AS other_count
18 FROM tblParks
19 WHERE STATE <> 'AK'
20 </cfquery>
```

**Figure 13.25** Your page's query block should look like this.

```
28 <body>
29 <hr size="1" noshade>
30 <cfdump var="#q_MyState#" label="Number of US Parks in Alaska"><br />
31 <cfdump var="#q_OtherStates#" label="Number of US Parks outside Alaska">
32 </body>
```

**Figure 13.26** Your page's body should look like this.

| Number of US Parks in Alaska - query | |
|---|---|
| MY_COUNT | STATE |
| 1  18 | AK |

| Number of US Parks outside Alaska - query |
|---|
| OTHER_COUNT |
| 1  371 |

**Figure 13.27** These two tables show the number of parks inside and outside Alaska.

6. Above the <hr> tag, type this code:

```
<cfchart showborder="yes"
→   show3d="yes" chartwidth="600"
→   chartheight="400"
→   pieslicestyle="sliced">
</cfchart>
```

You've already seen most of this code in action with static charts. The `pieslicestyle` attribute sets the appearance of the pie chart you are going to create next.

7. Within the <cfchart> container tags, create a new chart series:

```
<cfchartseries type="pie"
→   query="q_MyState" itemcolumn="STATE"
→   valuecolumn="my_count">
</cfchartseries>
```

You've already seen the **type** attribute; this time, you've specified that you want to create a pie chart.

**Table 13.1** identifies the three new attributes you've used in this tag in order to create a dynamic chart:

That's a lot of information to take in all at once.

8. Preview your page in a browser (**Figure 13.28**).

You'll see a pie chart showing the number of parks in Alaska.

But what's wrong with that chart? You already know the number of parks in Alaska by looking at the <cfdump> table. Your chart simply repeats the information in that table. Let's add one more piece of data to it.

*continues on next page*

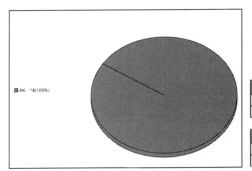

**Figure 13.28** This graph shows that the parks in Alaska make up 100 percent of the parks in Alaska. Hmm...

**Table 13.1**

| <cfchartseries> Attributes Used to Create a Dynamic Chart | | |
|---|---|---|
| **ATTRIBUTE** | **TELLS CHART** | **EXAMPLE FROM THIS CHART** |
| Query | Name of ColdFusion query from which to get data. | q_MyState |
| Itemcolumn | Name of a column in the query specified in the query attribute; contains the item label for a data point to graph. | STATE |
| Valuecolumn | Name of a column in the query specified in the query attribute; contains data values to graph. | query column my_count |

**9.** In between the opening and closing <cfchartseries> tags, add this code:

```
<cfchartdata item="Other States"
→ value="#q_OtherStates.other_count#">
```

Remember the recordset q_OtherStates that you created earlier? You've just told ColdFusion to add an item to your chart with the value of that query, and to label it Other States. Your <cfchart> tag, in its entirety, should look like the code in **Figure 13.29**.

**10.** Save your page and preview it in a browser (**Figure 13.30**).

Now that's a useful chart!

## ✔ Tips

■ You cannot combine a pie chart with any other type of chart.

■ As a rule of thumb, consider using a pie chart when you want to show the relative quantity of an item or group of items expressed as a number or percentage.

■ Don't use a pie chart when you need to show a quantity that changes over time.

```
29  <cfchart showborder="yes" show3d="yes" chartwidth="600" chartheight="400" pieslicestyle="sliced">
30      <cfchartseries type="pie" query="q_MyState" itemcolumn="STATE" valuecolumn="my_count">
31          <cfchartdata item="Other States" value="#q_OtherStates.other_count#">
32      </cfchartseries>
33  </cfchart>
```

**Figure 13.29** This code is a <cfchart> tag with dynamic chart series and chart data.

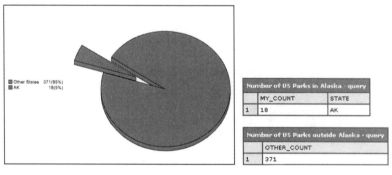

**Figure 13.30** This graph shows that the parks in Alaska make up 5 percent of all the parks in the United States.

# Building Dynamic Applications with Clickable Charts

In the preceding example, you learned how to show the proportion of national parks in Alaska to the number of parks in the rest of the United States. Assume that you run a Web site dedicated to parks and travel. Some of your visitors will care not a whit for grizzly bears and glaciers. In fact, it's simply not possible to guess the interests of each site user. With dynamic charts, you don't even have to try.

In previous chapters, you learned how to use a form to pass data to queries, whether you're building a simple search interface or updating a record. In this section, you use precisely the same skill to let your site's users specify a graph's query parameters.

You also can let your users explore your data by making your charts clickable. The `<cfchart>` tag includes the attribute URL, which allows you to specify the page your chart links to, as well as what dynamic data to pass along with the link.

## To create a dynamic chart using form data:

1. Create a new ColdFusion page, title it, and save it.

2. Build a simple form with a drop-down list populated by a recordset of the distinct national park regions.

   You can use the code listed in Figure **13.31** to create your page.

3. Save the page and then preview it in a browser.

   You will see a simple form with a drop-down list and Submit Query button (**Figure 13.32**).

```
1   <!--- get distinct list of regions --->
2   <cfquery datasource="exampleapps" name="q_DistinctRegions">
3   SELECT DISTINCT REGION
4   FROM tblParks
5   WHERE REGION IS NOT NULL
6   ORDER BY REGION
7   </cfquery>
8   <html>
9   <head>
10  <title>Select A Region</title>
11  <meta http-equiv="Content-Type" content="text/html; charset=iso-8859-1">
12  </head>
13  <body>
14  <h2>Select A Region</h2>
15  <p>Select a region from the dropdown list and click submit. The value you select
16    will be passed to the graph on the next page.</p>
17  <!--- create form to pass region to action page --->
18  <form name="form1" method="post" action="../ParksByRegion.cfm">
19    <select name="select">
20      <!--- loop through the list of regions --->
21      <cfloop query="q_DistinctRegions">
22        <cfoutput>
23          <!--- give each reach its own option --->
24          <option value="#REGION#">#REGION#</option>
25        </cfoutput>
26      </cfloop>
27    </select>
28    <input type="submit">
29  </form>
30  </body>
31  </html>
```

**Figure 13.31** This code queries a list of distinct regions and uses the recordset values in a simple form.

**Figure 13.32** This shows a select form control populated dynamically from a query.

4. Create a new page, title it, and save it. This page will be the action page for the form you created. Next you give the page a dynamic title.

5. In place of the standard &lt;title&gt; tags, type this code:

```
<cfoutput><title>US National Parks in
→ #form.select#</title></cfoutput>
```

6. At the top of the page, create a new recordset:

```
<cfquery name="q_ParksByRegion"
→ datasource="exampleapps">
SELECT STATE, COUNT(*) AS
→ state_count
FROM tblParks
WHERE REGION = '#form.select#'
→ AND STATE IS NOT NULL
GROUP BY STATE
ORDER BY STATE;
</cfquery>
```

This recordset is very similar to the other GROUP BY recordsets you've built in this chapter, with one exception: You want to gather data only in the region the user selected from the previous page. Let's give the page a dynamic header.

7. Immediately following the opening &lt;body&gt; tag, type this code:

```
<cfoutput><h2>US Parks in
→ #form.select#</h2></cfoutput>
```

8. Save the page, view your form page in a browser, and then select a Park region to test your pages.

You'll see the name of the region you selected appear in the title and header of the form's action page. All that remains is the build the chart.

*continues on next page*

BUILDING DYNAMIC APPLICATIONS

**9.** In the body of your action page, insert a pie chart that gets its data from the recordset q_ParksByRegion:

```
<cfchart showborder="yes"
→   show3d="yes" chartwidth="600"
→   chartheight="400"
→   pieslicestyle="sliced">
      <cfchartseries type="pie"
→   query="q_ParksByRegion"
→   itemcolumn="STATE"
→   valuecolumn="state_count">
      </cfchartseries>
</cfchart>
```

You don't need to learn any new tags for this chart; the query is doing all the heavy lifting. The <cfchartseries> tag simply shows a list of the states returned by q_ParksByRegion, and the number of parks within each state. Your code should look like **Figure 13.33**.

```
1  <!---- get the region's states and parks per state from the form data ----->
2  <cfquery name="q_ParksByRegion" datasource="exampleapps">
3  SELECT STATE, COUNT(*) AS state_count
4  FROM tblParks
5  WHERE REGION = '#form.select#' AND STATE IS NOT NULL
6  GROUP BY STATE
7  ORDER BY STATE;
8  </cfquery>
9  <html>
10 <head>
11 <!--- dynamic title --->
12 <cfoutput><title>US National Parks in #form.select#</title></cfoutput>
13 <meta http-equiv="Content-Type" content="text/html; charset=iso-8859-1">
14 </head>
15
16 <body>
17 <!--- dynamic head --->
18 <cfoutput><h2>US Parks in #form.select#</h2></cfoutput>
19 <!---- draw pie chart showing numbers of parks in my region relative to all the rest ----->
20 <!--- notice the url attribute that makes the chart clickable --->
21 <cfchart showborder="yes" show3d="yes" chartwidth="600" chartheight="400" pieslicestyle="sliced">
22     <!--- populate the series with a query --->
23     <cfchartseries type="pie" query="q_ParksByRegion" itemcolumn="STATE" valuecolumn="state_count">
24     </cfchartseries>
25 </cfchart>
26
27 <hr size="1" noshade>
28 <!--- display the data textually --->
29 <cfdump var="#q_ParksByRegion#" label="Number of US Parks in Selected Region"><br />
30 </body>
31 </html>
```

**Figure 13.33** Now you have all the code that's needed to build a dynamic chart.

**10.** Save the page, browse to the form page, select Pacific Northwest Region from the list of regions, and click Submit Query.

Presto! You have a dynamically generated chart of states within the region, along with the number of parks in each state (**Figure 13.34**).

## ✔ Tip

■ If you need a quick refresher on forms and working with form variables, see Chapter 7, "Inserting Data."

US Parks in PACIFIC NORTHWEST REGION

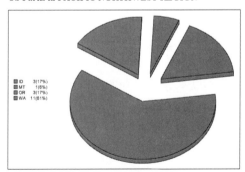

ID   3(17%)
MT  1(6%)
OR  3(17%)
WA  11(81%)

| | STATE | STATE_COUNT |
|---|---|---|
| 1 | ID | 3 |
| 2 | MT | 1 |
| 3 | OR | 3 |
| 4 | WA | 11 |

**Figure 13.34** This pie chart is built on the fly from form data.

## To make your charts clickable:

**1.** Open the form action page you created for the previous section.

You'll build upon the code you've already written.

**2.** Add the url attribute to the <cfchart> tag:

```
url="ParksByState.cfm?state=
→ $ITEMLABEL$"
```

In this case, the $ITEMLABEL$ will be the two digit abbreviation for the state that's clicked within the graph. This example shows a link to a page named ParksByState.cfm. You can use any URL you like; just ensure that the page you create in step 4 has the same name as the page in the URL.

**3.** Save your page.

**4.** Create a new page and save it with the name of the URL in step 3.

Don't give it a title yet since you're going to make the title dynamic.

**5.** Using the query builder or coding by hand, create this query at the top of the page:

```
<cfquery name="q_GetParks"
→ datasource="exampleapps">
SELECT PARKNAME, CITY, STATE
FROM tblParks
WHERE STATE = '#url.state#'
ORDER BY PARKNAME;
</cfquery>
```

This query looks for the variable state passed in the URL scope from the chart on the previous page. Because you specified the state as the $ITEMLABEL$ value in your graph, the query will show only those parks in the state you've selected. Now the only step that remains is to display the data on the page.

*continues on next page*

**Building Dynamic Applications**

**6.** Add this code to the `title` properties:

```
<cfoutput>Parks in
#url.state#</cfoutput>
```

Just like the query, our page's title will be dynamically set by the state you've selected.

**7.** If you like, you also can put a dynamic header just below the opening **<body>** tag:

```
<cfoutput><h2>Parks in
→ #url.state#</h2></cfoutput>
```

**8.** Place a `<cfdump>` tag in the page's body to show the query results:

```
<cfdump var="#q_getParks#" label="List
→ of Parks in Selected State">
```

Your page should look like **Figure 13.35**.

**9.** Save the page, browse to your form page, and test the complete application:

First, select Rocky Mountain Region from the drop-down list, and then click Submit Query (**Figure 13.36**).

```
1   <!--- get information for parks in desired state passed from graph --->
2   <cfquery name="q_GetParks" datasource="exampleapps">
3   SELECT PARKNAME, CITY, STATE
4   FROM tblParks
5   WHERE STATE = '#url.state#'
6   ORDER BY PARKNAME;
7   </cfquery>
8   <html>
9   <head>
10  <!--- dynamic page title --->
11  <cfoutput><title>Parks in #url.state#</title></cfoutput>
12  <meta http-equiv="Content-Type" content="text/html; charset=iso-8859-1">
13  </head>
14
15  <body>
16  <!--- dynamic header --->
17  <cfoutput><h2>Parks in #url.state#</h2></cfoutput>
18  <!--- output the results --->
19  <cfdump var="#q_getParks#" label="List of Parks in Selected State">
20  </body>
21  </html>
```

**Figure 13.35** Your page shows a query filtered from data passed by the URL.

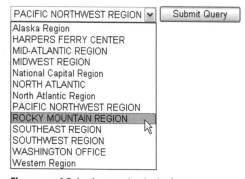

**Figure 13.36** Selecting a region in the form...

Next, when the Rocky Mountain Region graph appears, click the slice representing South Dakota, abbreviated as SD (**Figure 13.37**).

You'll see a table listing all the parks in the state of South Dakota (**Figure 13.38**).

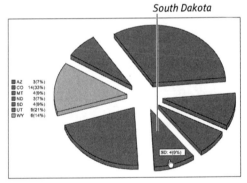

**Figure 13.37** ...reveals the states in the region. Clicking a state...

| | CITY | PARKNAME | STATE |
|---|---|---|---|
| 1 | INTERIOR | BADLANDS NATIONAL PARK | SD |
| 2 | CUSTER | JEWEL CAVE NATIONAL MONUMENT | SD |
| 3 | KEYSTONE | MOUNT RUSHMORE NATIONAL MEMORIAL | SD |
| 4 | HOT SPRINGS | WIND CAVE NATIONAL PARK | SD |

List of Parks in Selected State - query

**Figure 13.38** ...reveals the parks in the state.

## ✔ Tips

- The three variables used by the url attribute of the <cfchart> tag are the only standard ColdFusion variables that use the $ sign.

- In addition to the $ITEMLABEL$ variable, the URL attribute supports $VALUE$, to pass the value of the selected item, and $SERIESLABEL$, to pass the label of the selected series. To consider how you might use the $SERIESLABEL$ value, return for a moment to the demographic chart in the first half of this chapter. In order to make the chart clickable, you would want to pass the $SERIESLABEL$ along with the $ITEMLABEL$ so the application would know whether your user wanted to drill down to data about the United States (one series) or Western Europe (the other series) (**Figure 13.39**). Use this format to pass more than one variable with the URL attribute:

  ```
  url="drilldownpage.cfm?Series=$SERIES
  → LABEL$&Item=$ITEMLABEL$&Value=$VALUE$"
  ```

- Don't be afraid to experiment with your graphs as you develop other ColdFusion skills. For example, ColdFusion includes a tag called <cfschedule> that allows you to run your ColdFusion pages at regular intervals. You easily can build an application that stores a value in your database each day (for example, the price of a stock) and graphs the value on demand.

Address | http://localhost/showData.cfm?year=2015&region=United+States | Go

Address | http://localhost/showData.cfm?year=2015&region=Western+Europe | Go

**Figure 13.39** These links show the same year but different regions. Examine the URLs closely.

# APPLICATIONS AND SESSION MANAGEMENT

As you learned in Chapter 10, standard HTML pages are stateless. In other words, they do not track a user's movement from page to page. Compare this statelessness with the way many applications work: Each time you create a new document in Microsoft Word, for example, the program remembers your name. Word, when behaving properly, remembers your preferences as well, so you don't have to open each new document tabula rasa (as a clean slate).

ColdFusion MX provides a Web application framework to help you address the Web's inherent statelessness. In this chapter, you learn to think about your ColdFusion templates as an integrated application instead of a collection of various Web pages.

First, you learn how to initialize your ColdFusion applications with the Application.cfm file. Next, you learn how to use the <cfinclude> tag to assemble pages out of separate pieces of code. You also learn about *structures*, a powerful datatype. Finally, you learn to create and manage user sessions. Along the way, you learn about two new variable scopes: the application scope and the session scope.

# Initializing ColdFusion Applications

Many development languages support an *initialization routine*. In other words, when an application loads for the first time, a block of code sets global variables for use throughout the application. This code runs only when the application first loads, not when a user accesses each page. ColdFusion does not have an initialization feature per se, but by setting an application variable once and then checking for its existence thereafter, you can avoid setting the same global variables again and again.

## To test for the existence of an application variable:

1. Create a new ColdFusion page and save it as `Application.cfm`.

2. Name your application with the `<cfapplication>` tag and the `name` attribute:

   `<cfapplication name="myApp">`

3. Type this code to test for the existence of a variable:

   ```
   <cfif NOT isDefined("Application.Init")>
   </cfif>
   ```

   ColdFusion executes only the code within the opening and closing `<cfif>` tags if the variable `Application.Init` is not defined. Of course, we still need to define the variable.

4. In between the opening and closing conditional tags, set the application variable with this code:

   ```
   <cfset Application.Init = true>
   ```

   Your entire code block should look like the code listed in **Figure 14.1**. Now, instead of creating the `Application.Init` variable each time a page in your application loads, ColdFusion first checks for the existence of the variable and create it only if it hasn't already been defined.

```
1  <cfapplication name="myApp">
2  <cfif NOT isDefined("Application.Init")>
3      <cfset Application.Init = true>
4  </cfif>
```

**Figure 14.1** Check for the existence of application variables before setting them.

## Variable Locking

ColdFusion is a *multi-threaded* application; that is, the server can run several processes at the same time. While multi-threading is a great feature, it means you must be concerned about race conditions. A *race condition* can occur any time one user attempts to set a shared value while a second user attempts to access that value. ColdFusion provides the `<cflock>` tag for use any time a race condition could occur. A full discussion of the use of `<cflock>` is beyond the scope of this book, but if you plan to build applications that have any appreciable site traffic, you should read the section "Locking Code with `CFLOCK`" in the ColdFusion documentation. If you prefer not to work with `<cflock>` and run a site with low traffic, you can set the value of `Limit Simultaneous Requests` in the ColdFusion Administrator to 1.

## ✔ Tip

- There's nothing special about the variable name `Init` in the previous example. `Init` is simply short for "initialization," but you can name your variable anything that makes sense to you.

INITIALIZING COLDFUSION APPLICATIONS

```
1  <hr noshade size="1">
2  <p>&copy; 2003 Macromedia Press</p>
```

**Figure 14.2** Included footers should not have <html> and <body> tags.

# Including Pages with <cfinclude>

The <cfinclude> tag lets you include one ColdFusion page within another ColdFusion page. The tag takes only one attribute: template. The template attribute specifies the location of the ColdFusion page that you wish to include.

This tag is ideal for creating headers or footers: instead of typing the code for a footer in each of your site's pages, you can create a single footer and include it via <cfinclude>.

### To include a footer with <cfinclude>:

1. Create a new ColdFusion page, title it, and save it in your site folder.

   We saved the page as footer.cfm in our example.

2. Delete all the HTML code from the page so that it is blank.

   Because ColdFusion will include this page in another ColdFusion page, we don't want to end up with two sets of <html> and <body> tags.

3. Add a horizontal rule and a copyright notice to your footer with this code:

   ```
   <hr noshade size="1">
   <p>&copy; 2003 Macromedia Press</p>
   ```

   Note that this should be the only code on your page (**Figure 14.2**).

4. Save and preview the page.

   ColdFusion outputs a horizontal rule and a copyright notice.

5. Create a new ColdFusion page, title it, and save it.

6. Insert some text into the body of the new page.

   In our example, we inserted nonsense Latin text.

*continues on next page*

**7.** Immediately before the closing <body> tag of the new page, choose Insert > ColdFusion Basic Objects > Cfinclude to include your footer.

The Cfinclude Tag Editor opens (**Figure 14.3**).

**8.** Click the Browse button, choose footer.cfm in your site folder, and click OK. Click OK again to close the dialog.

ColdFusion inserts this code on your page:

```
<cfinclude template="footer.cfm">
```

**9.** Preview your page in a browser.

ColdFusion outputs the content of your main page and then includes the content of footer.cfm.

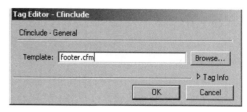

**Figure 14.3** The Cfinclude tag editor accepts only one attribute.

## ✔ Tip

■ You don't have to limit your use of <cfinclude> to building footers. Any code that appears on multiple pages is a good candidate for <cfinclude>.

### Templates, Library Items and <cfinclude>

You already may be familiar with Dreamweaver templates, which let you create pages with locked and editable regions, and library items, which store reusable page elements. Dreamweaver templates and pages built with <cfinclude> both have their strengths, but you should not confuse the two. Dreamweaver uses special comment code to recognize pages with templates or library items. When you change a Dreamweaver template, Dreamweaver updates every page based on that template. You must upload each changed page to the server. Conversely, changing an included ColdFusion page requires only that you upload the included page, and the server handles all changes to the output when Dreamweaver loads the page. To read more about Dreamweaver templates and library items, see the Dreamweaver MX documentation.

# Working with Structures

Structures allow you to store data within data. Think of a structure as a container for multiple pieces of data. Each new piece of data, called a *key*, should uniquely refer to a part of the structure.

You may not realize it, but you've already worked with ColdFusion structures extensively. Structures are so powerful that many ColdFusion features are built as structures. For example, <cfquery> returns its results as a structure. Think of the query name, for example q_Employees, as the structure, and the query's fields as the structure's keys.

## Building structures

Use the StructNew() function to create a new structure. After creating the structure, you can assign values to keys within the structure.

### To create a structure:

1. Create a new ColdFusion page, title it, and save it in your site's root folder.

2. Create a new structure above the opening <html> tag with this code:

   ```
   <cfset Employee=StructNew()>
   ```

   ColdFusion creates a new structure called Employee.

3. Create a new key in the structure called EmployeeID with this code:

   ```
   <cfset Employee.EmployeeID = "74DDD86E
   → -B0D0-14F2-D8EE1F2C8F353B45">
   ```

   That employee ID isn't user-friendly, so if you don't want to type it by hand simply cut and paste it from the cfexamples database. ColdFusion creates a new key called EmployeeID in the Employee structure.

4. Create FirstName, LastName, and Title keys within the structure with this code:

   ```
   <cfset Employee.FirstName = "Raymond">
   <cfset Employee.LastName = "Camden">
   <cfset Employee.Title = "Engineer">
   ```

   ColdFusion adds the three new keys to the structure and assigns values to them. Your code above the <html> tag should look like the code listed in **Figure 14.4**. Let's see how ColdFusion handles the data.

5. Dump the contents of the structure in the page body with this code:

   ```
   <cfdump var="#Employee#">
   ```

6. Preview the page in your browser.

   ColdFusion outputs the contents of the Employee structure (**Figure 14.5**). Does this output look familiar? If you had written an employee recordset with only one record, the output would look nearly the same.

7. Leave this page open in Dreamweaver to follow the steps in the next list.

```
1  <cfset Employee=StructNew()>
2  <cfset Employee.EmployeeID = "74DDD86E-B0D0-14F2-D8EE1F2C8F353B45">
3  <cfset Employee.FirstName = "Raymond">
4  <cfset Employee.LastName = "Camden">
5  <cfset Employee.Title = "Engineer">
```

**Figure 14.4** You can create a structure with StructNew(), then populate its keys.

| struct | |
|---|---|
| EMPLOYEEID | 74DDD86E-B0D0-14F2-D8EE1F2C8F353B45 |
| FIRSTNAME | Raymond |
| LASTNAME | Camden |
| TITLE | Engineer |

**Figure 14.5** Like any other variable, you can dump the contents of a structure.

# Accessing and updating structures

You can access and change the value of your keys within a structure, much as you would any normal variable. You even can delete a key from your structure with the StructDelete() function.

## To access a key within a structure:

1. Working with the same page you created in the previous section, type this code below the `<cfdump>` tag:

   ```
   <p>Employee First Name:<br />
   <cfoutput>#Employee.FirstName#</cfoutput>
   </p>
   ```

   ColdFusion outputs the contents of the key FirstName within the structure Employee. Again, this works just as if you wanted to output a field from a recordset.

2. Preview the page in a browser.

   ColdFusion outputs the name Raymond. Note that this value isn't static: You can change it, just like you would any other variable.

## To change a key's value within a structure:

1. Underneath the FirstName output from the previous steps, type this code:

   ```
   <cfset Employee.FirstName =
   → "ColdFusion Jedi Master">
   ```

   ColdFusion changes the value of FirstName.

2. Output the new first name with this code:

   ```
   <p>Employee New First Name:<br />
   <cfoutput>#Employee.FirstName#
   → </cfoutput></p>
   ```

   As with the previous set of steps, ColdFusion outputs the contents of the key FirstName.

3. Preview the page in your browser.

   ColdFusion outputs the original value of Raymond and the new value of ColdFusion Jedi Master.

## To delete a key from a structure:

1. Add this line of code to the page you worked on in the previous steps:

   ```
   <cfset StructDelete(Employee,
   → "FirstName")>
   ```

   ColdFusion deletes the key FirstName from the structure Employee.

2. Try to output the value of the key with this code:

   ```
   <p>Deleted First Name:<br />
   <cfoutput>#Employee.FirstName#
   → </cfouput></p>
   ```

3. Preview your page in a browser.

   ColdFusion generates an error, of course; you cannot output the value of the key FirstName because it no longer exists in the structure Employee. Let's clean the page up.

**4.** Insert this code to change the output block:

```
<p>Deleted First Name:<br />
<cfif isDefined('Employee.FirstName')>
<cfoutput>#Employee.FirstName#</cfoutput>
<cfelse>The First Name does not exist.
</cfif>
</p>
```

The entire code listing for the page appears in **Figure 14.6**.ColdFusion first checks whether Employee.FirstName is defined. If so, ColdFusion outputs the value of the key FirstName. If not, ColdFusion tells the user that the first name does not exist, and ColdFusion does not generate an error.

Why do structures belong in the middle of a chapter covering application and session variables? As you see in the next session, you can actually store your sessions as structures to achieve some very useful effects.

## ✔ Tip

- Structures are, by far, the most useful and powerful ColdFusion data type. We've just scratched the surface of structures. If you'd like to learn more, see the section "About Structures" in the ColdFusion MX documentation.

```
1  <cfset Employee=StructNew()>
2  <cfset Employee.EmployeeID = "74DDD86E-B0D0-14F2-D8EE1F2C8F353B45">
3  <cfset Employee.FirstName = "Raymond">
4  <cfset Employee.LastName = "Camden">
5  <cfset Employee.Title = "Engineer">
6  <html>
7  <head>
8  <title>Example of a Structure</title>
9  <meta http-equiv="Content-Type" content="text/html; charset=iso-8859-1">
10 </head>
11
12 <body>
13 <cfdump var="#Employee#">
14 <p>Employee First Name:<br />
15 <cfoutput>#Employee.FirstName#</cfoutput></p>
16
17 <cfset Employee.FirstName = "ColdFusion Jedi Master">
18 <p>Employee New First Name:<br />
19 <cfoutput>#Employee.FirstName#</cfoutput></p>
20
21 <cfset StructDelete(Employee, "FirstName")>
22 <p>Deleted First Name:<br />
23 <cfif isDefined('Employee.FirstName')>
24 <cfoutput>#Employee.FirstName#</cfoutput>
25    <cfelse>The First Name does not exist.
26 </cfif>
27 </p>
28 </body>
29 </html>
```

**Figure 14.6** You easily can set, change, and delete structure keys.

# Working with Sessions

The session variables are stored in the ColdFusion server's RAM and are unique to each user. Let's return for a moment to the scopes we discussed in Chapter 11. Variables in the `form`, `url`, and `variables` scope disappear almost as quickly as they are created. For instance, values in the `variables` scope are available only to the page on which they are created; values in the `form` scope are available only to the action page of a form.

The session variables, by contrast, persist roughly for the length of time a specific user is on your Web site. In other words, a user could create a variable in the session scope and have access to that variable on each of the pages in your site, until she closes her browser or the session expires.

## Managing sessions

You create a session variable as you would any other variable in ColdFusion: use `<cfset>` to create a new variable in the `session` scope, and assign a value to it. For example, this code block creates a new session variable called `myName` and assigns it the value `Marc`:

```
<cfset session.myName = "Marc">
```

You must enable session management with the `<cfapplication>` tag before ColdFusion will recognize session variables. The Dreamweaver User Authentication server behaviors, which you worked with earlier in this book, support session variables. In this section, we briefly return to the User Authentication server behaviors and examine the code they generate.

## To enable session management:

1. Create a new ColdFusion page and save it as `Application.cfm`.

2. Name your application, and include the `sessionmanagement` attribute with this code:

   ```
   <cfapplication name="myApp"
   → sessionmanagement="yes">
   ```

   ColdFusion enables session management when any page loads the `Application.cfm` file. It's that simple.

## ✔ Tip

■ If you received unexpected error messages when running code from this section, make sure you have enabled session variables in your application.

## To create a session variable:

1. Create a new ColdFusion page, title it, and save it.

   If you would prefer to simply follow along with the steps in this section, download the archive file that accompanies this chapter and extract the file `login.cfm`.

2. By hand, or with the Recordset server behavior, create this query:

   ```
   <cfquery name="q_Employees"
   → datasource="exampleapps">
   SELECT EmployeeID, FirstName,
   → LastName, Title FROM tblEmployees
   </cfquery>
   ```

   ColdFusion retrieves a list of employees.

3. Use code like this to add a form containing no assigned actions, two text inputs and a Submit button to the body of your page:

```
<form action="" method="POST"
→ name="form1">
<p>First Name:<br />
<input type="text" name="txtUsername">
</p>
<p>Password:<br />
<input type="password"
→ name="txtPassword">
</p>
<input type="submit" name="btnSubmit"
→ value="Submit">
</form>
```

4. Click the plus sign (+) in the Server Behaviors panel, and choose User Authentication > Log In User. Use the table tblEmployees from the exampleapps data source for your values. In this case, use the first name for the user name and the last name for the password. Restrict

Access based on the Title field of tblEmployees.

Your Log In User dialog should look like **Figure 14.7**.

5. Click OK.

Dreamweaver generates code to check the username and password of your user. Let's examine the code closely.

6. In the Dreamweaver Code view or Code and Design view, look for this line of code:

```
<cfset session.MM_UserAuthorization =
→ MM_rsUser.Title[1]>
```

With this code, ColdFusion creates the session variable MM_UserAuthorization and sets its value from the first title record returned in the query MM_rsUser. This session variable is available on subsequent pages of your site, and in the next section we use it to dynamically include information based on the employee's title.

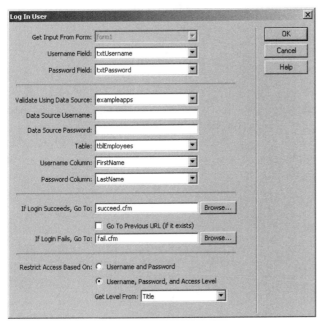

**Figure 14.7** This Log In User dialog gets its values from form1.

# Enhancing your applications with session management

Now that you understand the basics of creating and working with session variables, let's look at ways to apply them in your applications.

One common problem Web developers face is how to show the right content to the right person. Consider the distinction between *authentication* and *authorization*: when a server authenticates a user, the server has merely compared her username and password with values contained in a database, and then permits her access to certain pages in a site if those values match. Even though the server authenticates a user, the server still may need to authorize her to view certain privileged information on a site. For example, an intern and a CEO might encounter the same authentication routine, but surely the server authorizes the CEO to view more information about a company than the intern. Dreamweaver and ColdFusion make it easy to authorize users with session variables. As you saw in Chapter 10, you can restrict access to an entire page if a user isn't authorized to view that page. In this, section, you learn how to include sections of a page only if a user is authorized to view the information.

Other challenges developers often encounter are how to allow users to enter detailed form data without either confusing the user or losing the data. How many times have you visited a site, only to be put off by a lengthy sign-up form? One way to address this problem is to break your forms into multiple pages and to pass the values from page to page with session variables.

We next show you how to address these issues. Reminder: You must have `sessionmanagement` enabled in your `<cfapplication>` tag to run the examples in this section.

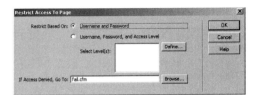

**Figure 14.8** This dialog restricts access based on Username and Password.

## To include code based on a session variable:

1. Create a new page, title it, and save it.

   In our example, we saved the page as `succeed.cfm`. You should name the page with whichever value you assigned to the If Login Succeeds, Go To field on your login page from the previous section.

2. From the Server Behaviors panel, choose User Authentication > Restrict Access To Page to add a server behavior to restrict access to the page unless the user is logged in. Restrict Access based on username and password, and don't forget to assign a failure page (**Figure 14.8**). Click OK. Dreamweaver inserts code to redirect the user to a failure page if she has not logged in.

3. In the body of the page, type this code to welcome the user by first name:

   ```
   <h2>Welcome
   → <cfoutput>#Session.MM_Username#
   → </cfoutput>!</h2>
   ```

   ColdFusion looks for a variable named `MM_Username` in the `session` scope and outputs its value. The Log In User server behavior created this variable on the login page.

4. In the body of the page, type this code:

   ```
   <cfif Session.MM_UserAuthorization IS
   → "Engineer">
   </cfif>
   ```

   ColdFusion compares the value of the variable `MM_UserAuthorization` in the `session` scope to the string `Engineer`. If the values match, ColdFusion executes any code within the opening and closing `<cfif>` tags.

   *continues on next page*

**5.** Within the conditional block, type this code:

`<cfinclude template="engineers.cfm">`

ColdFusion includes the document `engineers.cfm` if the user's `Title` is `Engineer`. The body of your page should look like the code listed in **Figure 14.9**.

**6.** Create a new ColdFusion page, title it, and save it with the value you used in the `template` attribute from the previous step.

In our example, we saved the page as `engineers.cfm`.

**7.** Delete all HTML code from the page, and type this code:

`<p>This page includes special information`
`→ for engineers.</p>`

**8.** Save all your pages.

Let's test the application.

**9.** Preview your login page in a browser. Provide the values `Raymond` and `Camden` for the username and password and submit the login form.

ColdFusion generates a page that welcomes Raymond by name and includes special information for engineers (**Figure 14.10**). Note our assumption that you still have a record in your table `tblEmployees` with the values `Raymond`, `Camden`, and `Engineer` in the fields `FirstName`, `LastName`, and `Title`. If you have changed the values in your database, your results will vary.

## ✔ Tips

■ For simple pages, it's just as easy to use `<cfoutput>` in a conditional block instead of `<cfinclude>`.

■ There's no reason to limit yourself to basic include pages. With `<cfinclude>` and switch-case logic, you easily could include dynamic tables based on a user's session variable. For example, a company intranet portal could dynamically include information specific to each employee's job title.

```
41  <body>
42  <h2>Welcome <cfoutput>#Session.MM_Username#</cfoutput>!</h2>
43  <p>You successfully logged in.</p>
44  <cfif Session.MM_UserAuthorization IS "Engineer">
45      <cfinclude template="engineers.cfm">
46  </cfif>
47  </body>
```

**Figure 14.9** This body dynamically includes a page based on the user's title.

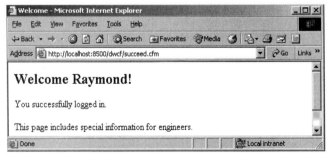

**Figure 14.10** Your users can't tell, but this page was assembled dynamically.

```
1  <cfif NOT isDefined("session.Employee")>
2      <cfset session.Employee = StructNew()>
3      <cfset session.Employee.FirstName = "">
4      <cfset session.Employee.LastName = "">
5      <cfset session.Employee.Title = "">
6      <cfset session.Employee.Email = "">
7  </cfif>
```

**Figure 14.11** Structures can be stored in the session scope.

## To create a multi-page form:

1. Create a new ColdFusion page, title it, and save it. Ensure that you are in the Dreamweaver Code or Code and Design view.

2. On the first line of the document, test for the existence of the structure Employee in the session scope with this code:

   ```
   <cfif NOT isDefined("session.Employee")>
   </cfif>
   ```

   ColdFusion checks for the existence of session.Employee and runs any code in between the opening and closing <cfif> tags if the expression evaluates as True.

3. In between the opening and closing <cfif> tags, type this code to create a new structure and four empty keys in the session scope, one each for FirstName, LastName, Title, and Email:

   ```
   <cfset session.Employee = StructNew()>
   <cfset session.Employee.FirstName = "">
   <cfset session.Employee.LastName = "">
   <cfset session.Employee.Title = "">
   <cfset session.Employee.Email = "">
   ```

   ColdFusion creates the new structure Employee in the session scope, and adds four empty keys to the structure. The code above your <html> tag should look like figure **14.11**.

*continues on next page*

**WORKING WITH SESSIONS**

4. In the body of the page, use code like this to insert a form with two text inputs (one for the first name and one for the last name):

```
<form action="multiForm2.cfm"
→ method="post" name="form1">
<p>
First Name:<br />
<input name="txtFirstName" type="text">
</p>
<p>Last Name:<br />
<input name="txtLastName" type="text">
</p>
<input type="submit" value="Continue"
→ name="btnSubmit">
</form>
```

Because we plan to build a multi-page form, it's better to assign a value of Continue instead of Submit to the button.

5. Save the first form page.

6. Create a new ColdFusion page, title it, and save it with the name you provided the form action of your first page.

For our example, we named the new page form2.cfm.

7. On the first line of the document, type this code:

```
<cfif isDefined("form.txtFirstName")>
<cfset session.Employee.FirstName =
→ form.txtFirstName>
<cfset session.Employee.LastName =
→ form.txtLastName>
</cfif>
```

ColdFusion checks whether txtFirstName is defined in the form scope, and if so, sets the FirstName and LastName keys to the values passed by the form.

| struct | |
|---|---|
| EMAIL | [empty string] |
| FIRSTNAME | Marc |
| LASTNAME | Garrett |
| TITLE | [empty string] |

**Figure 14.12** This structure has two empty keys.

8. In the body of the page, dump the contents of the session variable with this code:

```
<cfdump var="#session.Employee#">
```

9. Save the page and preview it in a browser. ColdFusion outputs the values for all keys in the structure (**Figure 14.12**). Email and Title still are empty, though.

10. Type code like this to insert a new form in the body of the page with two text inputs (one for Email and one for Title):

```
<form action="multiForm3.cfm"
→ method="post" name="form1">
<p>
Email:<br />
<input name="txtEmail" type="text">
</p>
<p>Title:<br />
<input name="txtTitle" type="text">
</p>
<input type="submit" value="Submit"
→ name="btnSubmit">
</form>
```

11. Save the page.

12. Create a new page, title it, and save it. We named our page multiForm3.cfm to correspond with the action attribute on the second form page.

*continues on next page*

WORKING WITH SESSIONS

**13.** On the first line of the new page, type this code:

```
<cfif isDefined("form.txtEmail")>
<cfset session.Employee.Email =
↪ form.txtEmail>
<cfset session.Employee.Title =
↪ form.txtTitle>
</cfif>
```

Much like the second form page, Cold-Fusion checks whether `txtEmail` is defined in the `form` scope, and if so, sets the `Email` and `Title` keys to the values passed by the form.

**14.** Type this code to dump the contents of the session variable in the body of the page:

```
<cfdump var="#session.Employee#">
```

**15.** Save your page, and test the first form page.

Each form page adds values to the keys in the structure, and ColdFusion populates all four keys after both forms have been filled out (**Figure 14.13**).

## ✔ Tip

■ For convenience, we've only dumped the results to the page. You easily could use the values in the `session` structure to insert a new record in the database.

| struct | |
|---|---|
| EMAIL | letters@since1968.com |
| FIRSTNAME | Marc |
| LASTNAME | Garrett |
| TITLE | Grand Poo-bah |

**Figure 14.13**
This structure has no empty keys.

# CUSTOMIZING MASTER/ DETAIL INTERFACES

# 15

In Chapter 3, "Customizing Data Display," you learned how to use Dreamweaver MX to help you generate a master/detail interface using the Master/Detail Page Set application object. This application object does have a few drawbacks:

◆ It requires a recordset on the master page that returns both the master and the detail data—thus returning more data than is necessary.

◆ It does not allow you to create a hyperlink on an image instead of text.

◆ It allows only limited formatting of both the master and detail page data.

◆ It allows for only one identifier (Unique Key) to be used when determining the row queried on the detail page. The Master/Detail Page Set application object does not allow for a database table that has a composite primary key.

◆ If your recordset returns data from more than one table, the Master/Detail Page Set does not currently generate the correct detail recordset.

In this chapter, you dig deeper into the CFML tags that it takes to create a Master/Detail interface to enable you to create a customized interface through a combination of code generation and hand coding.

# Creating the Master Page

To create the Master Page by hand, you must perform the following tasks:

1. Create a recordset that returns only the data you wish to display, plus the unique identifier for this information when the user drills in to find the detail.

2. Display the master recordset and format the data to your liking.

3. Create a hyperlink on a piece of information (or image) that you would like the user to click to get more details and pass a unique identifier on the URL to the detail page.

CREATING THE MASTER PAGE

## exampleapps Images

In order to use the images that are references in the tblItems table in the exampleapps database, copy the images from the following folder into your dwcf site that you created for this book:

```
C:\CFusionMX\wwwroot\cfdocs\
→ exampleapps\old\store\
→ images\products
```

This path assumes the default installation location, so alter the drive or path information if you installed ColdFusion MX elsewhere.

Also, you can download the exampleapps database and the images from the companion Website, as described in the Introduction.

Under the dwcf site, it is recommended to store the images in the \images\ products folder.

## To query and display the master recordset:

1. Create a new ColdFusion page.

2. Title the page and save it.

   Here, we are saving the page as Item_Master.cfm.

3. Create a recordset of the information you'd like to display on the master page. Do not forget to return the unique identifier for each row of data. If the primary key has multiple columns, return each column.

   In this example, we are returning items for sale in the tblItems table. Note the inclusion of the ItemID column to identify the item, even though we do not intend to display this information (**Figure 15.1**).

*continues on next page*

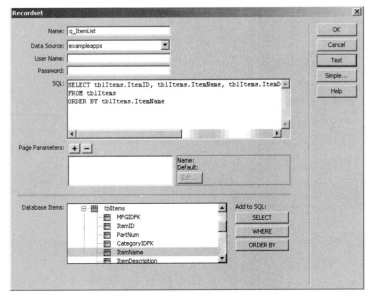

**Figure 15.1** Create a master recordset to return only what will be displayed, plus the identifying column(s).

CREATING THE MASTER PAGE

4. Display the results of the recordset on the page to your liking.

Here, for simplicity's sake, we are using the Dynamic Table application object to display the items in a table (**Figure 15.2**). We have removed the display of the `ItemID` column.

5. Save the page.

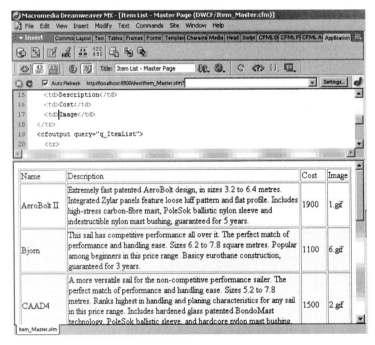

**Figure 15.2** Master page data looks like the data in this figure when viewed in Live Data view.

# Creating the Detail Link

Now that you have a page with the master recordset displayed, you can create a hyperlink on some information so that users can drill down and get more details about the chosen row.

To determine the chosen row in the detail page, you need to pass a unique identifier for the row on the URL in the query string.

You were first introduced to the query string in Chapter 3, "Customizing Data Display." *Query string* is the term for the portion of the URL where data is passed from the link to the linked page. A query string:

◆ Begins with a question mark (?).

◆ Contains name=value pairs of data, without spaces or special characters.

◆ Uses an ampersand (&) to separate more than one name=value pairs.

The following example passes a variable called name to the linkpage.cfm file and passes a value of Sue:

`<a href="linkpage.cfm?name=sue">`

## To link to the detail page:

1. Return to the master page and identify the data you wish to make a hyperlink.

   In our example, we will create a hyperlink on the ItemName column for the user to click and get more details about that item. Highlight the ItemName column in Code view or Design view.

2. In the Link textbox of the Property Inspector, type in the name of the detail page (yet to be created).

   Here we will name our detail page Item_Detail.cfm.

3. In Code view and at the end of the href attribute, type the question mark and an arbitrary variable name, and then drag in the ItemID column from the q_ItemList recordset in the Bindings panel to append the query string to pass the ItemID on the URL (**Figure 15.3**).

   The resulting <a> tag should be

   `<a href="Item_Detail.cfm?iid=`
   `→ #q_ItemList.ItemID#">`

4. Save the page and preview it in a browser.

   If you click a hyperlink, you will receive an error, since the detail page has not yet been created. However, you should see the iid variable passed on the URL.

CREATING THE DETAIL LINK

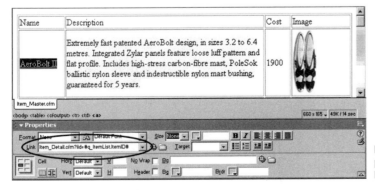

**Figure 15.3** Specify the detail page link in the Property Inspector.

255

# Creating Dynamic Image Tags

Images stored within database columns are not supported in ColdFusion MX. As a workaround, most developers store the filename of the image in a database column. This filename can then be used within an <img> tag to dynamically display the image when the page is requested.

In our examples, the ItemImage column contains the name of a GIF file that represents the item.

In order to display the actual image instead of the image name, you can use the ItemImage recordset variable within an <img> tag.

It is a best practice not to store the full path to the image in the database because later you may wish to move the images to another directory. If the images are not in the same directory as the page that displays them, you must specify the path to the image as well as the filename of the image in the <img> tag.

## To display an image using a variable:

1. Highlight the ItemImage variable either within Code view, Design view or Live Data view.

2. On the Common toolbar of the Insert bar, choose the Image icon (**Figure 15.4**). The Select Image Source dialog displays.

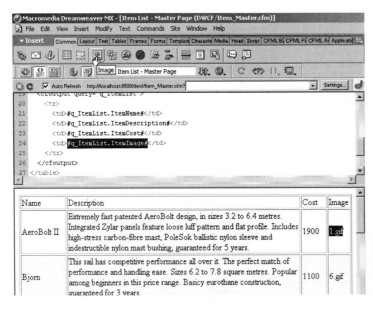

**Figure 15.4** Highlight the variable that represents the image file name and choose Image from the Common toolbar.

**3.** Change the Select File Name From dialog to Data Sources (**Figure 15.5**).

**4.** Select the column from the desired recordset to be used as the image filename.

Here, we are selecting the ItemImage column from the q_ItemList recordset.

**5.** In the URL textbox, prefix the existing variable name with the relative path to the image.

Here we are assuming the item images are stored in the \images\products subdirectory under the dwcf site root folder. The resulting URL should be as follows:

./images/products/#q_ItemList.ItemImage#

*continues on next page*

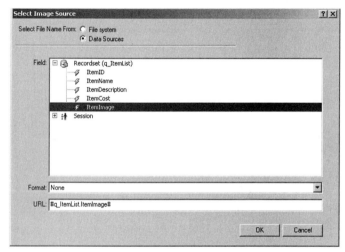

**Figure 15.5** The Select Image Source dialog enables you to choose a file from a data source.

**6.** Click OK.

**7.** Remove the display of the ItemImage column.

**8.** Save the page and preview it in a browser.

You should see the images displayed in the output in the final master page display (**Figure 15.6**).

## ✔ Tip

■ If your images don't show up or show up as broken links, either the path to your images isn't correct, or the images don't exist in the location you're specifying.

**Figure 15.6** ColdFusion dynamically determines the image filename and uses it in the <img> tag to display the image.

# Creating the Detail Page

When you are ready to create a detail page, you need to perform the following tasks:

1. Create a recordset to retrieve all column information desired about the chosen row.

2. Use the URL variable that was passed as a filter on the detail recordset.

3. Display the detail recordset.

## To create the detail page:

1. Create a new ColdFusion page.

2. Title the page and save it under the same name as the link you used in the master page, here `Item_Detail.cfm`.

3. Create a query that returns all relevant detail information.

   In this case, we join the `tblItems` table to the `tblCategories` and `tblManufacturers` tables to retrieve all information about an item. The static portion of the resulting `SELECT` statement is:

```
SELECT tblItems.PartNum,
tblItems.ItemName,
tblItems.ItemDescription,
tblItems.ItemCost,

tblItems.ItemImage, tblItems.Teaser,

tblManufacturers.Name,
    tblCategories.CategoryName

FROM tblItems, tblManufacturers,
    tblCategories

WHERE tblCategories.CategoryID =
    tblItems.CategoryIDFK

AND tblManufacturers.ManufacturerID =
    tblItems.MFGIDFK
```

*continues on next pge*

CREATING THE DETAIL PAGE

**4.** Add a Page Parameter called `URL.iid` and give it a blank default value.

**5.** Add an `AND` clause to filter on the `ItemID` using the `URL.iid` parameter. Do not forget to use pound signs and single quotes since this is a text column. The `AND` statement should be as follows:

```
AND tblItems.ItemID = '#URL.iid#'
```

**6.** Click OK to close the recordset builder.

**7.** Display the detail rows.

Here, we are displaying the data within a vertical table (**Figure 15.7**).

**8.** Save the page.

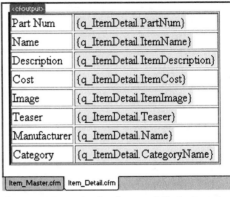

**Figure 15.7** Query the detail row and display it on the Web page.

## To ensure a user came from the Master page:

1. Place your cursor in Code view at the top of the page, right below the <cfparam> for URL.iid, and open a new line.

   If the user did not come from the master page (URL.iid is blank), you redirect the user back to the Master page.

2. On the CFML Flow toolbar of the Insert bar, choose the if icon.

3. Inside the <cfif>, create a condition to test to see if URL.iid is blank.

4. Within the <cfif> and </cfif> tags, open a new line.

5. On the CFML Basic toolbar on the Insert bar, choose the <cflocation> icon.

6. Click Browse and choose the Item_Master.cfm file.

7. Click OK (**Figure 15.8**). Click OK again to close the dialog.

   The final code should look like this:

   ```
   <cfif URL.iid IS "">
       <cflocation url="Item_Master.cfm"
                   addtoken="yes">
   </cfif>
   ```

*continues on next page*

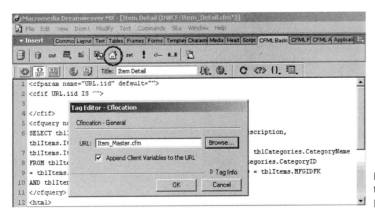

**Figure 15.8** The <cflocation> tag redirects the user to another page.

CREATING THE DETAIL PAGE

**8.** Save the page and preview it in a browser.

Since you have not gone through the master page, ColdFusion should redirect you back to the master page instead of showing results.

**9.** In the master page, choose a hyperlink of a row.

You should get the detail page with only that row's information (**Figure 15.9**).

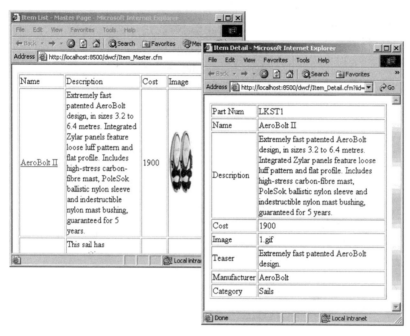

**Figure 15.9** The solution comes together when you choose a master hyperlinked row and receive the row's detail page.

# BUILDING AN ADVANCED SEARCH INTERFACE

As you learned in Chapter 9, you easily can build search interfaces in ColdFusion using Dreamweaver's code generation tools. For simple searches, Dreamweaver does all the work for you after you've responded to a few dialogs.

But what if your users want to search by multiple parameters and you don't know which parameters your users will choose?

In this chapter, you revisit much of the same ground you covered in Chapter 9. This time, however, the emphasis is on building searches by hand. First, you learn how to search text by using wildcards. Next, you learn how to search when using more than one parameter. Then you learn how to build and evaluate dynamic form controls using database results. Last, you learn how to search for data from more than one table by using a subquery.

This chapter builds on most of the coding skills you've developed in the previous sections of the book. At a minimum, you should ensure that you understand the concepts of variables and lists covered in Chapter 11. Finally, you should ensure that you're familiar with SQL SELECT and WHERE clauses.

# Searching Text

As you learned in Chapter 9, a search result page simply filters a recordset by one or more parameters specified by the user. You may have discovered, though, that SQL can be maddeningly literal. Without help, your database doesn't know that a user searching for "Island National" actually might want to find "Assateague Island National Seashore" or "Cumberland Island National Seashore."

The operators you've seen so far (such as = and IS NOT) compare a field against a precise value. Either National Seashore equals National Seashore, or it does not.

The LIKE operator searches for patterns instead of precise matches and allows you to use wildcards to build those patterns. *Wildcards* take the place of one or more characters in a value.

The two most common operators are the percent sign (%) and the underscore (_). A percent sign matches any number of characters in place of the percent, while an underscore matches only one character in place of the underscore. Let's see it in action.

## To search text with the underscore wildcard:

1. From this book's companion Web site, download the zip file that contains the code for this chapter. Extract the zip file and locate searchEmployee.cfm. Save it in your Dreamweaver site folder.

2. Open the file in Dreamweaver and preview it in your browser.

   This page is a simple search form that submits to itself; notice that the form has no action specified in the Property Inspector (**Figure 16.1**). The text input searches against the field `FirstName` in `tblEmployees` and dumps the result of the search if there's an exact match. Try it.

3. In your browser, type the name `Vicki` and submit the form.

   ColdFusion returns the result `Vicki`. Had you misspelled `Vicki` as `Vicky`, however, ColdFusion would have returned no results.

   The underscore character enables you to guess the spelling.

4. In Dreamweaver's Code view, add an underscore at the end of the search term. To do so, change the WHERE clause from this:

   ```
   WHERE FirstName LIKE
   → '#form.txtFirstName#'
   ```

   to this:

   ```
   WHERE FirstName LIKE
   → '#form.txtFirstName#_'
   ```

   Note the added underscore at the end of the form variable. Your query should look like the code listed in **Figure 16.2**.

5. Preview the page and search for `Vick`.

   ColdFusion returns `Vicki`. Had there been an employee named `Vicky`, ColdFusion would have returned her name as well: The pattern `Vick_` matches both `Vicki` and `Vicky`.

**Figure 16.1** The Property Inspector shows a form with no action.

```
3  <cfif isDefined('form.submit')>
4      <cfquery datasource="exampleapps" name="q_employees">
5      SELECT FirstName
6      FROM tblEmployees
7      WHERE FirstName LIKE '#form.txtFirstName#_'
8      ORDER BY LastName
9      </cfquery>
10 </cfif>
```

**Figure 16.2** An underscore replaces a single character in a search string.

## ✔ Tips

- If you have updated the sample ColdFusion database, your search results may vary from the ones described in this book.

- The underscore doesn't have to be placed at the end of the pattern. You can place an underscore at the beginning, the end, or anywhere in between.

- Remember that each underscore always matches only one character. You can specify two characters with two underscores (\_\_), three characters with three underscores (\_\_\_), and so on.

### To search text with the percent wildcard:

1. With the same searchEmployee.cfm file you used in the last example, add a percent sign to the WHERE clause:

   ```
   WHERE FirstName LIKE
   → '#form.txtFirstName#%'
   ```

   Note the percent sign at the end of the form variable.

2. Preview the page in a browser.

3. Enter the letter J and submit the form.

   ColdFusion returns Joe, Jacob, Joel, and two James. The percent sign matched any number of characters following the search string J. In other words, ColdFusion also would have matched Josephine, Jehosaphat, and Jocularity had they existed in the database. The length of the string does not matter when you use the percent operator.

   But what if you wanted to find employees with the letter e appearing anywhere in their first name?

4. Add a percent operator to the beginning of your search string:

   ```
   WHERE FirstName LIKE
   → '%#form.txtFirstName#%'
   ```

   Note the percent operators now surround the search string.

5. Preview the page.

6. Search for the letter e.

   ColdFusion returns sixteen names, including Eve, Ben, and Siouxsie. As you can see, ColdFusion looked for the letter e anywhere within the FirstName field.

## ✔ Tips

- Experiment with the percent operator to achieve different search results. For example, you can place the operator only at the beginning of the string, and then search for ing if you want to find only words ending with "ing."

- Use multiple percent operators only when absolutely necessary because doing so uses quite a bit of processing power.

### Searching Text with Verity

ColdFusion includes a powerful built-in search engine called Verity that allows you to index and search documents, databases, and Web pages. Verity is beyond the scope of this book, but you should be aware that it's included for free with each installation of ColdFusion. If you find yourself searching lots of documents or want to permit your users to write their own complex searches, consider using Verity. For more information, see the entry "About Verity" in the ColdFusion MX documentation.

# Searching with More than One Parameter

As you saw in Chapter 9, Dreamweaver makes it very easy to build a search result page using the recordset builder in the Bindings panel. You even can let Dreamweaver generate code to search for more than one parameter. The results, however, are not as flexible as they would be if you built the search code by hand. (If you'd prefer to stick with Dreamweaver's code generation tools, see "Searching with multiple search parameters" in Dreamweaver's online help documents.)

Assume that you don't know which parameters your user will pass from the form to the search page. Dreamweaver addresses this issue by setting default values for all form fields with `<cfparam>`. But another way to tackle the problem is to search only those fields that your user wants and to leave the others entirely out of the SQL statement with conditional processing.

Your strategy, in part, depends on understanding how form fields are passed to a result page. When you submit a text input or select control, form variables are created for those inputs whether they have a value or not. Thus, when you construct your dynamic SQL statement, you merely have to check for a form variable's *value*, and not the form variable's *existence*.

## Microsoft Access Wildcards

ANSI SQL, as you learned in Chapter 2, is a standard on which everyone agrees, but no one wholly implements. The standard wildcard characters in ANSI SQL are percent (%) and underscore (_), as covered in this chapter.

Microsoft Access actually uses different wildcard characters. Instead of using a percent sign to match any number of characters, Access uses an asterisk (*), and in place of an underscore, Access uses a question mark (?). You should be aware of this difference if you ever write your queries directly within Access instead of creating them via `<cfquery>`.

## To build a dynamic SQL statement with two parameters:

1. From this book's companion zip file, extract the document submitTitle.cfm and save it in your Dreamweaver site folder.

2. Preview the page in a browser.

   You will see a simple form, with a text input for the employee's first name and a select control with a list of titles. The page has two form controls: txtName, a text input for a first name; and selectTitle, the dynamic select control (**Figure 16.3**). The page was built entirely with Dreamweaver's visual tools; even the dynamic list box was created with the Property Inspector (**Figure 16.4**).

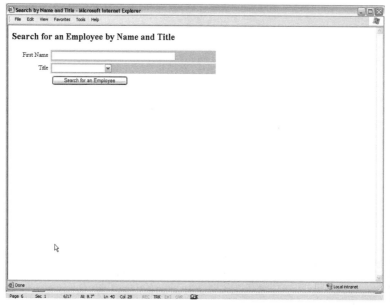

**Figure 16.3** Including a select control on your search page can help users narrow search terms.

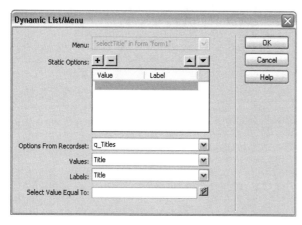

**Figure 16.4** The Dynamic List/Menu dialog quickly builds data-driven lists.

**3.** Create a new ColdFusion page, title it, and save it.

In our example, we have saved the page as searchTitle.cfm. This page will display the results of your search.

**4.** Ensure that you are in Code view. At the top of the page, enter a new SQL query:

```
<cfquery datasource="exampleapps"
→ name="q_getEmployees">

SELECT EmployeeID, FirstName, LastName,
→ Title

FROM tblEmployees

</cfquery>
```

Of course, the query is not complete without a WHERE clause. You want to instruct ColdFusion to search on a field only if the user has specified a value for that field.

**5.** Between the opening and closing `<cfquery>` tags, insert this code:

```
<cfif form.txtName NEQ "">WHERE
FirstName
→ LIKE '%#form.txtName#%'</cfif>

<cfif form.selectTitle NEQ "">AND
→ TITLE =
'#form.selectTitle#'</cfif>
```

Your entire query should look like the code listed in **Figure 16.5**. ColdFusion will now check the form variable txtName, and if it is not equal (NEQ) to null, the SQL query will compare the form's text value to the field FirstName. The conditional clause for the select control works precisely the same way.

If you're considering taking a break now, don't put this code on a production Web site! There's a serious flaw in the WHERE clause that we'll examine in a moment.

*continues on next page*

```
1  <cfquery datasource="exampleapps" name="q_getEmployees">
2  SELECT FirstName, LastName, Title
3  FROM tblEmployees
4  <cfif form.txtName NEQ "">WHERE FirstName LIKE '%#form.txtName#%'</cfif>
5  <cfif form.selectTitle NEQ "">AND TITLE = '#form.selectTitle#'</cfif>
6  </cfquery>
```

**Figure 16.5** Conditional processing allows you to search only the parameters your users specify, but this code isn't quite complete ...

**6.** Add this code to dump the query results into the body of the page:

```
<cfdump var="#q_getEmployees#"
→ label="Employees">
```

Your page, in its entirety, should look like the code listed in **Figure 16.6.**

**7.** Save the page and preview the form page, submitTitle.cfm, in a browser.

**8.** In the FirstName field, enter the letter e, and in the drop-down list, select Marketing Drone. Submit the form.

ColdFusion returns Alice Bluetooth and Lee Alister, two employees in search of better job titles. Can you guess what's wrong with the code?

**9.** Return to the form page, clear any letters from the name input, and submit the form again.

ColdFusion returns a database error (**Figure 16.7**).

**10.** Examine the WHERE clause again:

```
<cfif form.txtName NEQ "">WHERE
→ FirstName
→ LIKE '%#form.txtName#%'</cfif>
<cfif form.selectTitle NEQ "">AND
→ TITLE =
→ '#form.selectTitle#'</cfif>
```

```
1  <cfquery datasource="exampleapps" name="q_getEmployees">
2  SELECT FirstName, LastName, Title
3  FROM tblEmployees
4  <cfif form.txtName NEQ "">WHERE FirstName LIKE '%#form.txtName#%'</cfif>
5  <cfif form.selectTitle NEQ "">AND TITLE = '#form.selectTitle#'</cfif>
6  </cfquery>
7  <html>
8  <head>
9  <title>Search Results</title>
10 <meta http-equiv="Content-Type" content="text/html; charset=iso-8859-1">
11 </head>
12
13 <body>
14 <cfdump var="#q_getEmployees#" label="Employees">
```

**Figure 16.6** This code searches the recordset and dumps the results.

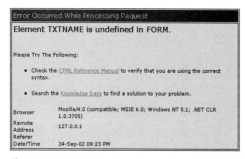

**Figure 16.7** ColdFusion generates an error when form elements are undefined.

As you can see, the code assumes that a user *always* will provide a value for the txtName form field. But users may simply want to search against the title field.

You must not only ensure that the WHERE clause is outside the conditional code, but also that it always returns true. To solve this problem, use a "dummy" WHERE clause.

**11.** Insert a new WHERE clause above the conditional clauses in your query:

WHERE 0=0

No matter which form fields are selected, this condition always will be true. Now you can check as many additional parameters as you wish.

**12.** In the first conditional clause of your query, change the WHERE to AND.

```
<cfif form.txtName NEQ "">AND FirstName
→ LIKE '%#form.txtName#%'</cfif>
```

Your entire query should look like the code listing in **Figure 16.8**. ColdFusion now treats the form fields as additional parameters of the WHERE clause.

**13.** Save the page and test your form in a browser. Leave the name field blank and select Engineer from the title list.

This time, ColdFusion doesn't generate an error, instead returning several engineers.

### ✔ Tip

■ If you've forgotten how to build a dynamic list control, see Chapter 9 of this book.

```
1  <cfquery datasource="exampleapps" name="q_getEmployees">
2  SELECT FirstName, LastName, Title
3  FROM tblEmployees
4  WHERE 0=0
5  <cfif form.txtName NEQ "">AND FirstName LIKE '%#form.txtName#%'</cfif>
6  <cfif form.selectTitle NEQ "">AND TITLE = '#form.selectTitle#'</cfif>
7  </cfquery>
```

**Figure 16.8** The dummy WHERE clause helps to keep your pages error free.

# Working with Dynamic Checkbox Controls

You've already seen how to assess the value of form variables created by select and text input controls. In this section, you learn two new skills: testing for the existence of a form variable using the `isDefined()` function, and searching for a list of values using the SQL keyword `IN`.

A text input field is defined by virtue of its existence in a form. Even if a user does not type any text into an input named `txtName`, the variable `form.txtName` is created and passed to the action page when the form is submitted.

A checkbox, on the other hand, is not defined unless a user actually checks the box before submitting the form. Before attempting to work with a checkbox value, you must check for its existence. **Table 16.1** shows the differences between a checkbox and a text input when each is submitted in a form.

In Chapter 11, you learned to use the `<cfparam>` tag to test for the existence of a variable. As you saw in the previous section, however, you don't always want to assign a default value to a variable. In the previous search example, you used conditional processing to ignore a variable that was created but held no value.

The `isDefined()` function allows you to test for the existence of a variable. Since `isDefined()` returns `TRUE` if the variable in question exists, it is often used in conjunction with conditional processing. For example, you can test for the existence of a variable like this:

```
<cfif isDefined('myVariable')>
<!-- run this code if the variable
→ exists -->
</cfif>
```

Don't overuse `isDefined()`. As we mentioned in passing in Chapter 11, it's easy to use `isDefined()` to write bad code. Try to limit your use of `isDefined()` to special circumstances like the one discussed here.

The SQL keyword `IN` matches your search value with any value in a subquery or list. For instance, compare these two queries, one in English, the other in SQL.

English:

```
I want to find my term if it matches this
→ term, or that term, or the other term.
```

SQL:

```
WHERE myTerm IN ('this term', 'that
→ term', 'the other term')
```

In the following two exercises, you use the function `isDefined()` and the keyword `IN` to search a recordset using dynamic checkboxes. Remember to always enclose your variable names in quotes when using `isDefined()`.

**Table 16.1**

| Text Inputs and Checkboxes | |
|---|---|
| FORM CONTROL | STATUS ON SUBMIT |
| Text input with no text | Form variable created but no value supplied |
| Text input with text | Form variable created with a value supplied |
| Checkbox not selected | Form variable not created |
| Checkbox selected | Form variable created with a value supplied |

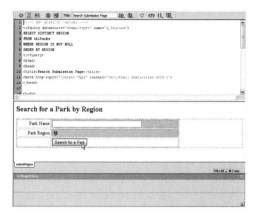

**Figure 16.9** This page has a recordset that will dynamically populate checkboxes.

## To build a list of dynamic checkboxes:

1. From this book's companion Web site, download the file submitRegion.cfm and save it in your site folder.

2. Open the document in the Dreamweaver Code and Design view and examine it.

   The page contains a query that lists each distinct region from tblParks in the exampleapps data source. There's also a form to allow users to submit both park name and park region (**Figure 16.9**).

   In the next step, you write code to dynamically create a list of checkboxes, one for each region. The task is very similar to creating a dynamic select control.

3. Locate the table cell with the ColdFusion comment insert checkboxes here. If you have difficulty finding it, Dreamweaver helpfully inserts an icon for each comment in the Design view. Choose Insert > ColdFusion Basic Objects > CFoutput.

   Dreamweaver opens the cfoutput Tag Editor.

4. In the Query Name textbox, type q_Regions and click OK.

   Dreamweaver inserts a <cfoutput> tag in the table cell.

5. In between the opening and closing <cfoutput> tags, choose Insert > Forms Objects > Check Box.

   The Input Tag Editor opens.

*continues on next page*

**SEARCHING WITH MORE THAN ONE PARAMETER**

**6.** In the Type drop-down list, accept the default value checkbox. Name your checkbox checkRegion, and give it a value of #q_Regions.REGION#. Click OK.

Dreamweaver inserts a checkbox that will get its value from the REGION column in your q_Regions recordset.

Your page is not quite finished, however. If you were to test it, you would see a string of unlabeled checkboxes running across the width of the table cell.

**7.** Next to the checkbox, insert this code to output the Region's name and a line break:

#q_Regions.REGION#<br />

The code for your entire table cell should look like the code listed in **Figure 16.10**. Dreamweaver also represents the dynamic actions of the page in the Design view (**Figure 16.11**).

**8.** Save the page and then preview it in a browser (**Figure 16.12**).

ColdFusion displays a list of park regions, each one with its own checkbox. To better understand the page, examine the HTML that ColdFusion generated.

```
25  <td valign="top" bgcolor="#CCCCCC">
26  <cfoutput query="q_Regions">
27      <input type="checkbox" name="checkRegion" value="#q_Regions.REGION#">
28      #q_Regions.REGION#<br />
29  </cfoutput>
30  </td>
```

**Figure 16.10** Output a query to create dynamic checkboxes.

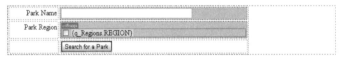

**Figure 16.11** Dreamweaver shows the dynamic elements of a form.

**Figure 16.12** ColdFusion generates checkboxes, one per region.

9. View the page's source code. In Internet Explorer, for example, choose View > Source.

Here is a sample line:

```
<input name="checkRegion"
→ type="checkbox" value=
→ "Alaska Region">Alaska Region<br />
```

As you can see, each checkbox has the value of a region from the recordset. When you check a box and submit the form, this value is passed to the form's action page. In the next section, you learn how to process these dynamic values.

## To search with values from dynamic checkboxes and the keyword IN:

1. Create a new ColdFusion page, title it, and save it.

   In our example, we have named the page searchRegion.cfm. It's important that you give the page the same name you assigned to the search form you created in the previous section.

2. If you skipped the last section, you can extract the completed page submitRegionComplete.cfm from this chapter's zipped file.

3. Create a new recordset named q_getParks based on the datasource exampleapps. Retrieve your data from the table tblParks, and filter the recordset on the value of the park's name passed from the form on the previous page:

```
<cfquery datasource="exampleapps"
→ name="q_getParks">
SELECT PARKNAME, ParkType, STATE, REGION
FROM tblParks
WHERE 0=0
<cfif form.txtName NEQ "">AND
→ PARKNAME LIKE
→ '%#form.txtName#%'</cfif>
ORDER BY PARKNAME
</cfquery>
```

Notice that the query uses the dummy WHERE clause and searches against the PARKNAME field only if the user has entered a name in the field txtName.

4. Following the first conditional AND clause of the SQL query, add a <cfif> statement to check for the existence of the checkbox:

```
<cfif
→ isDefined('form.checkRegion')>
</cfif>
```

The isDefined() function checks to determine whether the variable form.checkRegion is defined, and if so, executes any code within the opening and closing <cfif> tags.

As you might guess, you use the SQL keyword IN to determine whether your user's search value matches a list of regions. If the search were static, your SQL AND clause might look like this:

```
AND REGION IN ('Alaska Region', 'Midwest
→ Region', 'North Atlantic Region')
```

But you want to offer your users the chance to specify the region or regions in which they wish to search.

*continues on next page*

**5.** Within the opening and closing `<cfif>` tags, type this code:

```
AND REGION IN
(<cfloop index="i"
→ list="#form.checkRegion#">
<cfoutput>'#i#',</cfoutput>
</cfloop>)
```

Your entire SQL query should look like the code listed in **Figure 16.13**. What's going on here?

Checkboxes pass their values as a list. As you learned in Chapter 11, ColdFusion handles lists with ease and lets you loop through list content with `<cfloop>`. Line by line, here's how the `AND` clause works:

```
AND REGION IN
```

This line simply specifies that ColdFusion should try to match `REGION` with a list of values.

```
(<cfloop index="i"
→ list="#form.checkRegion#">
```

This line begins with a parenthesis to enclose the SQL list. Next, the `<cfloop>` tag sets the index to i and tells ColdFusion to loop through the list passed in the `form.checkRegion` variable. Remember, ColdFusion passed all the values from the checkboxes on the form page in a list.

```
<cfoutput>'#i#',</cfoutput>
```

This line simply outputs the contents of the list, enclosed in single quotes and followed by a comma.

```
</cfloop>)
```

This line closes the loop and encloses the SQL list with a closing parenthesis.

```
1   <cfquery datasource="exampleapps" name="q_getParks">
2   SELECT PARKNAME, ParkType, STATE, REGION
3   FROM tblParks
4   WHERE 0=0
5   <cfif form.txtName NEQ "">AND PARKNAME LIKE '%#form.txtName#%'</cfif>
6   <cfif isDefined('form.checkRegion')>
7   AND REGION IN
8   (<cfloop index="i" list="#form.checkRegion#">
9                       <cfoutput>'#i#',</cfoutput>
10                  </cfloop>)
11  </cfif>
12  ORDER BY PARKNAME
13  </cfquery>
```

**Figure 16.13** Search a ColdFusion list with the keyword IN.

**6.** In between the opening and closing <body> tags, dump the contents of your query:

`<cfdump var="#q_getParks#" label="Parks">`

Your page should look like the code listed in **Figure 16.14**.

**7.** Preview the form submission page in a browser to test the search page; if you preview the result page in a browser you'll receive an error because the form variables aren't defined.

**8.** Type the word monument in the Park Name textbox, select the Southeast Region checkbox, and submit the form.

ColdFusion finds fewer than ten records matching your search query.

**9.** Click your browser's Back button to return to the search page. Perform the same search, but add the Rocky Mountain Region to your selected regions.

ColdFusion finds over 20 records matching your search. Now that you understand how ColdFusion recognizes a set of values passed from checkboxes as a list, let's take one more step to tighten up your code.

**10.** In the query q_getParks, delete the final AND clause and replace it with this code:

```
AND REGION IN
→ (#ListQualify(form.checkRegion,
→ "'")#)
```

ColdFusion includes the ListQualify() function, which inserts a string at the beginning and end of list elements. In this example, ListQualify() uses two parameters, form.checkRegion, the variable containing the list; and ', the delimiter that separates the list elements.

**11.** Test the form submission page again in your browser. The ListQualify() function generates the same results as the <cfloop>, but with fewer lines of code.

*continues on nex page*

```
1  <cfquery datasource="exampleapps" name="q_getParks">
2  SELECT PARKNAME, ParkType, STATE, REGION
3  FROM tblParks
4  WHERE 0=0
5  <cfif form.txtName NEQ "">AND PARKNAME LIKE '%#form.txtName#%'</cfif>
6  <cfif isDefined('form.checkRegion')>
7  AND REGION IN
8  (<cfloop index="i" list="#form.checkRegion#">
9                  <cfoutput>'#i#',</cfoutput>
10                 </cfloop>)
11 </cfif>
12 ORDER BY PARKNAME
13 </cfquery>
14 <html>
15 <head>
16 <title>Park Results</title>
17 <meta http-equiv="Content-Type" content="text/html; charset=iso-8859-1">
18 </head>
19
20 <body>
21
22 <cfdump var="#q_getParks#" label="Parks">
23 </body>
24 </html>
```

**Figure 16.14** This page queries a list of regions and dumps the result.

## ✔ Tips

- If you're confused by the dummy WHERE clause and the conditional AND clause, review the previous sections of this chapter.

- By including the multiple attribute to a select control, you also can pass values in a list to a form action page.

- If you passed integer values from a form to an IN clause, looping through a list would be overkill. You do not have to wrap integers in single quotation marks to use them with an IN clause. Here are some examples.

  This is a valid IN clause:

  ```
  WHERE myField IN (1, 2, 3, 4)
  ```

  This is **not** a valid IN clause:

  ```
  WHERE myField IN (Ben, Sue, Marc,
  → Angela)
  ```

  This is a valid IN clause:

  ```
  WHERE myField IN ('Ben', 'Sue', 'Marc',
  → 'Angela')
  ```

- As with all SQL select queries, don't be afraid to experiment with the IN clause. The worst that can happen is that Cold-Fusion will generate an error, and even the errors are instructive.

- The real power of the IN clause lies in its ability to handle subqueries. You learn about subqueries later in the next section.

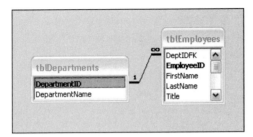

**Figure 16.15** One department can have many employees.

## Searching with Subqueries

As you learned in Chapter 2, databases often contain normalized data in relational tables. For example, the `cfexamples` database used throughout this book stores a list of employees in `tblEmpoyees` and a list of departments in `tblDepartments`. Each department can contain more than one employee: thus a department has a one-to-many relationship with employees (**Figure 16.15**). Each employee's department data is stored as a string of letters and numbers; thus, if you were to examine the database you would find an employee's department listed as `BA1EA73F-7D79-11D3-A928005004218998` instead of `Development`.

Assume that you want to allow your users the opportunity to narrow an employee search by department, and that you want to show the user-friendly department name instead of the incomprehensible string of digits. You easily can solve this problem using a subquery.

In the previous section, you used the SQL keyword `IN` to search from a list of comma-delimited values. You also can use `IN` to search the results of a query, and this section shows you how.

## To narrow your search with a subquery:

1. From this chapter's zipped file, extract the document submitDepartment.cfm and save it in your site folder.

2. Preview the page in your browser (**Figure 16.16**).

   ColdFusion generates a search form with a text input for the employee's first name, and a drop-down list to choose the employee's department. For your reference, the drop-down list contains both the department name and department ID.

   The drop-down list, built using the Dreamweaver Dynamic List/Menu dialog, is populated by a distinct list of department names and ID numbers. In our example, we assigned searchDepartment.cfm as the form's action, but you can specify any name for the file you create in the next step.

3. In the Dreamweaver Code and Design view, create a new ColdFusion page, title it, and save it.

4. At the top of the page in Code view, type this query:

   ```
   <cfquery datasource="exampleapps"
   → name="q_getEmployees">
   SELECT DeptIDFK, EmployeeID, FirstName,
   → LastName
   FROM tblEmployees
   WHERE 0=0
   <cfif form.txtName NEQ "">AND firstName
   → LIKE '%#form.txtName#%'</cfif>
   </cfquery>
   ```

   As you know by now, ColdFusion retrieves all records in the table matching the WHERE clause. Now you need to narrow the search by the department. Note, though, that you can retrieve only one column with a subquery.

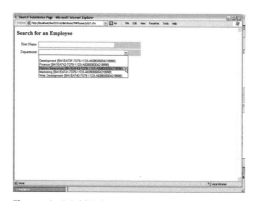

**Figure 16.16** ColdFusion populates a drop-down list dynamically.

```
1  <cfquery datasource="exampleapps" name="q_getEmployees">
2  SELECT DeptIDFK, EmployeeID, FirstName, LastName
3  FROM tblEmployees
4  WHERE DeptIDFK IN (SELECT DeptIDFK
5      FROM tblDepartments
6      WHERE DeptIDFK = '#form.selectDepartment#')
7  </cfquery>
```

**Figure 16.17** This query includes a subquery.

## Subqueries vs. Joins

Use subqueries judiciously because they're not always the most efficient way to retrieve recordset data. A subquery is easy to read, but a join often retrieves the data faster. You were introduced to joins in Chapter 4. While a full discussion of joins is beyond this book, you should be aware that most subqueries can be rewritten as joins, and you should consider comparing the performance of the two before you decide to rely exclusively on subqueries.

✔ **Tip**

■ Sometimes it's hard to know where a drill-down ends and a search begins. If you have a small number of items in your table (say, 50 or fewer) and the search is too open-ended, your users can become frustrated by empty results. Consider helping your users find the results they want by providing drop-down lists and checkboxes.

5. Add a second conditional **AND** clause to search for the department with this code:

```
<cfif form.selectDepartment NEQ "">
DeptIDFK IN (SELECT DeptIDFK
   FROM tblDepartments
   WHERE DeptIDFK =
→ '#form.selectDepartment#')
</cfif>
```

Your entire query should now look like the code listed in **Figure 16.17**.

You already know that the `<cfif>` statement checks whether the `selectDepartment` variable submitted by the form has a value. To understand how the **IN** clause works, first examine the **SELECT** clause within the parentheses:

```
(SELECT DeptIDFK
   FROM tblDepartments
   WHERE DeptIDFK =
→ '#form.selectDepartment#')
```

This clause simply retrieves the field `DeptIDFK` from `tblDepartments` if the `DeptIDFK` matches the value submitted by the form. ColdFusion stores the results of that query in a list and then uses the **IN** clause to search the list, just as it searched the comma-delimited list you saw in the previous section.

6. In between the opening and closing `<body>` tags, dump the query results:

```
<cfdump var="#q_getEmployees#"
→ label="Employees">
```

7. Save the page, and test your form submission page in a browser.

If the user selects a department on the submission page, ColdFusion narrows the results accordingly.

# BUILDING AND USING COMPONENTS

As you've worked through the previous chapters, you may have wondered why you ever should have to type the same bit of code more than once. Wouldn't it be nice if your server stored functions that you could call from within your ColdFusion applications?

ColdFusion MX introduces ColdFusion components (CFCs), a new feature that provides a simple and flexible way to maintain and reuse your code as you work. CFCs are ColdFusion files saved with a .cfc file extension that encapsulate application functionality and make that functionality available to browsers, Macromedia Flash Players and Web services. CFCs may be the single most powerful new feature in ColdFusion MX. Fortunately, Dreamweaver MX provides visual tools that make creating and consuming CFCs almost as easy as drag and drop.

In this chapter, you first learn how to use an existing CFC through the Dreamweaver Components panel. Next, you learn how to create your own CFC using Dreamweaver's Create Component wizard. Finally, you learn how to document and consume the new CFC, and then integrate it into an application.

We've saved this chapter for last because it builds on many of the concepts presented in previous chapters. While creating and consuming CFCs might be slightly more complex than writing a cfquery, they're worth the trouble. Let's get started.

# Working with an Existing ColdFusion Component

Components package application functionality into a single reusable software unit written in CFML (ColdFusion Markup Language). Instead of having multiple pages or custom tags that perform similar functions and reside in separate files and directory structures, you now have the ability to organize this functionality into a single CFC. As a rule of thumb, consider using a component any time you have a piece of business logic or application logic that you want to reuse.

"Application logic" sounds a bit abstract. In practical terms, when might you want to use a CFC? Recall the search interfaces you built in Chapters 9 and 16. What if you wanted to offer the same functionality at different places in your application? You could rewrite the search code each time, or copy and paste it from one template to another. But that method will quickly prove unmanageable. You also could use `<cfinclude>` to store your search query; prior to the introduction of CFCs many developers did precisely that. But a CFC is more flexible than simply using `<cfinclude>` to manage your code, and allows you to pass data to other applications outside of ColdFusion.

Admittedly, it all sounds a bit confusing at first. As with any ColdFusion topic, CFCs will become much clearer when you start coding.

You can use Macromedia Dreamweaver MX to consume CFCs that already exist on your network. The Components panel allows you to introspect components for their methods and arguments. In the following steps, you'll select a CFC from the Components panel and simply drag it onto your page.

## ✔ Tip

■ In the context of Dreamweaver, "introspection" isn't something you do when you're feeling sensitive or lonely. In this case, it means that you can examine a self-describing component and find out details about how it operates.

## Custom Tags

If you've used an earlier version of ColdFusion, you already may be familiar with custom tags. Custom tags are ideal for processing input such as text and numerical values, and returning output such as HTML. You specify the input values in one or more of the tag's attributes. The code that processes the input values is contained in a separate file. The code's output, not the code itself, is passed back to the original page, replacing the custom tag.

CFCs supplement, but do not replace, custom tags in ColdFusion MX. Because custom tags have been a popular feature of ColdFusion for several versions, there are thousands of tags available at the Macromedia developer's exchange. Although custom tags are beyond the scope of this book, you can learn more about them by searching for "Custom Tags" in the ColdFusion MX Documentation included with Dreamweaver MX.

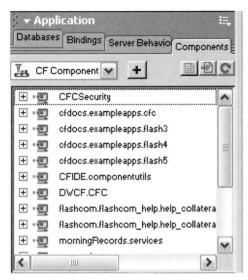

**Figure 17.1** The Components panel lists the components available to your network.

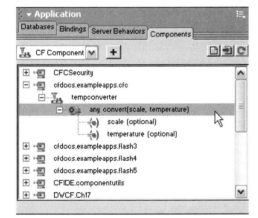

**Figure 17.2** In this figure, the component package is fully expanded.

## To add an existing CFC to your page:

1. Create a new ColdFusion page, title it, and save it.

2. To open the Components panel, do one of the following:

   ▲ Choose Window > Components.

   ▲ Press Ctrl+F7 (Windows) or

   ▲ Command+F7 (Mac).

   The Components panel may open either to CF Components or Web Services.

3. Ensure that CF Components is selected in the drop-down list.

   Dreamweaver shows a list of the components available to you (**Figure 17.1**). This may take some time, depending on your system speed and network configuration.

4. Click the plus sign (+) to expand all the tree nodes underneath the component package cfdocs.exampleapps.cfc until you can see the function convert(scale, temperature) (**Figure 17.2**).

   Don't worry for the moment what all the nodes on the tree mean; you explore them later in this chapter.

*continues on next page*

**5.** With your mouse, click the function convert(), drag it between the <body> tags of your page, and drop it.

You will see a plus sign underneath your mouse pointer (**Figure 17.3**). When you release the mouse, Dreamweaver automatically will generate most of the code necessary to invoke the function. (**Figure 17.4**). From the name of the component, you can guess that it takes a temperature value and converts it from Celsius to Fahrenheit or vice versa.

**6.** Add these attributes to the <cfinvoke> tag to provide the function with a scale and a temperature to convert:

```
scale="Celsius"
temperature="35"
```

Again, you learn more about the syntax later in this chapter. Your code should look like **Figure 17.5**.

**7.** After the closing <cfinvoke> tag, add a <cfoutput> tag to display the temperature you retrieved from the function:

```
<cfoutput>35 Celsius =
→ strong>#convertRet#</strong>
→ Fahrenheit</cfoutput>
```

**8.** Save the page and preview it in your browser.

You should see text stating that "35 Celsius = 95 Fahrenheit." You've just successfully invoked your first ColdFusion component.

**9.** Optional: If you're curious to see the code that you invoked, right-click on the tempconverter component and choose the Edit the code option (**Figure 17.6**).

The component opens within Dreamweaver, and you can see how the conversion actually takes place. You learn about the tags used to assemble the component in the next section.

**Figure 17.3** Dragging a function onto your page...

**Figure 17.4** ... tells Dreamweaver to automatically generate the code to invoke the function.

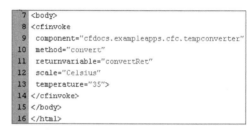

**Figure 17.5** Invoking a CFC is as simple as dragging and dropping.

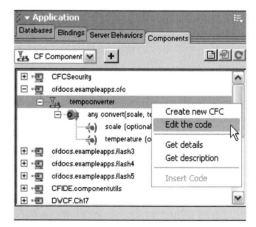

**Figure 17.6** Choose Edit the code to edit a CFC within Dreamweaver.

WORKING WITH A COLDFUSION COMPONENT

Here are two key points you should take away before moving on to the next section, in which you learn about creating and consuming components in detail:

- CFCs can work like a "black box." All you have to know to use a component in Dreamweaver is how to drag it onto the page and which values to pass to it. You don't have to know how to convert Celsius to Fahrenheit. This means that you can include complex business logic in your components and invoke them simply within Dreamweaver. This feature is useful if you work in a team.

- Invoking a CFC is as easy as drag and drop. Simply browse a list of existing components and apply the one you want to your page.

## Editing Components

Dreamweaver offers an easy way to add, delete, or edit ColdFusion Components defined within your site. To use these features, however, your development environment must be set up as follows.

- ColdFusion MX must be running locally.

- In the Advanced Site definition, the Access type on the Testing Server must be Local/Network.

- The path of your local root folder must be the same as the path of the testing server folder.

- The component must be stored in the local site folder or any of its subfolders on your hard disk.

For more information on installing and configuring Dreamweaver and ColdFusion, please see the Appendix.

## ✔ Tips

- If you have not already specified an RDS password for Dreamweaver, you will need to do so before you can browse components on the ColdFusion server. The RDS is the same password you use to log in to the ColdFusion administrator. If you do not know this value, you can obtain it from your administrator. For more information on RDS, please see the Appendix, "Installation."

- Make sure you have a site defined before you start working with CFCs. Dreamweaver does not let you introspect a CFC unless your file is saved in a Dreamweaver ColdFusion site.

- There's not much to see when you're building and consuming CFCs, so consider switching to the Dreamweaver Code view.

- Components are stored on the ColdFusion server. An installation can have many different configurations. In this chapter, we'll use the word network to refer to any location you've defined that you can connect to via Dreamweaver.

- The component package `cfdocs.exampleapps.cfc` is installed by default with ColdFusion MX. If it does not exist on your network, your system administrator may have decided not to install the ColdFusion docs for security purposes. If the component isn't available to you, just follow along for now. You'll build a new component from scratch in the next section.

WORKING WITH A COLDFUSION COMPONENT

# Creating ColdFusion Components

As we noted earlier, you can use Macromedia Dreamweaver MX to build a ColdFusion component and its functions visually. Creating a CFC requires that you learn two new tags: `<cfcomponent>` and `<cffunction>`.

♦ `<cfcomponent>` encapsulates all code in the CFC. It also accepts attributes such as `displayname` and `hint` that help to document the component's uses.

♦ `<cffunction>` surrounds the code for each of the component's methods. The component's actual programming logic is stored within `<cffunction>` blocks.

Dreamweaver's Create Components wizard creates a .cfc file and inserts the necessary CFML tags for you. (Of course, as with all CFML, you can write the code by hand as well.)

In this section, you use code that's very similar to the query you created in the last chapter, "Building an Advanced Search Interface," to build your own search CFC.

## Application Architecture

If you write applications long enough, you will eventually care deeply about how you manage your code, and how you structure your Web site. Developers have religious wars over this subject, known as "application architecture." (Incredibly, developers also have religious wars over what "application architecture" actually means).

One of the few subjects almost all developers agree on is that separating content from presentation is vastly preferable to mixing everything together as "spaghetti code." (All developers use the term "spaghetti code" dismissively. If you learn to throw around the words "spaghetti code" and "application architecture" in debates, you'll be speaking like a developer in no time).

CFCs are a gentle introduction to this concept: With a component, you can handle business or application logic, pass the data back to a relatively clean presentation page, and send the HTML to the browser. You also will find that by embracing a consistent architecture, your code will be easier to debug and reuse.

If you'd like to learn more about the subject, Macromedia has several excellent articles in its Designer & Developer Center (`http://www.macromedia.com/desdev/`).

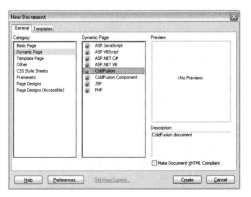

Figure 17.7 Use the New Document dialog to create a CFC.

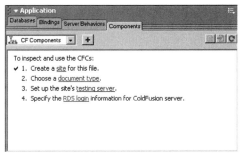

Figure 17.8 The CFC checklist identifies the task needed to be completed.

## To create a new CFC skeleton:

1. Within the root folder of your site, create a new folder and name it **CFC**.

2. Press Ctrl+N (Windows) or Command+N (Mac).

   The New Document dialog appears (**Figure 17.7**).

3. Select Dynamic Page and choose ColdFusion.

   A new ColdFusion page is created.

4. To open the Components panel, do one of the following:

   ▲ Choose Window > Components.

   ▲ Press Ctrl+F7 (Windows) or

   ▲ Command+F7 (Mac).

   The Components panel appears.

5. Complete any outstanding steps required for CFC inspection (**Figure 17.8**).

6. On the Components panel, click the plus (+) button to enter the Create Component dialog.

   The Create Component dialog appears (**Figure 17.9**).

*continues on next page*

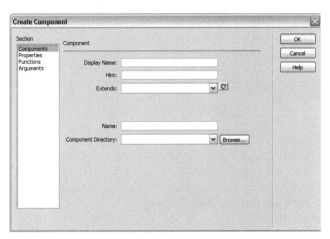

Figure 17.9 The Create Component dialog is where you actually begin creating the CFC.

CREATING COLDFUSION COMPONENTS

7. In the Display Name textbox in the Create Component dialog, type parkSearch, the component name that you reference when you call the CFC.

8. In the Name field, type parkSearch, the name of the file in the file system.

9. For the Component Directory, select the CFC folder you created at the beginning of this section.

10. Leave all other fields empty (**Figure 17.10**).

11. In the Section area, click Function.

The Functions section appears.

12. In the Functions section, click the + sign to add a function.

13. Name the function listParks.

14. Set access to public.

15. Set the returnType to query.

16. Click OK.

Dreamweaver generates the code shown in **Figure 17.11** and creates the file parkSearch.cfc within your CFC folder.

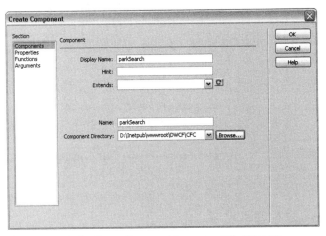

**Figure 17.10** Display Name, Name, and Component Directory are specified in the Create Component dialog.

```
1  <!---- Generated by Dreamweaver MX 6.0.1722 [en] (Win32) - Mon Sep 09 15:50:02 GMT+0800 (Malay Peninsula
   Standard Time) 2002 --->
2
3  <cfcomponent displayName="parkSearch">
4      <cffunction name="listParks" access="public" returnType="query" output="false">
5          <!---- listParks body ---->
6          <cfreturn >
7      </cffunction>
8  </cfcomponent>
```

**Figure 17.11** Dreamweaver creates the skeleton code for your component...

## ✔ Tips

- It is a quirk of Dreamweaver that if you select ColdFusion Component from the New Document dialog, Dreamweaver creates a component skeleton without giving you the benefit of the Create Component Wizard. For now, you may find it easier to create a ColdFusion page and then use the Create Component dialog.

- You can either put the CFC and Cold-Fusion pages in a separate folder, like an asset, or in the same folder with the group of CFML pages that use the CFC. Regardless, Dreamweaver MX can locate them and make all CFCs in your defined site available to all other CFML pages in the Web site. You can store CFCs anywhere in your Webroot, but it is a best practice to keep them in a separate folder.

- See this book's Appendix if you need help configuring your development environment.

- Remember that you can use CFCs with ColdFusion MX only. CFCs are not supported in ColdFusion 5 or below.

- The Component Directory textbox specifies where the component will be saved.

- Dreamweaver adds a function with the name Function by default. When you change the default name by editing the Name field, and Dreamweaver changes the default name automatically.

- Setting the `access` attribute to `public` ensures that the component can be used by any of the ColdFusion pages in your application. If you were to set the access attribute to remote, the CFC would become available as a Web service. Although a detailed discussion of Web services and remote access are beyond the scope of this book, see the sidebar "Flash Remoting and Web Services" for a quick introduction.

- You can add methods to your component with the Create Component dialog, but we'll do so by hand in the next section.

## To add logic to your CFC:

1. From the Site panel, open parkSearch.cfc if it is not already open.

2. Insert a few blank lines after the opening `<cffunction>` tag.

3. Within the `<cffunction>` tag, type this code to create a query to obtain the Park Name and State of all parks in tblParks:

```
<!-- query the list of parks -->
<cfquery name="getParks"
→ datasource="exampleapps">
SELECT PARKNAME, STATE
FROM tblParks
<!-- dummy where clause -->
WHERE0=0
</cfquery>
```

Dreamweaver closes the `<cfquery>` tag automatically. This query retrieves all records from tblParks (recall from the last chapter that the dummy WHERE clause is always true). But we want to let the users narrow the search results to match only the states and park names they desire. First, provide optional arguments for the function.

4. Above the opening `<cfquery>` tag, insert these arguments:

```
<cfargument name="parknameString"
→ required="false" default="">
<cfargument name="stateString"
→ required="false" default="">
```

This code specifies that your function will take two arguments, both optional: an argument for the park name, and an argument for the state.

5. Add two conditional WHERE clauses to the query:

```
<cfif ARGUMENTS.parknameString NEQ "">
AND PARKNAME LIKE
→ '%#ARGUMENTS.parknameString#%'
</cfif>
<cfif ARGUMENTS.stateString NEQ "">
AND STATE = '#ARGUMENTS.stateString#'
</cfif>
```

As with the conditional search query from the previous chapter, you have specified that you want the query to search against certain fields only if the user desires those fields. Finally, you must tell the component how to return the data to the page that invokes it.

**6.** After the closing `<cfquery>` tag, insert this code:

`<cfreturn getParks>`

The `<cfreturn>` tag simply returns values from a component method. You can have only one `<cfreturn>` tag for each function. In this case, you have specified that the function will return the data from the query getParks. The function in its entirety should look like **Figure 17.12**.

```
4  <!----- listParks() method ---->
5  <cffunction name="listParks" access="public" returnType="query" output="false">
6      <!----- listParks body ---->
7      <!---- optional arguments ---->
8      <cfargument name="parknameString" required="false" default="">
9      <cfargument name="stateString" required="false" default="">
10
11         <!---- query the list of parks ---->
12         <cfquery name="getParks" datasource="exampleapps">
13         SELECT  PARKNAME, STATE
14         FROM    tblParks
15         <!---- dummy where clause ---->
16         WHERE   0=0
17         <!---- search for park name if it's defined in the form ---->
18         <cfif ARGUMENTS.parknameString NEQ "">
19         AND PARKNAME LIKE '%#ARGUMENTS.parknameString#%'
20         </cfif>
21         <!---- search by state if it's defined in the form ---->
22         <cfif ARGUMENTS.stateString NEQ "">
23         AND STATE = '#ARGUMENTS.stateString#'
24         </cfif>
25         </cfquery>
26
27      <!---- return the recordset ---->
28      <cfreturn getParks>
29  </cffunction>
```

**Figure 17.12** The listParks() function returns the data from the query getParks.

Your new component is complete. If you save your code and refresh the Components panel, you should see the parkSearch component, along with its single function and two arguments, in the components list. Look for it under the node DWCF.CFC (**Figure 17.13**).

### ✔ Tip

- Don't forget that you can build your query by pulling database fields from the data Bindings panel if you prefer not to type them by hand.

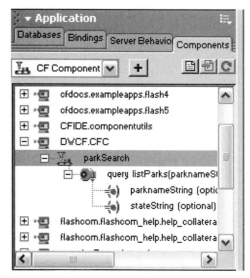

**Figure 17.13** The new parkSearch component appears in the Components panel.

## CFC Best Practices

When writing CFCs, you should assume that you know nothing about the application that will call your CFC. What does that mean in practice?

Always use the arguments scope when building components. (For a refresher on variable scopes, see Chapter 11). Take another look at the query code in the listParks() function. As you can see, you could have written the conditional WHERE clauses to check for the existence of form variables instead of argument strings. Had you done so, however, you would have limited the utility of the component.

Remember, one of the primary goals of writing a component is code reuse. If your component accesses form variables directly, you cannot call it from a page that handles its data from URL or session variables. It's much better to work with arguments, as you have seen in this section, and to pass those arguments to the component via the <cfinvoke> tag.

CREATING COLDFUSION COMPONENTS

# Consuming Components

In the previous section, you created a component that lists all parks in tblParks from the cfexamples database. Optionally, you can limit the recordset by state and by searching against the park name. Of course, you still need to invoke the component before you can view its output in an application. In this section, you learn how components describe their own methods. You also learn how to integrate the component into a form page, using the same invocation technique that you encountered briefly at the beginning of this chapter.

## To document a CFC in your browser:

1. Open your browser and point it to the URL of the searchPage component.

   This URL varies, depending on your installation. If you have a default installation of ColdFusion MX connected to IIS on your local machine, you can reach the CFC with this URL:

   `http://localhost /DWCF/ cfc/parkSearch.cfc`

2. Depending on your ColdFusion configuration, you probably will encounter the Component Browser login screen (**Figure 17.14**) and must provide your RDS or Admin password and login.

You will see documentation for the parkSearch component in your browser window. The features of this page are generated automatically by ColdFusion. As you can see (and as you already know), the component has only one method, listParks, which returns a query. The listParks method accepts two optional parameters, parknameString and stateString. This is a good beginning, but a developer who encounters your component for the first time still will have to make some guesses as to how precisely it should be used.

3. Within the Dreamweaver Components panel, right-click on the parkSearch component and choose Edit the code (**Figure 17.15**).

   The CFC opens in the Dreamweaver Code view.

*continues on next page*

**Figure 17.14** If the ColdFusion MX Component Browser screen appears, you must log in.

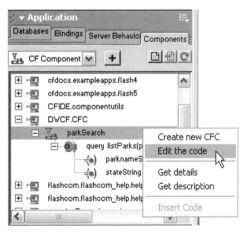

**Figure 17.15** Use the Dreamweaver Components panel to access the component-editing menu.

**4.** Add this hint attribute to the
<cfcomponent> tag:

hint="Retrieves data for US National
Parks"

**5.** Add another hint of your choosing to the
<cffunction> tag and then save the CFC
and view it in your browser.

Notice that your new hints now appear
with both the component and its
method (**Figure 17.16**). The component
now has enough information for a developer who has never used it before to
begin programming with it.

## ✔ Tips

■ Be sure to use the hint attribute of components, especially when more than one
developer works on a project or when a
component has more than one method.
You'll be amazed at how much of your
own code you forget after a few months.
When you return to a component to
debug it or add a new feature, the hint
can save a tremendous amount of time.

■ If you're on a Macintosh, remember that
the actual component will be somewhere
on your network. You cannot browse a
component stored on your machine.

**Figure 17.16** Including hints can make your components much easier to understand.

CONSUMING COMPONENTS

## To invoke a component in your application:

**1.** Create a new ColdFusion page, title it, and then save it in your site directory.

Next, in the Dreamweaver Code view, you define two form parameters and create a query to retrieve a list of states.

**2.** Type this code above the opening <html> tag:

```
<!-- FORM parameters -->
<cfparam name="FORM.parkname"
default="">
 → <cfparam name="FORM.state"
 → default="">
<!-- get the list of states to
 → populate dropdown list -->
```

```
<cfquery name="getStates"
 → datasource="exampleapps">
  SELECT DISTINCT STATE
  FROM tblParks
  ORDER BY STATE
</cfquery>
```

**3.** In between the opening and closing <body> tags, build a form that submits the page to itself. Add two form inputs: a **text** input for the Park Name and a **select** control that loops through the list of states.

Your page's body should look like the code listed in **Figure 17.17**.

*continues on next page*

CONSUMING COMPONENTS

```
18  <body>
19  <h2>Search for Parks by Park Name and State</h2>
20  <cfform>
21      <p>
22      Park Name<br />
23      <cfinput name="parkname" value="#FORM.parkname#">
24      </p>
25      <p>
26      State<br />
27      <select name="state">
28          <cfloop query="getStates">
29              <cfoutput><option value="#getStates.STATE#" <cfif getStates.STATE EQ FORM.STATE>selected
</cfif>>#getStates.STATE#</option></cfoutput>
30          </cfloop>
31      </select>
32      </p>
33      <input type="submit" value="Search">
34  </cfform>
35
36  </body>
```

**Figure 17.17** This dynamic form submits the page to itself.

**4.** Open the page in the Dreamweaver Code view and preview it in your browser (**Figure 17.18**).

You will see a search form with an input field for Park Name and a select control for State. If you view the page code, you'll see the page simply submits to itself. You will now invoke the parkSearch component and pass the form data to it.

**5.** In the Components panel, expand the node DWCF.CFC if it is not already expanded, and then expand the parkSearch component.

You will see the listParks() function.

**6.** Expand the listParks() node.

You will see the function's optional parameters.

**7.** Drag the listParks() function into the Dreamweaver Code view below the closing <cfform> tag.

Dreamweaver generates the code shown in **Figure 17.19**. You should take note of several features in the code.

First, the component isn't invoked as parkSearch. Instead, ColdFusion refers to it as DWCF.CFC.parkSearch. Using dot notation, this means that from the root of your Web directory, ColdFusion will look in the \DWCF folder, then in the \CFC folder for the file parkSearch.cfc.

Next, Dreamweaver calls the method listParks, the only method in your component.

Finally, Dreamweaver assigns the variable listParksRet as your returnvariable. This means that the information generated by the component will be stored in a variable called listParksRet that may be referred to like any other ColdFusion variable.

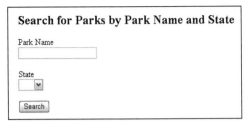

**Search for Parks by Park Name and State**

Park Name

State

Search

**Figure 17.18** This simple search form has an input field for Park Name and a select control for State.

```
36 <cfinvoke
37   component="DWCF.CFC.parkSearch"
38   method="listParks"
39   returnvariable="listParksRet">
40 </cfinvoke>
```

**Figure 17.19** This code invokes the listParks() method.

CONSUMING COMPONENTS

```
37  <cfinvoke
38  component="DUCF.CFC.parkSearch"
39  method="listParks"
40  returnvariable="listParksRet"
41  parkNameString = "#FORM.parkname#"
42  stateString = "#FORM.state#">
43  </cfinvoke>
```

**Figure 17.20** Use parameters to pass values to a CFC.

**8.** If you have forgotten the parameters of your component, look them up in the Components panel.

As you recall, our parameters are **parknameString** and **stateString**. These parameters function just like optional attributes to a CF tag.

**9.** Add this code to your <cfinvoke> tag:

```
parkNameString = "#FORM.parkname#"
stateString = "#FORM.state#"
```

Your code should look like **Figure 17.20**. Invoking a component on your page is analogous to running a <cfquery>: ColdFusion retrieves the data, but you still need to output it to your page.

**10.** Below the closing <cfinvoke> tag, add this code:

```
<cfoutput query="listParksRet">
#PARKNAME# (#STATE#)<br />
</cfoutput>
```

This code outputs the contents of the variable **listParksRet**. Remember, you specified that you wanted your data returned as a query when you created the component.

**11.** As a finishing touch, add this code to let the user know when there are no matches to the search:

```
<cfif listParksRet.recordcount IS 0>
There are no parks that match your
→ search terms. Please try again.
</cfif>
```

*continues on next page*

12. Save the page and test it in a browser. You will see that simply loading the page generates the form and lists all the parks in the database—more than 300 records. This result makes sense if you think about it for a moment: you have written a component that simply lists all the parks in the table `tblParks`. Optionally, you can limit that list be searching for specific parks.

13. Still in your browser, type `monument` in the Park Name field, select CA from the drop-down list, and click Search.

    You will see a list of six California monuments displayed in the browser window (**Figure 17.21**).

### ✔ Tips

- It's a bit confusing, but ColdFusion refers to the same piece of code as both a function and a method.

- If you move your CFC to a new folder, the name of the CFC will change accordingly. For example, if you move the CFC created in this section from the \CFC folder to the \DWCF folder, refer to it as `DWCF.parkSearch`.

**Search for Parks by Park Name and State**

Park Name
monument

State
CA

Search

CABRILLO NATIONAL MONUMENT (CA)
DEVILS POSTPILE NATIONAL MONUMENT (CA)
JOSHUA TREE NATIONAL MONUMENT (CA)
LAVA BEDS NATIONAL MONUMENT (CA)
MUIR WOODS NATIONAL MONUMENT (CA)
PINNACLES NATIONAL MONUMENT (CA)

**Figure 17.21** Here parks are filtered by a search criteria.

## Flash Remoting and Web Services

In this chapter, you learned how to build a simple ColdFusion component and invoke it to retrieve data, just as you would with the `<cfquery>` tag. In fact, you might conclude that it's not worth the trouble of writing the extra code in order to wrap a query in a component.

But in making your component available remotely, you can interact with Macromedia Flash MX as well as applications on other computers a world away via Web services.

Flash MX introduces Flash Remoting, a method of letting Flash communicate easily with your ColdFusion applications. Instead of plain-vanilla HTML, you can build a Flash interface and populate it with data via ColdFusion.

Web services, on the other hand, allow computers to pass data back and forth automatically, without human intervention. Google.com and Amazon.com have recently introduced services that allow developers to access their information from remote computers. For example, you can now add a book to a customer's Amazon shopping cart directly from your Web site.

Dreamweaver MX and ColdFusion MX make it very easy to consume Web services or to use CFCs to produce your own.

As you move beyond the skills introduced in this book, you might consider delving deeper into components and Web services. When you do, you'll understand why so many developers, both beginning and expert, embrace ColdFusion MX: No other platform lets you develop advanced Web applications quicker and easier than ColdFusion. Happy coding.

# INSTALLATION AND CONFIGURATION

Dreamweaver MX and ColdFusion MX both offer relatively easy, straightforward methods of installation. This appendix walks you through the steps to install each program and points out some of the common pitfalls highlighted along the way. You also learn how to configure ColdFusion Administrator options to get the most out of your ColdFusion server.

# Installing Dreamweaver MX

Although Dreamweaver MX runs equally well on both Windows and Mac computers, each operating system has its own requirements. In this section, you learn the requirements and installation steps for each OS.

## Windows requirements and tips

Prior to installing Macromedia Dreamweaver MX on Windows, you should ensure that computer meets these minimum system requirements recommended by Macromedia:

- Intel Pentium II processor or equivalent 300+ MHz

- Windows 98, 2000, NT, ME, or XP

- Microsoft Data Access Components (MDAC) 2.6 or later

- Netscape Navigator or Internet Explorer 4.0 or later

- 96 MB of available RAM (128 MB recommended)

- 275 MB of available disk space

- 256-color monitor capable of 800 x 700 resolution (1024 x 768, millions of colors recommended)

### ✔ Tips

- When Macromedia says minimum, it means minimum. Consider installing Dreamweaver MX on a Pentium III or higher with at least 512 MB of RAM for best performance.

- Dreamweaver does not interact well with ZoneAlarm, a popular freeware personal firewall. If you encounter problems, configure ZoneAlarm to allow Dreamweaver MX to act as a server and to be able to access the Internet.

## Macintosh requirements and tips

Prior to installing Macromedia Dreamweaver MX on a Macintosh, you should ensure that computer meets these minimum system requirements recommended by Macromedia:

- A Power Macintosh G3 or better

- Mac OS 9.1 or higher, or Mac OS X 10.1 or higher

- Apple Macintosh Runtime for Java (MRJ) 2.2.5 or later

- Netscape Navigator 4.0 or Internet Explorer 4.0 or later

- 96 MB of RAM (128 MB recommended)

- 275 MB available disk space

- 256 color monitor capable of 800 x 600 resolution (1024 x 768, millions of colors recommended. Thousands of colors required for OS X)

### ✔ Tips

- You will happier with the visual display of Dreamweaver MX if you use a monitor 1024 x 768 or larger.

- If you're having problems getting Dreamweaver MX up and running on Mac OS X, see Macromedia TechNote 16471, "Troubleshooting Dreamweaver MX on Macintosh OS X."

## About MDAC

If you have problems connecting Dreamweaver to a database, an older version of Microsoft Data Access Components (MDAC) is often the culprit. As of this writing, MDAC 2.7 is the current version, but that may change by the time the book is published. Dreamweaver should work properly as long as you have MDAC 2.6 or later installed on your system.

If you're not sure which version of MDAC you have, Microsoft offers a Component Checker that scans your system and reports your MDAC version (**Figure A.1**). You can download it at this URL: http://microsoft.com/data/download.htm. Microsoft changes its URLs frequently, so if you find only a broken link at the page listed above, just go to Microsoft's home page and search for "MDAC Component Checker."

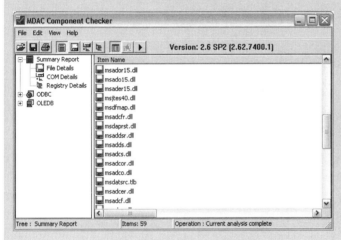

**Figure A.1** The MDAC Component Checker checks your system's MDAC version.

# Installing on Windows or Macintosh

When you've ensured that your system meets the minimum requirements, you can safely install Dreamweaver MX. The installation process is very similar on both systems.

## To install Dreamweaver MX:

1. Close all open applications.

2. Insert the Dreamweaver MX CD into your computer's CD-ROM drive.

3. Do one of the following:

   If you are installing Dreamweaver MX on a Windows system, choose Start > Run. Click Browse and choose the Dreamweaver MX Installer.exe file on the Dreamweaver CD. When the Run dialog appears, click OK to start the installation.

   If you are installing Dreamweaver MX on a Macintosh system, double-click the Dreamweaver MX Installer icon.

4. Accept the license agreement and click Next.

5. Do one of the following:

   Accept the default installation folder.

   Specify your own folder.

6. Click Next.

   Dreamweaver asks whether it should be the default editor for a number of file types (asp, jsp, cfm, and so on).

7. Unless you have a separate editor you wish to use for a particular file type, allow Dreamweaver to set itself as the default editor (**Figure A.2**). Click Next.

8. Confirm your installation selections and click Next to complete the installation.

9. If prompted, restart your computer.

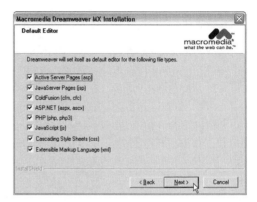

**Figure A.2** Dreamweaver sets itself as default editor for most Web documents.

## ✔ Tip

- Dreamweaver supports multi-user environments in Windows NT, Windows 2000, Windows XP, and Mac OS X. This means that different developers on the same system can have their own Dreamweaver configurations. Ensure that you install Dreamweaver MX as a user with administrative privileges.

# Installing ColdFusion MX Application Server

ColdFusion MX comes in four editions: Developer, Professional, Enterprise, and ColdFusion MX for J2EE. This appendix assists you with installing the Developer and Professional editions. For help installing the Enterprise or J2EE editions, please see the Macromedia Web site or the documentation included with your software.

The Developer and Professional editions can be installed on Windows and Unix systems. This book assists you with installing ColdFusion MX on a Windows server. For help with installing ColdFusion MX on Unix (including Linux, Solaris, and HP-UX), please see the Macromedia documentation.

If you work on a Mac and you've read this far, you know that ColdFusion MX cannot be installed on a Macintosh. You must install ColdFusion MX on a Windows or Unix machine on your network.

## ColdFusion MX system requirements

Macromedia has these minimum requirements for installing ColdFusion MX on Windows:

♦ Intel Pentium processor

♦ Windows 98, ME, NT4, 2000 SP2, and XP

♦ Netscape Navigator 4 or later, or Internet Explorer 5 or later

♦ 128 MB of available RAM (256 MB recommended) for the Developer Edition, or 256 MB of available RAM (512 MB recommended) for the Professional Edition

♦ 400 MB of available disk space to install, 250 to run

♦ Any one of the following Web servers: Microsoft IIS 4 or later, Netscape Enterprise Server 3.6x, iPlanet Enterprise Server 4.x or 6.x, or Apache Web server 1.3.12–1.3.22, 2.x. ColdFusion MX also includes a stand-alone Web server for testing (see below)

♦ A Java Virtual Machine: either the Sun JDK/JRE 1.3.1 or later, or IBM JVM 1.2.2–1.3 or later

♦ Any one of the following databases: Oracle 8.1.7 or 9i, Sybase 11.9.2 or 12, DB2 6.2 or 7.2, Informix 9.x, MS SQL Server 7.x or 2000, MySQL, or Microsoft Access. ColdFusion MX also supports SQLAnywhere and PostGreSQL but does not include drivers for those two databases

Finally, you either can upgrade from ColdFusion 5 or install a fresh copy of ColdFusion MX on your server. Upgrading from a previous version of ColdFusion is beyond the scope of this book; please see the Macromedia documentation.

## Considerations before you install

Before you install ColdFusion MX, you should consider how you plan to use it in your work environment. Three major factors affect your installation and configuration: whether you intend to use CF MX as a development or production server; which edition of CF MX Server you install; and whether you use the stand-alone MX Web server or connect CF MX server to an external Web server.

A development server is a server used for writing and testing code; think of the development server as the place to make mistakes, where only your coworkers and clients have access to your code. In contrast, a production server is the face you show the world; use a production machine to serve code that you have thoroughly tested and debugged. The production server should host the pages your users see when they visit your Web site. As you see below, whether you intend to build a production or development server affects your choice of both ColdFusion edition and mode.

As noted earlier, ColdFusion MX comes in several editions. Any edition you install, however, times out after 30 days and reverts to the Developer edition if you do not provide a serial number. The Developer Edition supports requests from only the local host and one remote IP address that you must specify. In other words, you cannot use the Developer Edition as a full Web server that supports public requests for pages. This is an important consideration, especially if you want to work on a Macintosh with the Developer edition. To do so successfully, you must specify the IP address of the machine on which Dreamweaver is installed in order to browser ColdFusion pages.

Also, ColdFusion MX offers a stand-alone Web server. With the stand-alone server, ColdFusion can handle Web requests on port 8500 without ever accessing popular Web servers such as IIS or Apache. To access the default ColdFusion server with a stand-alone installation, enter the following URL:

`http://localhost:8500/`

The stand-alone server is appropriate only for development purposes, not production. You always can run the server connector in the ColdFusion Administrator after installation if you want to connect ColdFusion's server to IIS or Apache, but if you want to run the ColdFusion server in stand-alone mode, you must specify this option during installation. When you select stand-alone mode, your default Web root directory for ColdFusion pages is `C:\CFusionMX\wwwroot`.

### ✔ Tip

- Windows 98, ME, and XP Home Edition do not include IIS. Thus, you must install ColdFusion MX in stand-alone mode on these operating systems.

# Installing ColdFusion MX on Windows

When you've ensured that your system meets the minimum requirements and you've decided how to configure your Web server, you're ready to install ColdFusion MX.

### To install ColdFusion MX:

1. Close all open applications.

2. Insert the ColdFusion MX CD into your computer's CD-ROM drive.

   The installation wizard starts.

3. Accept the license agreement and follow the installation wizard instructions.

4. When prompted, do one of the following:

   Choose to connect ColdFusion MX to a Web server already installed on your system.

   Choose to install ColdFusion MX in stand-alone mode.

   Upon successful installation of CF MX Server, the ColdFusion Administrator opens and confirms your installation. ColdFusion MX should now be ready to serve ColdFusion pages.

### ✔ Tips

- For security purposes, you should not install the sample applications and documents on a production server.

- The installation wizard will ask you for a RDS password and a CF Admin password. You must supply a RDS password to access a ColdFusion server from Dreamweaver MX. You must supply the CF Admin password to access the CF Admin. These passwords are critical to the security of your ColdFusion server, and you should choose them with care.

- For tips on configuring your ColdFusion Administrator, see the next section.

INSTALLING COLDFUSION MX APPLICATION SERVER

# Configuring ColdFusion Administrator

The ColdFusion Administrator is your window into the health and status of your ColdFusion MX system. You could write a book about the ColdFusion Administrator—in fact, Macromedia has. See the file *Administering ColdFusion MX* in your ColdFusion MX documentation folder for detailed help on the Administrator. This section covers some of the most common administrative tasks.

You access the ColdFusion Administrator via the following URL:

```
http://localhost/CFIDE/administrator/
⤳ index.cfm
```

If you have installed ColdFusion MX in stand-alone mode, access the Administrator at port 8500:

```
http://localhost:8500/CFIDE/
⤳ administrator/index.cfm
```

# Checking server settings

ColdFusion can generate a report of all configuration settings. This can be especially useful when you need to troubleshoot application errors.

## To generate a setting summary report:

1. Log in to the ColdFusion Administrator.

2. In the Server Settings menu, choose Settings Summary.

   ColdFusion generates a lengthy settings summary report (**Figure A.3**). Be patient; sometimes this can take a minute or two to produce.

## ✔ Tip

- You can select groups within the report to display the relevant section of the ColdFusion Administrator.

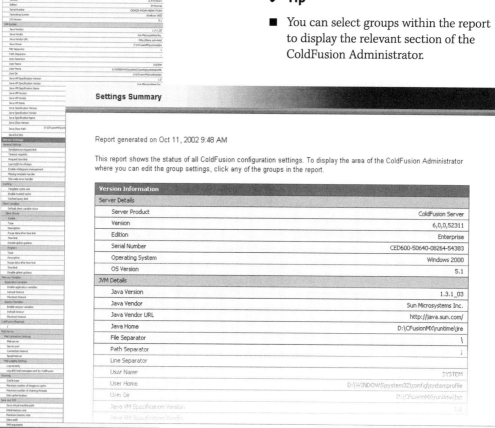

**Figure A.3** ColdFusion generates a very long settings summary report.

## Using RDS and Admin Passwords

As long as you are using the Professional edition of ColdFusion MX, you can access the Administrator from any computer on the Internet (assuming, of course, that your server is connected to the Internet):

```
http://yourIPaddress/CFIDE/
→ administrator/index.cfm
```

Now you can see why you need to choose your CF Admin password with care; anyone on the Internet can access your Administrator!

### ✔ Tip

■ ColdFusion system administrators tend to jealously guard access to the ColdFusion Administrator. You should not attempt to make changes to a production server unless you run the server yourself, or unless you have permission from the system administrator.

## To change your CF Admin password:

1. Use the password you specified during installation to log in to the ColdFusion Administrator.

2. In the Security menu, choose CF Admin Password.

   ColdFusion opens the ColdFusion Administrator Password page (**Figure A.4**).

3. Ensure that you've selected the Use a Cold-Fusion Administration Password option.

4. Provide a new password, confirm the password, and click Submit Changes.

   ColdFusion updates your password.

## ✔ Tips

■ Always specify a password that isn't easily guessed by either outsiders or coworkers. This means no pet names, no birthdays, and no words that come straight from the dictionary. A ColdFusion Administration password is case-sensitive, so try to include a combination of mixed case letters and numerals.

■ The process for changing the RDS password is almost the same. In the Security menu, choose RDS Password.

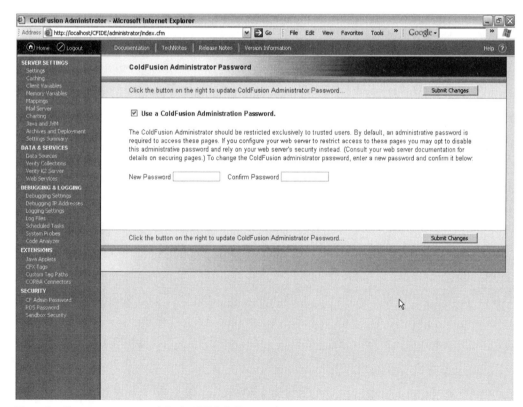

**Figure A.4** Change your password via the CF Admin Password page.

CONFIGURING COLDFUSION ADMINISTRATOR

# Debugging ColdFusion

Don't forget that you learned in Chapter 5 how to turn on the ColdFusion Debugging feature! You should get in the habit of using this feature regularly; it's an excellent way to find out what's wrong with your applications. In addition to turning on Debugging, you can specify which IP addresses receives debugging messages. You should consider strictly limiting these IP addresses because debugging information tends to contain sensitive data about your system and database.

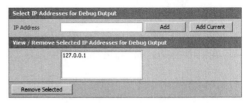

**Figure A.5** ColdFusion allows you to specify which IP addresses receive debugging information.

## To specify debugging IP addresses:

1. Log in to the ColdFusion Administrator.

2. In the Debugging & Logging menu, choose Debugging IP Addresses.

   The Select IP Address for Debug Output dialog appears (**Figure A.5**).

3. If your localhost IP address is not already listed, type 127.0.0.1 in the IP Address textbox and click Add.

   Assuming you have turned on Debugging, ColdFusion now shows debugging information only to the localhost.

We've scratched only the surface of the Cold-Fusion Administrator functions. As long as you're not on a production system, don't be afraid to experiment with different settings.

# INDEX

**INDEX**

INDEX

INDEX

# X – Z

INDEX

# Macromedia Press...helping you learn what the Web can be

## *Reality*

Macromedia Press proudly introduces the Reality series–this is your invitation to join a crack team of experts as they confront real-world development problems and work out practical solutions. As a virtual member of these development teams, you'll create a series of complete, configurable, high-quality applications that are defined, discussed, used, and then analyzed. Not only do you get an insider's view of real world case studies, but you also learn best practices and create complete applications that you can use or adapt for your own work.

**Reality Macromedia ColdFusion MX: Intranets and Content Management**
By Ben Forta, et al
ISBN 0-321-12414-6 • 528 • $39.99

**Reality Macromedia ColdFusion MX: J2EE Integration**
By Ben Forta, et al
ISBN 0-321-12948-2 • 576 pages • $39.99

**Reality Macromedia ColdFusion MX: Flash MX Integration**
By Ben Forta, et al
ISBN 0-321-12515-0 • 432 pages • $39.99

**Reality J2EE: Architecting for Macromedia Flash MX**
By Steven Webster
ISBN 0-321-15884-9 • 504 pages • $39.99

## *Other Macromedia Press Titles*

**ColdFusion MX Web Application Construction Kit**
By Ben Forta, et al
ISBN 0-321-12516-9 • 1536 pages • $54.99

**Advanced ColdFusion MX Application Development**
By Ben Forta
ISBN 0-321-12710-2 • 1200 pages • $49.99

**Macromedia Flash MX Creative Web Animation and Interactivity**
By Derek Franklin
ISBN 0-321-11785-9 • 952 pages • $44.99

**Certified Macromedia Flash MX Designer Study Guide**
By Christopher Hayes
ISBN 0-321-12695-5 • 408 pages • $35.00

**Macromedia Flash MX: Creating Dynamic Applications**
By Michael Grundvig, et al
ISBN 0-321-11548-1 • 504 pages • $44.99

**Macromedia Showcase: Flash Interface Design**
By Darci DiNucci
ISBN 0-321-12399-9 • 304 pages • $34.99

**Macromedia Flash MX Accelerated Learning Workbook**
By MD Dundon
ISBN 0-321-12398-0 • 448 pages • $44.99

**Certified Macromedia Flash MX Developer Study Guide**
By John Elstad, et al
ISBN 0-321-15730-3 • 304 pages • $35.00

# Macromedia Press...helping you learn what the Web can be

## *Training from the Source*

Macromedia's Training from the Source series is the only series on the market that was created by insiders at Macromedia and modeled after Macromedia's own training courses. This series offers you a unique training approach that introduces you to the major features of the software you are working with and guides you step by step through the development of real-world projects.

Each book is divided into a series of lessons. Each lesson begins with an overview of the lesson's content and learning objectives and is divided into short tasks that break the skills into bite-size units. All the files you need for the lessons are included on the CD that comes with the book.

**Macromedia Authorware 6:**
**Training from the Source**
By Orson Kellogg and Veera Bhatnagar
ISBN 0-201-77426-7 • 568 pages • $49.99

**Macromedia ColdFusion MX:**
**Training from the Source**
By Kevin Schmidt
ISBN 0-321-16224-2 • 304 pages • $44.99

**Macromedia Director 8.5 Shockwave**
**Studio 3D: Training from the Source**
By Phil Gross and Mike Gross
ISBN 0-201-74164-4 • 800 pages • $44.99

**Macromedia Dreamweaver MX:**
**Training from the Source**
By Khristine Annwn Page
ISBN 0-201-79929-4 • 560 pages • $44.99

**Macromedia MX eLearning Advanced:**
**Training from the Source**
By Jeffrey Bardzell
ISBN 0-201-79536-1 • 488 pages • $44.99

**Macromedia Fireworks MX:**
**Training from the Source**
By Patti Schulz
ISBN 0-201-79928-6 • 312 pages • $44.99

**Macromedia Flash MX ActionScripting:**
**Advanced Training from the Source**
By Derek Franklin and Jobe Makar
ISBN 0-201-77022-9 • 616 • $44.99

**Macromedia Flash MX:**
**Training from the Source**
By Chrissy Rey
ISBN 0-201-79482-9 • 472 pages • $44.99

**Macromedia Flash MX FreeHand 10**
**Studio: Training from the Source**
By Brad Kozak
ISBN 0-201-77502-6 • 304 pages • $44.99

**Macromedia FreeHand 10: Training**
**from the Source**
By Tony Roame and Subir Choudhury
ISBN 0-201-75042-2 • 472 pages • $44.99

## *Other Macromedia Press Titles*

**Advanced ColdFusion MX**
**Application Development**
By Ben Forta
ISBN 0-321-12710-2 • 1200 pages • $49.99

**Macromedia Flash MX Creative Web**
**Animation and Interactivity**
By Derek Franklin
ISBN 0-321-11785-9 • 952 pages • $44.99

**Macromedia Flash MX: Creating**
**Dynamic Applications**
By Michael Grundvig, et al
ISBN 0-321-11548-1 • 504 pages • $44.99

**Macromedia Showcase:**
**Flash Interface Design**
By Darci DiNucci
ISBN 0-0-321-12399-9 • 304 pages • $34.99

*www.peachpit.com*